GAME OF THRONES

AND

PHILOSOPHY

The Blackwell Philosophy and Pop Culture Series

Series Editor: William Irwin

24 and Philosophy
Edited by Jennifer Hart Weed, Richard Davis, and Ronald Weed

30 Rock and Philosophy
Edited by J. Jeremy Wisnewski

Alice in Wonderland and Philosophy
Edited by Richard Brian Davis

Arrested Development and Philosophy
Edited by Kristopher Phillips and J. Jeremy Wisnewski

The Avengers and Philosophy
Edited by Mark D. White

Batman and Philosophy
Edited by Mark D. White and Robert Arp

Battlestar Galactica and Philosophy
Edited by Jason T. Eberl

The Big Bang Theory and Philosophy
Edited by Dean Kowalski

The Big Lebowski and Philosophy
Edited by Peter S. Fosl

The Daily Show and Philosophy
Edited by Jason Holt

Family Guy and Philosophy
Edited by J. Jeremy Wisnewski

Final Fantasy and Philosophy
Edited by Jason P. Blahuta and Michel S. Beaulieu

Game of Thrones and Philosophy
Edited by Henry Jacoby

The Girl with the Dragon Tattoo and Philosophy
Edited by Eric Bronson

Green Lantern and Philosophy
Edited by Jane Dryden and Mark D. White

Heroes and Philosophy
Edited by David Kyle Johnson

House and Philosophy
Edited by Henry Jacoby

The Hunger Games and Philosophy
Edited by George Dunn and Nicolas Michaud

Inception and Philosophy
Edited by David Johnson

Iron Man and Philosophy
Edited by Mark D. White

Mad Men and Philosophy
Edited by James South and Rod Carveth

Metallica and Philosophy
Edited by William Irwin

The Office and Philosophy
Edited by J. Jeremy Wisnewski

South Park and Philosophy
Edited by Robert Arp

Spider-Man and Philosophy
Edited by Jonathan Sanford

Terminator and Philosophy
Edited by Richard Brown and Kevin Decker

True Blood and Philosophy
Edited by George Dunn and Rebecca Housel

Twilight and Philosophy
Edited by Rebecca Housel and J. Jeremy Wisnewski

The Ultimate Harry Potter and Philosophy
Edited by Gregory Bassham

The Ultimate Lost and Philosophy
Edited by Sharon Kaye

Watchmen and Philosophy
Edited by Mark D. White

X-Men and Philosophy
Edited by Rebecca Housel and J. Jeremy Wisnewski

GAME OF THRONES

AND

PHILOSOPHY

LOGIC CUTS DEEPER
THAN SWORDS

Edited by
Henry Jacoby

WILEY

John Wiley & Sons, Inc.

For general information about our other products and services, please contact our Customer Care Department within the United States at (800) 762-2974, outside the United States at (317) 572-3993 or fax (317) 572-4002.

Wiley also publishes its books in a variety of electronic formats and by print-on-demand. Some content that appears in standard print versions of this book may not be available in other formats. For more information about Wiley products, visit us at www.wiley.com.

ISBN 978-1-118-16199-9 (paper); ISBN 978-1-118-20605-8 (ebk);
ISBN 978-1-118-20606-5 (ebk); ISBN 978-1-118-20607-2 (ebk)

Printed in the United States of America

10 9 8 7 6 5 4 3 2 1

CONTENTS

FOREWORD

Elio M. Garcia and Linda Antonsson

"The man who passes the sentence should swing the sword."

"Love is the bane of honor, the death of duty."

"When you play the game of thrones, you win or you die."

With phrases like these, George R. R. Martin's *A Game of Thrones* reveals not only a powerful sense of drama, a rich setting, and complex characters, but an understanding that at the heart of his story—of any great story—lies conflict. Martin often cites William Faulkner's statement that the only story worth telling is that of "the human heart in conflict with itself," and that conflict appears again and again throughout the Song of Ice and Fire series in a way that seemed unprecedented in the epic fantasy genre back in 1996 when the first novel was published. Whether the conflict entailed one lonely, misshapen dwarf's efforts to survive in a society that looks down on him, a friend's struggle to keep an irresponsible king on his throne, or a mother's choice between her family and her duty, Martin presented the moral complexity of people and societies that breathed reality. Though inspired by the likes of J. R. R. Tolkien—father of the epic fantasy—Martin took a different path, and opened the door for a wave of new writers who explore characters and settings with an eye toward the darker side of human nature and society.

When it was announced that George R. R. Martin's series of fantasy novels, A Song of Ice and Fire, would be adapted by HBO in *Game of Thrones*, it caused a great deal of excitement and speculation among fans who had been following the saga for a decade. Casting, budgets, shooting locations, special effects—these subjects and more were up for discussion. Yet at the heart of all of these questions was a single, overriding concern for most fans: How much fidelity would the show maintain to Martin's novel, not only in terms of plot and characters, but in tone and themes? The first season came and went, and now we know that the producers largely stayed faithful on all levels, weaving together a drama that combined elements of the heroic epic with a moral scale that covered the range from the saintly to the monstrous.

Readers often cite the moral complexity of the novels as being a key part of their enjoyment, alluding to characters painted in "shades of gray." Previous works of epic fantasy tended to operate with a straightforward moral compass where the antagonist was some variety of evil "Dark Lord" and the protagonists were defined by their opposition to this evil character based on their obvious moral goodness. In contrast, Martin's series has been written with no dark lord to speak of, instead focusing the narrative on the dynastic conflicts that rend the Seven Kingdoms apart beneath the shadow of a looming catastrophe. That catastrophe may be created by nefarious creatures and it may be the ultimate end point of the narrative, but Martin's choice to keep his eyes on the very human characters, with their very human flaws, was done well enough to win him legions of fans who appreciated the so-called "gritty realism" of the narrative.

Some of the post-Martin fantasists seem to pursue "grittiness" for the sake of grittiness—and that certainly is one approach among many. But it's hard to find in some of these works the human core of the story. In contrast, Martin keeps a sharp focus on his characters, and though they suffer greatly at times, it tastes all the sweeter when they triumph. When they struggle, we struggle with them: Eddard Stark's struggle with questions of honor and honesty, Jon Snow's struggle to choose between vows and love, Tyrion Lannister's effort to win his father's approval because he has so little else. The inner conflict is absolutely integral to the weight of the story, to making A Song of Ice and Fire—and now *Game of Thrones*—such popular works. These and other questions—of ethics, political philosophy, and more—are the fulcrum on which the entire story turns. Despite the fact that many of the problems presented in the novel and on the screen are couched in the quasi-medieval context of lords and castles and personal honor, there's a relevance to the way the characters wrestle with choices that do not seem so dissimilar to choices that we are faced with on a daily basis.

George R. R. Martin's writing is ripe for introspection and consideration, not merely as examples of masterfully told popular literature, but as a genuine exploration of human nature in uncertain times. To provide some avenues for illumination, *Game of Thrones and Philosophy* presents essays on topics that run the gamut of philosophical topics, from ethics to metaphysics to political philosophy. Eric Silverman interrogates Plato's views on virute and happiness, seen through the lense of Ned Stark's and Cersei Lannister's very different life strategies. Henry Jacoby explores the topic of consciousness in a series where magically created wights and supernatural direwolves exist. Richard Littman imagines Hobbes as a maester, looking on Westeros and considering the question of who should rule. These essays are just a few examples, of course; as Martin might write, there are "many and more" to engage with.

And all this, thanks to the sudden image Martin received one day back in 1991, while trying to write a science fiction novel: a huge wolf, found dead amidst summer snow. From such small beginnings, something great came, something worth reading, worth enjoying, worth examining.

A RAVEN FROM
HOUSE WILEY

Editor's Note on Spoilers

Many of the philosophical quandaries of this series cannot be discussed without looking at events across the five books of the Song of Ice and Fire series that have been published at the time of this writing. However, we understand that some readers are fans of the HBO series and don't want to be spoiled for events beyond the first season. Therefore, with that in mind, you may wish to delay reading chapters 3, 11, 12, 14, 18, and 20 until you've read further into the series; the rest are safe and relatively spoiler-free.

All citations for the first four books are from the Bantam Dell mass market paperback editions, and, of course, the citations for the fifth book are from the 2011 hardcover edition.

Episodes from the television series are referenced by their titles in the text.

ACKNOWLEDGMENTS

How I Was Spared from Having to Take the Black

If it had not been for all the generous help I received while working on this book, my honor surely would have been compromised. Therefore, I wish to thank the following:

First, Ser William Irwin, the Lord of Pop Culture, provided constant support, encouragement, and maesterly advice throughout. Without him, there would be no *Game of Thrones and Philosophy*; I can't imagine anyone doing a better job as series editor. Great to work with you, as always, Bill.

Also from House Wiley, I was fortunate to work with, first, Lady Ellen Wright, whose in-depth knowledge of *A Song of Ice and Fire* made for much enjoyable speculation on what might happen next in the series. Then, I was happy to be able to finish the project with Lady Connie Santisteban and Ser John Simko, who were wonderful to work with on *House and Philosophy* and continued to be so here. Thank you all.

My fellow philosophers—true maesters all—authored terrific essays that reflect both their expertise and their love of the source material. I'm proud to have worked with them.

My longtime friend, Ser Robin of House Riebe in the North (it's been how long since I've seen you?), read everything I wrote and improved everything I wrote with detailed comments and suggestions. I looked forward to reading every raven he sent—always fun and instructive, as he is himself.

My good friend and colleague Ser John of House Collins provided helpful suggestions on my mind and metaphysics chapter and was always willing to listen and help out with any difficulties I had while working on this volume. I always appreciate and benefit from our discussions.

I want to thank two long-distance friends and colleagues as well. Ser David Kyle of House Johnson, a trusted associate of the Lord of Pop Culture, contributed valuable suggestions on Lord Schoone's chapter on evil. And Lady R. Shannon of House Duval, "The Wonderninja," not only wrote a very fine chapter of her own, but graciously shared her wisdom concerning Eastern philosophy and martial arts, and in so doing, enabled my Water Dance chapter to go on dancing.

I'm especially grateful to Lord Elio M. Garcia and Lady Linda Antonsson for contributing their beautifully written foreword. They perfectly captured why the works of George R. R. Martin are, in their words "worth reading, worth enjoying, and worth examining." Their wonderful website, westeros.org, as well as another great site, winter-is-coming.net, entertained me, kept me updated on all the *Game of Thrones* news while I was working on this volume, and were there for me to always make sure I had my facts straight!

And speaking of George R. R. Martin, without him there would, of course, be no book to write. Thank you, ser, for my all-time favorite books. And further thanks go to everyone at HBO who bought it all to life, better than I could have imagined or hoped for.

My brother Alan, now a retired Lord, provided good humor and enthusiastic support throughout, and I thank him for that and for everything else he does for me. Like Tyrion (his favorite character), he's exceedingly clever; I doubt that I could beat him at *cyvasse*.

Finally, my wife, Kathryn, the Lady of the Looms. Born in Craven County (I'm not making this up), but certainly no craven. As proof, she puts up with me. As long as I have you, it matters not that winter is coming.

INTRODUCTION

So What if Winter Is Coming?

Henry Jacoby

Winter is coming; the Wall may not hold, and the Others may kill us all. Yes, all men must die—*valar morghulis*, as they say in Braavos.

In Braavos, they also tell us *valar dohaeris*—all men must serve. So shall we serve the gods? Or those who rule? What good is serving anyone if winter is indeed coming? Maybe we should just drink wine and sing a few choruses of "The Bear and the Maiden Fair."

The House Words of the Starks remind us that we must be vigilant, and even though the future may be grim, we should hold our heads high . . . at least while we still have them. We have our honor, our duty; we can yet lead meaningful lives. As Ygritte told Jon Snow, all men must die, but first we'll live. He knows nothing, that Jon Snow.

"Fear cuts deeper than swords." This is a lesson Arya learned well from her Braavosi sword master. The words become a recurring refrain in her mind whenever she needs to find some inner strength and push on. They can help us, too. And here's another lesson: "Logic cuts deeper than swords." When wielded properly, swords can be used against an enemy. Logic, likewise, can be a powerful weapon. When applied correctly, logic can disarm or defeat opponents—or at least their arguments—and usually without too much loss of blood. While swords can defend our bodies, logic indeed goes deeper, defending our ideas, our beliefs, our values—the things that define who we are and how we see ourselves in relation to the rest of reality. Socrates said that no evil can befall a good person. One's body can be harmed easily enough by swords, but not the inner self. The person of virtue and integrity has a soul in harmony that stands steadfast against desires and influence.

Yes, fear cuts deeper than swords, but so does logic. In philosophy, one has to learn not to fear where logic leads. All men must serve, and philosophers serve the truth. The authors in this volume have done just that. No tongues were ripped out, no fingers removed; the truth was fearlessly pursued. Maybe Hobbes would've made a great maester; maybe chivalry is a bad thing; maybe Robb's war isn't so just after all; maybe Arya can teach us about Zen; and you know, Ned really would have benefited from reading Machiavelli. Speaking of reading, in *A Dance with Dragons*, the master himself tells us that "a reader lives a thousand lives. . . . The man who never reads only one."[1]

So get to it. Winter will be here before you know it.

NOTE

1. George R. R. Martin, *A Dance with Dragons* (New York: Bantam Books, 2011), p. 452.

PART ONE

"YOU WIN OR YOU DIE"

MAESTER HOBBES GOES TO KING'S LANDING

Greg Littmann

Who should rule in the Seven Kingdoms of Westeros? It's the fundamental question underlying *Game of Thrones* and the entire Song of Ice and Fire saga. Lannister armies, bristling with pikes, march north from Casterly Rock in support of young King Joffrey. The royal House Baratheon divides against itself, as the brothers Stannis and Renly each lay claim to the Iron Throne. In Winterfell Robb Stark is declared king in the North, subject to none, and in the Iron Islands, the grim fleets of the Greyjoys sail out to take the North for themselves. Meanwhile, in the distant eastern lands of the Dothraki, Daenerys Targaryen, last survivor of a dynasty that has ruled the Seven Kingdoms for three hundred years, raises a horde of fearless mounted nomads to reconquer her homeland and restore the Targaryen dragon to the throne.

Considering the issue of who should sit on the Iron Throne is not just an excuse for a self-indulgent wallow in the world of A Song of Ice and Fire. The question has real philosophical importance because we, like the warring peoples of Westeros, must decide who is to rule us. Philosophers have been theorizing about politics for at least two and a half thousand years, and one way to test their theories is to consider how well they work in hypothetical fictional situations, called "thought experiments." All that it takes to turn any fictional state of affairs, like the world of A Song of Ice and Fire, into a thought experiment is to ask what the implications of our theories would be if this state of affairs were real.

One such theory comes from the English philosopher Thomas Hobbes (1588–1679) and his masterpiece, *Leviathan*. What would Hobbes think of the political situation in Westeros? How would he advise the nobility of the great houses? What makes the perspective of Thomas Hobbes particularly fascinating is that he lived through the game of thrones *for real*. Hobbes, a professional tutor by trade, was a loyal supporter of the great House Stuart. The Stuarts not only reigned over England (once seven kingdoms itself!), but were kings of Scotland and Ireland as well. Like the Targaryens, the Stuarts were overthrown by their subjects in a terrible civil war. King Charles I of House Stuart, like Mad King Aerys II of House Targaryen, was put to death in the revolt, but Prince Charles, his son, like Viserys and Daenerys Targaryen, escaped into exile to plot a return to power. We readers are yet to learn whether Daenerys will finally sit upon the Iron Throne, but Hobbes's student Charles Stuart returned to England to become Charles II. Hobbes was an avid reader of history, an experienced traveler, and a careful observer of his times. As he watched Britain's bloody game of thrones unfold, he came to some very definite conclusions about the nature of human beings and how they should be governed.

You Are Selfish and Dangerous

"Grand Maester Aethelmure wrote that all men carry murder in their hearts."

—Grand Maester Pycelle[1]

Hobbes believed that people act only out of personal self-interest, claiming that "no man giveth, but with intention of good to himself."[2] People often *pretend* to have loftier goals, of course; passionate oaths of loyalty to the crown were as common in Stuart England as they are in King's Landing. Beneath the facade, however, we are motivated by selfishness—we are all Lord Littlefinger under the skin. Because we are fundamentally selfish, our behavior is bound only by what we can get away with. Where people are not forced to obey rules, there is nothing but violent anarchy, a "war of every man against every man."[3]

According to Hobbes, conflict arises for three reasons: People fight to gain their neighbor's possessions, like the barbarous clans who prey on travelers through the Mountains of the Moon. People fight to defend themselves from danger, even if it means striking preemptively against potential threats, as when Robert Baratheon seeks to assassinate Daenerys Targaryen just in case she ever becomes dangerous. And people fight just for the glory of it, like Khal Drogo, who slaughters his foes as much to satisfy his pride as his greed for treasure.

When everyone can do what they want, life, according to Hobbes, is "solitary, poor, nasty, brutish and short."[4] Nobody is safe in such chaos. Even mighty champions like the Mountain That Rides, Ser Gregor Clegane, must sleep sometimes, and when they do, even a poor warrior like Samwell Tarly could kill them. Our only recourse is to establish a set of rules that we will agree to live by, mutually giving up freedoms for the sake of mutual benefit. For example, you agree not to stick a battle-axe in my head and in return, I agree not to stick a battle-axe in yours. Being part of such a social contract is in everyone's self-interest. Of course, since humans are driven only by self-interest, we won't keep such promises unless it is in our own interest to do so. You may promise to keep your axe to yourself, but as soon as my back is turned, you will break your promise if it is in your best interest to do so, giving me a swift chop and making off with my lunch. What people need to do, then, is set up an authority to make sure that everyone obeys the rules. Once there is someone watching us to make sure that if you give *me* the axe, *you* get the axe, it will be in your best interest not to strike as soon as my back is turned.

The Realm Needs a King

> When Joffrey turned to look out over the hall, his eye caught Sansa's. He smiled, seated himself, and spoke. "It is a king's duty to punish the disloyal and reward those who are true. Grand Maester Pycelle, I command you to read my decrees."
>
> —*A Game of Thrones*[5]

Given all of this talk about social contracts, Hobbes might sound like a champion of democracy. In fact, he was anything but. So great is the need to contain human selfishness by making sure that there are always negative consequences for breaking the rules, that we must be ruled by an all-powerful dictator to whom we give complete obedience. Hobbes called such an absolute ruler a *Leviathan*, taking the name of the huge fire-breathing sea monster of Hebrew mythology. I assume that George R. R. Martin's use of the dragon to symbolize the (once) all-powerful House Targaryen is a nod to Hobbes's *Leviathan* (although it's also possible that Martin, like the rest of us, just likes dragons). Hobbes understood that being all-powerful includes having the power to appoint your own successor. Holding elections to appoint the next dictator would be as alien to Hobbes's ideal government as it would be to the kings of Westeros. But how does such a totalitarian system jibe with a social contract, according to which the power of the leaders is derived from the will of the people?

Hobbes believed that the social contract he recommends was already made long ago in all civilized, organized nations. The monarchies of Europe existed because Europeans' barbarous and disorganized ancestors had tired of living in a hellish state of anarchy. They had agreed to submit to authority for the sake of their mutual good, and agreed on behalf of their descendants as well. The social contract having been made, there is no need for further input from the common people, who are born into the social contract and need only obey authority without question. Hobbes recognized that not all states were ruled by a monarch, and in that case, the people have a duty to establish a monarchy to rule them, but once the monarchy is in place, no more input from the common people is desirable.

As an analogy, consider the manner in which Robb Stark is declared the King in the North. He achieves this position of authority because his bannermen call on him to rule them. "[Greatjon Umber] pointed at Robb with the blade. 'There sits the only king I mean to bow my knee to, m'lords,' he thundered. 'The King in the North!' And he knelt, and laid his sword at . . . [Robb's] feet."[6] The other assembled lords follow suit, and the rafters of the great hall in Winterfell ring with their shouts of "The King in the North!" However, once the lesser houses have declared Robb the King in the North, they no longer have the right to *undeclare* him the King in the North. If they withdraw support from him at a later date, they become oathbreakers, devoid of honor. As for trying to tell a Stark ruler whom he may have as his successor, the lords of the north would have a better chance trying to teach a direwolf to dance.

Hobbes Takes the Maester's Chain

"So many vows . . . they make you swear and swear.
Defend the king. Obey the king. Keep his secrets.
Do his bidding. Your life for his."

—Jaime Lannister[7]

So what would Hobbes think about the situation in Westeros? How would he advise the nobility? Let's make Hobbes a court adviser like Maester Luwin and Grand Maester Pycelle. He can drop by Oldtown first for several years of maester training at the Citadel. Having won enough links for his chain to wind around his neck, Hobbes sets sail for King's Landing in 273, ten years into the reign of the last Targaryen king, Aerys II. He's to be employed as a tutor, instructing noble Targaryen children just as he instructed the young prince Charles Stuart, and we'll let him become a valued member of court with the ear of the king, as he was in Charles's court.

When Maester Hobbes first arrives at the court of Aerys, he would find much to admire. Here is a king who understands the importance of centralizing power! The Leviathan Aerys rules his kingdom with an iron fist and crushes those he considers enemies. The rules in the court of Aerys are whatever Aerys says they are. Even a King's Hand stands only one step from execution—Aerys goes through five of them in twenty years. Serious miscreants are burned alive with wildfire, while Ser Ilyn Payne has his tongue ripped out with hot pincers just for making a tactless jest. At the court of Lady Lysa Arryn, Tyrion Lannister is able to thwart Lysa's will to kill him by insisting on a trial by combat. Lysa gives in to his demand because she is not an absolute dictator and places the authority of tradition over her own authority. Conversely, at the court of Aerys, when Eddard Stark's father Lord Rickard demanded *his* right to trial by combat, Aerys simply chose fire as his champion and had Rickard roasted alive. The Targaryen words are "Fire and Blood." These are kings who rule by force, not by negotiation and consensus.

It must be admitted, Aerys was not merely strict and authoritative, as a Leviathan should be, but was harsh, dangerous, and erratic, particularly toward the end of his reign. His judgments were often more than a little cruel and unfair. When Aerys's son Rhaegar abducts Lyanna Stark, and Brandon Stark rides to King's Landing with a group of young noblemen to protest, Aerys executes the lot of them for treason *and* executes all their fathers for good measure. They didn't call him "Mad King Aerys" for nothing.

What are Aerys's subjects supposed to do in the face of such tyranny? Should they simply obey the king in order to maintain the implicit social contract? Or should they rebel as Robert Baratheon and Eddard Stark do, in an attempt to replace him with someone better? For Robert and Ned, honor and reason alike demand that they resist Aerys, but Maester Hobbes would continue to counsel obedience to the king. Why should the people of the Seven Kingdoms endure such a ruler? The answer is that the alternative is civil war, and civil war is so much worse.

The Horrors of War

The northerners broke into a run, shouting as they came, but the Lannister arrows fell on them like hail, hundreds of arrows, thousands, and shouts turned to screams as men stumbled and went down.

—*A Game of Thrones*[8]

Civil wars are easily romanticized. The tales of King Arthur's knights are often glamorized stories of civil war as Arthur's realm crumbles, and Shakespeare's historical plays make England's Wars of the Roses seem a glorious triumph of good over evil. However, England went through a civil war in Hobbes's lifetime, making the grim reality all too clear to him. It had been a century and a half since the Wars of the Roses, in which the lords of York and Lancaster contested for the English crown just as the lords of Stark and Lannister contest for the Iron Throne. At stake in the English Civil War (1642–1651) was not just *who* should rule England, but also *how* it should be ruled. Charles I of the Stuarts, like Aerys Targaryen, believed that the king should hold the reins of power tightly, ruling as an absolute dictator unhampered by the judgments of his subjects. Indeed, his father, James I of England, had declared that the power of a king should be that of a god on earth! Many of Charles's subjects, on the other hand, believed that there should be limitations on the power of the king and, in particular, that only the elected parliament should be able to levy new taxes. If only Charles had compromised and shared power, he would almost certainly have kept both his throne and his life. Instead, he was determined to crush all resistance and was eventually captured and beheaded.

The English Civil War was a time of terrible slaughter, with brutal clashes like the battles of Edgehill, Naseby, and Preston. Well over one hundred thousand soldiers were killed at a time when the population of Britain was less than six million. That's like the modern United States fighting a war in which it loses five million soldiers—and that doesn't even factor in the wounded! The horrors of this war only confirmed for Hobbes what he had already concluded from historical studies: civil war is so awful that it is never worth fighting. *Any* alternative is better as long as it keeps the peace. Hobbes wrote, "the greatest [harm], that in any form of Government can possibly happen to the people in general, is scarce sensible, in respect of the miseries, and horrible calamities, that accompany a Civil War."[9]

Maester Hobbes would urge the people of the Seven Kingdoms to endure the eccentricities of Aerys the Mad (and to stop *calling* him that); he'd insist that they show some sense of perspective. So a few Starks and other nobles get dispossessed, kidnapped, roasted, strangled, and otherwise treated with a brutality normally reserved for the common people. What is that compared with the suffering in a realm that is at war with itself?

Robert's Rebellion

> They had come together at the ford of the Trident
> while the battle crashed around them, Robert
> with his warhammer and his great antlered helm,
> the Targaryen prince armored all in black. On his

breastplate was the three-headed dragon of his
House, wrought all in rubies that flashed like fire in
the sunlight.

—*A Game of Thrones*[10]

Robert Baratheon, of course, is not the sort of fellow who
would be calmed by Maester Hobbes's appeals to the good of
the realm. Hobbes's worst fears come to pass, and the houses
Baratheon, Arryn, and Stark rise up against Aerys Targaryen.
Thousands die in bloody clashes like the battles of Summerhall,
Ashford, and the Trident, while the great city of Kingsport is
sacked by the Lannisters and comes within a hair's breadth of
being burned to the ground.

After Robert's final triumph at the Trident in 283, in which
he slays Rhaegar in single combat and puts the loyalist army
to flight, Maester Hobbes has an important choice to make:
he could either flee into exile with the surviving Targaryens,
like Ser Jorah Mormont, or remain in King's Landing to try
to persuade the new king to let him keep his old job, like the
spider Varys and Grand Maester Pycelle. Pragmatist that he
was, Hobbes's usual response to danger was to flee. When his
political writings upset supporters of parliament, he fled to
Paris. When his political writings upset other royalists in Paris,
he fled back to London again. If there were two things Hobbes
was good at, they were annoying people and fleeing. It might
be tempting, then, to believe that Hobbes would escape with
the last Targaryens into the lands of the Dothraki, there to try
to explain social contracts to Khal Drogo. Besides, it seems
natural to suppose that if subjects owe their king complete
loyalty, they should maintain that loyalty if the king is driven
into exile. Indeed, that is *exactly* what Hobbes did in the case
of young Charles Stuart.

For all that, I believe that Hobbes would remain in Kingsport
and transfer his loyalty to Robert. He would do this not because
he is a craven or an oathbreaker, but because the same principles
that led him to support the Leviathan Aerys so wholeheartedly

would lead him to desire a replacement. Remember, the entire point of giving our complete loyalty to an all-powerful dictator is that we are driven to seek safety, and only an all-powerful dictator can offer us the best protection. But a so-called king like the exiled Viserys Targaryen can't offer anyone any protection. He's only got one knight, and even *he* won't do as he's told. Hobbes wrote: "The obligation of subjects to the sovereign is understood to last as long as, and no longer, than the power lasteth by which he is able to protect them."[11] The Targaryens' power to protect is gone and so is any reason to support them. Hobbes supported young Charles Stuart because the only alternative was to support a *republican government*. In the person of Robert Baratheon, Hobbes has a perfectly good king to support, and will concentrate on serving his new monarch loyally and tutoring Prince Joffrey to be a great dictator in his own turn.

In Hobbes's view, despite the fact that Robert should never have rebelled in the first place, it is now King Robert who must never be rebelled against. It is just as wrong for Queen Cersei to defy the usurper Robert by plotting to place a Lannister on the throne as it would have been if she'd tried that on Aerys, who was heir to a three-hundred-year dynasty. It goes without saying that her *murder* of the king is even worse! Such an act puts the entire realm in terrible danger. Yet once again, just as in the case of Aerys, once Robert is gone, the important thing is not bringing the perpetrators to justice but making sure that there is someone sitting on the Iron Throne to keep the peace. Hobbes would be as eager to transfer his loyalty from King Robert to King Joffrey as he had been to transfer it from King Aerys to King Robert, even if he knew of Joffrey's true heritage. Targaryen, Baratheon, Lannister—it really doesn't matter very much as long as *nobody breaks the peace*. It isn't even particularly important that Joffrey is so incompetent a ruler that he thinks disputes over real estate should be settled by combat to the death. The harm the little git can inflict is minimal compared to the carnage of a civil war.

The eunuch Varys would agree absolutely. He works desperately to keep King Robert alive, but when Eddard threatens the peace of the realm by preparing to reveal that Joffrey is not Robert's rightful heir, Varys conspires to have him executed. He cannot allow Ned to undermine the power of Joffrey, regardless of his lineage, because to do so would plunge the Seven Kingdoms once more into civil war. When Ned asks Varys to at least smuggle a message to his family, Varys replies that he will read the message and deliver it if it serves his own ends to do so. Ned asks, "What ends are those, Lord Varys?" and without hesitation, Varys answers, "peace." Like a true Hobbesian, he explains, "I serve the realm, and the realm needs peace."[12]

Lion and Direwolf, Dragon and Leviathan

"The High Septon once told me that as we sin, so do we suffer. If that's true, Lord Eddard, tell me . . . why is it always the innocents who suffer most, when you high lords play your game of thrones?"

—Varys[13]

Hobbes's way of thinking about politics differs greatly from that of most of the nobility of Westeros. Who is right—Hobbes, or the great houses, or neither? Hobbes would view himself as a realist who is willing to face some hard truths—truths that are dangerous to ignore. To his mind, ambitious nobles like Tywin Lannister endanger the realm by defying the will of the king. It may seem that such nobles are simply being selfish, as Hobbes recommends, but a sensible selfish person would realize that they put their own safety in great danger by playing the game of thrones, and would opt for obedience to the Leviathan instead. Honorable nobles like Eddard Stark endanger the realm no less than plotters like Tywin. Their obsessive concern with the rules of honor leads to the War of the Five Kings just as surely as Lannister greed.

Hobbes was right to recognize that political theory must take into account the degree to which people are motivated by self-interest rather than duty. The Starks in particular could have used some instruction from Maester Hobbes on this point. When Ned comes to King's Landing, he tragically puts his trust in Littlefinger to do the right thing, when it should have been obvious that Littlefinger's interests would be served by betraying Ned to Queen Cersei. When Robb first marches against the Lannisters, he expects his bannerman Lord Frey to answer his call to arms because that is Frey's sworn duty, while Catelyn understands that Frey will be moved only by his self-interest, including an advantageous marriage for his daughter.

On the other hand, Hobbes was surely mistaken that people are *only* motivated by self-interest. Like Eddard, whose attachment to honor is so great that he dies rather than serve an illegitimate king, people in real life sometimes die for what they believe in. Similarly, like Jon Snow, who gives up home, safety, and luxury for a life of hard service on the Wall, people sometimes make extraordinary sacrifices for the benefit of others. Tales of courage, honor, and self-sacrifice in fiction ring true for us when they capture something of the best in real humanity. If we were all motivated by self-interest alone, stories about people like Ned and Jon would be absurd, even incoherent. We understand the motivations of characters like these precisely because we understand that a human being can be motivated by higher concerns.

Perhaps it is his oversimplification of human psychology that leads Hobbes to miss the way that overcentralization of power can weaken, rather than stabilize, a state. When Aerys went insane, it was the very fact that he held the reins of power so tightly that left civil war as the only alternative to enduring his abuses. After all, he could not be voted out, forced to abdicate, or restrained by law in any way. Perhaps Robert's rebellion could have been avoided if only the Targaryen Leviathan had not been so powerful! The same problem arises under the reign of Joffrey. The War of the Five Kings erupted because the only way to replace Joffrey was to rebel. Hobbes really ought to have learned from events in Britain that flexibility in a ruler can be more important than the will to dominate. Few supporters of the English parliament even *wanted* to get rid of the monarchy, until Charles I made it so clear that he would never share power that the parliamentarians were left with a choice between servility and civil war.

For all his failings, Hobbes understood the horrors of war a little more clearly than the scheming nobility of Westeros. The War of the Five Kings was every bit as terrible as Maester Hobbes feared it would be. Tully forces are slaughtered at Riverrun and Mummer's Ford, Lannister forces at Whispering Wood and the Battle of the Fords, and Stark forces at the Green Fork and at the Red Wedding. From Stannis Baratheon's terrible defeat against the Lannisters at King's Landing to Loras Tyrell's Pyrrhic victory against Baratheon defenders at Dragonstone, from Ramsay Bolton's murderous sacking of Winterfell to the terrible carnage inflicted by Greyjoy Ironmen invading across the north and west of Westeros, the history of the war is a tale of shocking loss and human suffering. Worse yet, all of this happens when the realm is most in need of a unified response to external threat. Winter is coming and the Others are returning to reclaim their old stalking grounds, while in the east, a Targaryen *khaleesi* with a sideline in hatching dragons prepares to reclaim the Iron Throne. Wherever we situate the point at which a people simply *must* rise in rebellion against dishonest, vicious, or incompetent rulers, surely the cost of the War of the Five Kings is so great that the decision to go to war should have depended on more than a matter of principle regarding legitimate succession.

The lesson that the nobles of Westeros should have learned from Maester Hobbes is not that they should never rebel, but that civil war is so horrific that it must be avoided at almost any cost. Appeals to lofty principles of justice and honor that are never to be violated are all very well, but these principles must always be weighed against the consequences our actions will have for human lives. Our most fundamental need as humans is not justice; our most fundamental need as humans is avoiding having a greatsword inserted up our nose. As citizens of Western democracies with the duty to vote for our leaders, we are all, in a way, required to play the game of thrones, in our own nation and across the world. When we forget the cost of our principles in terms of human suffering, to ourselves, or to those who fight for us, or even to those we fight for and those we fight *against*, then we are in danger of doing more harm with our good intentions than any Targaryen tyrant ever inflicted with his greed for power.

NOTES

1. George R. R. Martin, *A Game of Thrones* (New York: Bantam Dell, 2005), p. 253.

2. Thomas Hobbes, *Leviathan*, ed. J. C. A. Gaskin (Oxford: Oxford Univ. Press, 2009), p. 100.

3. Ibid., p. 85.

4. Ibid., p. 84.

5. Martin, *A Game of Thrones*, p. 620.

6. Ibid., p. 796.

7. George R. R. Martin, *A Clash of Kings* (New York: Bantam Dell, 2005), p. 796.

8. Martin, *A Game of Thrones*, p. 687.

9. Hobbes, *Leviathan*, p. 122.

10. Martin, *A Game of Thrones*, p. 44.

11. Hobbes, *Leviathan*, p. 147.

12. Martin, *A Game of Thrones*, p. 636.

13. Ibid.

IT IS A GREAT CRIME
TO LIE TO A KING

Don Fallis

"It is one thing to deceive a king, and quite another to hide from the cricket in the rushes and the little bird in the chimney."

—Lord Varys[1]

Despite King Robert Baratheon's warning that "it is a great crime to lie to a king," Prince Joffrey lies to him.[2] He claims that Arya Stark and the butcher boy, Mycah, attacked him and "beat him with clubs," when, in fact, Joffrey was the instigator of the conflict. His lie costs the innocent lives of the butcher boy and Sansa's direwolf, Lady. Although Joffrey is never punished for it, the vast majority of moral philosophers would agree that he has committed a serious crime here. But is Joffrey's crime morally worse because his lie is addressed to *the king* rather than to someone else? And is it morally worse because he explicitly *lies* instead of merely trying to deceive the king in some other way?

Lying and Deceiving in Westeros

While deception is the order of the day in *Game of Thrones*, the citizens of Westeros usually try to adopt more subtle means of deceit than simply lying like Joffrey does. For instance, Robb Stark fools the Lannisters by sneakily splitting the forces of the North, and as a result, he is able to capture the Kingslayer and break the siege on Riverrun. Mirri Maz Duur leads Daenerys Targaryen to believe that her bloodmagic will return Khal Drogo to health, but all that she explicitly claims is that she can keep him alive.[3] Lord Varys, the master of whisperers, often moves about the Red Keep in disguise. And most notably, Queen Cersei tricks almost everyone, including the king, into believing that Prince Joffrey is the true heir to the Iron Throne, without having to actually say so. Are such deceivers morally better off for having avoided outright lies?

First of all, though, what is the difference between lying and deceiving in general? Almost all philosophers (from Saint Augustine [354–430] in his *De Mendacio* to Bernard Williams [1929–2003] in his book *Truth and Truthfulness*) think that you *lie* if you *intend to deceive* someone into believing *what you say*.[4]

Lying is not just saying something false. For instance, even though Tyrion Lannister, the Imp, is innocent, Catelyn Stark is not lying when she claims that he "conspired to murder my son."[5] She actually believes that Tyrion is guilty. (She has been told that Tyrion won the knife used by the assassin in a bet with Littlefinger at "the tourney on Prince Joffrey's name day."[6]) Thus, when Catelyn accuses Tyrion, she is not trying to deceive anyone at the inn by the crossroads. If they were to find out that Tyrion was innocent, Ser Willis Wode, Marillion the singer, and the others who were present that night *might* say that there is a sense in which she "lied" to them. But accusing someone of "lying" when she just inadvertently says something false is a loose way of speaking.

Of course, Prince Joffrey is not the only liar in the Seven Kingdoms. There is actually quite a bit of lying in Westeros.

According to Lady Lysa Arryn, at least, "The Lannisters are all liars."[7] In addition, Tyrion seems to be correct when he claims that "lying comes as easily as breathing to a man like Littlefinger."[8] Lord Petyr Baelish, master of coin, certainly lies to Eddard Stark, Lord of Winterfell and Hand of the King, when he says, "I will go to Janos Slynt this very hour and make certain that the City Watch is yours."[9] (When the gold cloaks turn against Eddard at the crucial moment, Littlefinger says to him, "I *did* warn you not to trust me, you know."[10]) In fact, after she takes Tyrion hostage, Catelyn herself *is* lying when she tells everyone "often and loudly" that she is taking him to Winterfell.[11] She knows that they will be heading for the Eyrie instead. But she wants everyone to believe otherwise so that the Lannisters will go the wrong way if and when they try to follow.

Lord Stark's Lies

Even Eddard Stark, who is renowned for his honesty, lies. King Robert tells him, "You never could lie for love nor honor, Ned Stark,"[12] but Eddard actually lies on several occasions. For instance, he tells Ser Jaime Lannister that "your brother has been taken at my command, to answer for his crimes."[13] Of course, his wife was acting on her own initiative and took advantage of the opportunity to capture Tyrion at the inn. In fact, in an attempt to protect his wife, Eddard even lies directly *to the king* about this when he says, "My lady wife is blameless, Your Grace. All she did she did at my command."[14] But most notably, at the Great Sept of Baelor the Beloved, Eddard proclaims falsely to the people of King's Landing that "I plotted to depose and murder Robert's son and seize the throne for myself."[15]

Some philosophers might claim, though, that Eddard's false confession is not really a lie. As Paul Grice (1913–1988) pointed out in his *Studies in the Way of Words, saying* something—at least in the sense required for lying—demands more than simply uttering some words. In particular, the speaker has to make a certain sort of "commitment" to those words. For instance, when Catelyn finally gets Tyrion to the Eyrie, Lady Lysa accuses him of murdering her husband, Jon Arryn, the previous Hand of the King, in addition to attempting to murder Catelyn's son, Bran. In response to this second false accusation, Tyrion sarcastically utters the words, "I wonder when I found the time to do all this slaying and murdering."[16] Even though he is not really wondering about this, he is not lying because (given the sarcasm) he has not committed himself to the literal meaning of his words.

It could be argued that Eddard is not really *saying* that he is a traitor, not because his utterance is not serious like Tyrion's, but because his utterance is coerced. In *How to Do Things with Words*, the philosopher J. L. Austin (1911–1960) suggested that one does not actually *say* something if one utters the words "under duress." So, the idea is that Eddard was not really lying because he had no choice but to give a false confession. In fact, though, he did have a choice.[17] After all, Sir Thomas More (1478–1535) was under just as much pressure as Eddard to say something that he believed to be false, that King Henry VIII had absolute authority over the Church of England. More, however, chose *not* to lie, and he accepted the consequences of his refusing to do so.[18] It seems that, unlike Tyrion, Eddard has committed himself to the literal meaning of his words. In fact, this is precisely what the queen is counting on. So, while the coercion may make him less blameworthy for lying, it does not mean that he is not lying.

Note also that Eddard sometimes thinks that he's lying when he really isn't. When Robert is on his deathbed, Eddard decides not to tell the king what he has learned about Joffrey's parentage. ("*Joffrey is not your son*, he wanted to say, but the words would not come."[19]) It is pretty clear that Eddard thinks that he is lying to the king by keeping his mouth shut. ("The deceit made him feel soiled. *The lies we tell for love*, he thought. *May the gods forgive me*.") But Eddard is not lying to the king in this case because he does not *say* something that he believes to be false. Admittedly, there is a sense in which we might say of anyone who is trying to deceive that he is "lying." For instance, the American humorist and pundit Mark Twain (1835–1910) claimed that "almost all lies are acts, and speech has no part in them."[20] But again, this is just a loose way of speaking.

One might go even further and argue that Eddard isn't attempting to *deceive* the king, but is just trying to *keep him in the dark*. Indeed, it is true that simply withholding information does not necessarily count as deception. In particular, it is not deception if your goal is simply to keep someone ignorant of something rather than to make sure that he has a false belief.[21] However, as contemporary philosopher Thomas Carson points out, "withholding information can constitute deception if there is a clear expectation, promise, and/or professional obligation that such information will be provided."[22] As the Hand of the King, Eddard clearly has such an obligation to reveal to the king information that is critical to the governance of the realm. In fact, the queen presumably has the same obligation. Thus, both of them *are* deceiving the king by keeping the identity of Joffrey's father secret.

Is Lying Worse than Deceiving?

Some cases of deception are clearly morally worse than some lies. For instance, in comparison with the deceptions perpetrated by the queen to gain control of the Iron Throne, Eddard's confession of treason (in order to save the lives of his daughters and to preserve the king's peace) is actually quite commendable. However, several prominent philosophers, including Immanuel Kant (1724–1804) and Roderick Chisholm (1916–1999), have claimed that, *all other things being equal*, lying to someone's face is worse than deceiving him in some other way.[23] Indeed, most people seem to have the intuition that if you are going to deceive someone about something, it is morally better to do it without telling a lie, like Queen Cersei, who simply keeps her affair with her brother secret and lets people draw their own conclusions about the identity of Joffrey's father. Many philosophers, like Kant and Chisholm, agree that if she had tried to promote the same false belief by explicitly assuring people that Joffrey is Robert Baratheon's son, she would have done something (at least somewhat) worse.

Almost all moral philosophers think that the main reason it is wrong to lie is that lying involves intentionally deceiving someone. But while Kant and Chisholm think that there is something extra wrong with lying, other prominent philosophers disagree (including Bernard Williams, mentioned above, and T. M. Scanlon in his book *What We Owe to Each Other*). While they grant that there are differences between lying and other forms of deception, they claim that these differences do not show that lying is morally worse. In other words, they essentially agree with the English poet William Blake (1757–1827) that "a truth that's told with bad intent beats all the lies you can invent."

Betraying Trust and Shifting Responsibility

Perhaps the extra thing wrong with lying is that liars *invite us to trust* them and they *betray* that trust. As Roderick Chisholm and Thomas Feehan put it, "Lying, unlike other types of intended deception, is essentially a breach of faith."[24] For instance, Eddard explicitly invites the people of King's Landing to believe (falsely) that he is a traitor. By contrast, Robb does not invite Lord Tywin Lannister to trust him that *all* of his troops are marching south down the kingsroad. So, he does not betray any trust when he leads "nine tenths of their horse"[25] across the Green Fork at the Twins.

But even if we assume that inviting trust makes deception worse, it will not explain why lying is morally worse than *all* other forms of deception. It is possible for a deceiver to invite trust and to betray that trust without telling an outright lie. For instance, Mirri Maz Duur implies that she can return Khal Drogo to health. Also, when she merely says that "only death may pay for life,"[26] she leads Daenerys to believe that the price will be the life of Drogo's great red stallion rather than that of her unborn child. But despite not having actually lied, it still seems that she invites Daenerys to trust her and that she betrays her trust. (Daenerys, of course, pays the *maegi* back for that betrayal by binding her to Drogo's funeral pyre.)

Many philosophers claim that it is better to deceive without lying because you bear less of the *responsibility* for your audience's being deceived. If you lie to them outright, you are solely responsible for their being deceived. Your audience really has no choice but to take you at your word. (Of course, if someone is sufficiently skeptical, she could question your sincerity. But because it's such a serious allegation, most people are loath to call someone a liar unless they are absolutely sure.)

By contrast, if you deceive them in some other way, your audience has to draw an inference on their own in order to end up with a false belief. In other words, your audience makes a choice about what to believe, and people are clearly responsible for the choices that they make. For instance, although the *maegi* does not specify which life will pay for Drogo's life, Daenerys jumps to the conclusion that it will be the life of Drogo's horse. Thus, Daenerys seems to bear some responsibility for being deceived about the outcome of the bloodmagic. When Daenerys says, "You warned me that only death could pay for life. I thought you meant the horse," Mirri Maz Duur plausibly replies, "No. That was a lie you told yourself. You knew the price."[27]

Of course, Daenerys concludes that the death of the horse will restore Drogo to health only because Mirri Maz Duur intends her to reach this conclusion and says just the right things to lead her to it. So, does the fact that Daenerys deceives herself lessen the *maegi*'s moral responsibility for the deception? Consider the following analogy inspired by an example from contemporary philosopher Jennifer Saul.[28] Suppose that you walk around Flea Bottom showing off your expensive dagger with its Valyrian steel blade and its dragonbone hilt instead of keeping it hidden under your cloak. When your dagger is finally stolen, there is a sense in which you are partly to blame. The theft would have been much less likely if you had been more careful. But does this diminish the thief's responsibility? Presumably, he deserves to be sent to the king's dungeons—or to the Wall—as much as a thief who steals from more cautious citizens.

It might be better to deceive without lying because *even if* the responsibility that your audience bears does not lessen yours, you have at least preserved more of their autonomy.[29] A person is *autonomous* if she can freely make her own choices about what to do; and the more choices she has, the more autonomous she is. Both Kant in his *Groundwork for the Metaphysics of Morals* and the British philosopher John Stuart Mill (1806–1873) in his *On Liberty* have emphasized the important moral value of autonomy.

As noted, if you lie to them, your audience has few options. For instance, they can believe what you say (or at least pretend to do so), or they can directly question your sincerity. Thus, they have very little autonomy. By contrast, if you simply imply something that you believe to be false, your audience has additional options and somewhat greater autonomy. For instance, without having to question the *maegi*'s sincerity, Daenerys could have easily clarified matters by asking, "Do you really mean that you can return Drogo to health and that only his horse will have to die?"

But do the victims of other forms of deception always have more options than the victims of lies? For instance, after he was "savaged by a boar whilst hunting in the kingswood," Robert asks Eddard to take care of his children when he dies.[30]

The words twisted in Ned's belly like a knife. For a moment he was at a loss. He could not bring himself to lie. Then he remembered the bastards: little Barra at her mother's breast, Mya in the Vale, Gendry at his forge, and all the others. "I shall . . . guard your children as if they were my own," he said slowly.[31]

In this case, while Eddard intends to convey something that he believes to be false, he believes what he actually says. So, he is not lying. But is Robert really going to think to ask, "Okay, but are we in agreement as to who my children are?" In other words, does the king really have more options than he would have had if Eddard had lied? In fact, since Robert has no choice but to believe that Eddard is going to take care of Joffrey, Myrcella, and Tommen, does he really bear any of the responsibility for having been deceived?

The Ruses of War

Whether or not deceiving is just as bad as lying, is it worse to lie to (or to deceive) *the king* than to lie to someone else? And Joffrey's lie is not our only motivation for addressing this important issue. As noted, many people in the "game of thrones," including Eddard and the queen, lie to the king or try to deceive him in other ways.

There are, of course, certain situations in which it is clearly acceptable to try to deceive a king. For instance, it is okay to bluff when you play poker with a king. Also, you can try to trick him on the battlefield when you are at war with him. As the Dutch philosopher Hugo Grotius (1583–1645) wrote, "the general sense of mankind is that deceiving an enemy is both just and lawful."[32] So, for instance, it is okay for Robb Stark to try to fool the Lannisters by splitting his forces. (Of course, according to Barristan the Bold, Lord Commander of the Kingsguard, "there is small honor in tricks."[33] So perhaps it would have been more honorable for Robb to follow the

Dothraki practice and braid his hair with "bells so his enemies would hear him coming and grow weak with fear."[34])

But poker games and battles are special situations where deception is an accepted part of the strategy, in which even a king essentially gives people permission to lie to him. By contrast, in most situations, no such permission is granted. In fact, in many situations, such as when the king holds court—which is where Joffrey tells his lie—it is made quite explicit that lying will not be tolerated. Then again, maybe the king tacitly gives people permission to lie to him simply by virtue of playing the *game* of thrones?

By the way, I do not want to leave the impression that "*all* is fair in love and war." Some types of deception are morally unjustified even in battle. For instance, in our world, the Geneva Conventions condemn "the feigning of civilian, noncombatant status." Similarly, it is questionable practice for Ser Gregor Clegane, bannerman of House Lannister, to destroy villages in the Trident while masquerading as an outlaw raider. And while he definitely overreacts, Ser Gregor himself has some reason to be upset when Ser Loras Tyrell rides a mare in heat to distract the Mountain's horse during the Hand's tourney. Such ruses are not the accepted norm whether in battle and or in jousts.

Bad Consequences and Broken Oaths

Outside of poker games and battles, it is probably not morally acceptable to try to deceive the king. But is it worse to try to deceive *the king* rather than someone else? Traditional ethical theories provide some potential explanations for why this might be the case.

According to *consequentialism*, when deciding what to do, we should consider what the consequences of our actions are likely to be. And we should not do things that are likely to have bad consequences. Now, the consequences of misleading a person as powerful as the king can be extremely dire. For instance, King Robert Baratheon orders the deaths of an innocent person and an innocent animal as a result of Joffrey's lie. The queen's deception of the king arguably leads to the dissolution of the realm. So we will usually have more reason to avoid lying to the king than we have to avoid lying to the smallfolk.

However, consequentialist considerations do not show that it is *always* worse to lie to a king. For instance, Eddard deceives Robert about Joffrey's parentage only when Robert is already on his deathbed. Since he is about to die, there is little opportunity for Robert to take any further unwise actions as a result of his false belief. Knowing the truth would just cause him additional pain. ("The agony was written too plainly across Robert's face; he could not hurt him more."[35]) So it seems that the benefits of deceiving Robert in this case were likely to outweigh the costs.[36]

But we might also try to appeal to *nonconsequentialist* considerations to show that it is worse to lie to a king. Many philosophers, including Kant, think that we have an obligation to behave in certain ways—and an obligation *not* to behave in other ways—regardless of what the consequences might be. In particular, in *The Right and the Good*, W. D. Ross (1877–1971) claims that we have a duty of *fidelity* or *truthfulness*. In other words, we are obliged not to lie or to deceive people in other ways. Of course, this is a duty that we owe to everyone and not just to kings. However, subjects arguably have a special obligation not to deceive their king. Doing so would break an "oath of fealty" taken before the old and/or new gods.[37]

Unfortunately, not everyone in Westeros has explicitly sworn an oath to the king. The lords and the knights certainly have, but the smallfolk probably have not. In addition, it is not clear that Joffrey—being only twelve years old—had yet sworn such an oath to Robert Baratheon. And in any event, as Lord Varys points out, "we all know what a Lannister's oath is worth."[38]

30 DON FALLIS

But we might nevertheless argue that all subjects have this special obligation to their king by appealing to the doctrine of the "divine right of kings." The idea is that a king has god-given authority over his subjects just like the authority that parents have over their children. And it would clearly be especially bad to try to deceive someone who legitimately has this sort of authority over you.

Admittedly, Robert Baratheon seized the Iron Throne in battle rather than inheriting it from his father. But this does not mean that he does not have the backing of the gods. In a similar vein, Tyrion is presumably found innocent in his "trial by combat" at the Eyrie—championed by the sellsword Bronn—because the gods really control the outcome.[39]

But while the divine right of kings would explain why it is worse to lie to a king, it is by no means clear that there really is a divine right of kings. The English philosopher John Locke (1632–1704) gave an influential argument against this doctrine in his *Two Treatises of Government*. As Thomas Jefferson (1743–1826) wrote in the Declaration of Independence—which is cribbed from Locke—"all men are created equal" and political authority derives only from the "consent of the governed." Or as a peasant in another medieval fantasy famously put it, "strange women lying in ponds distributing swords is no basis for a system of government. Supreme executive power derives from a mandate from the masses, not from some farcical aquatic ceremony."[40] Thus, nonconsequentialist considerations may not show that it is invariably worse to lie to a king either. So, while you may very well receive greater punishment for lying to the king than for lying to someone else, it is not clear that you have necessarily done something morally worse.[41]

NOTES

1. George R. R. Martin, *A Clash of Kings* (New York: Bantam Dell, 2005), pp. 241–242.

2. George R. R. Martin, *A Game of Thrones* (New York: Bantam Dell, 2005), p. 155. Plato (429–347 BCE) claimed in *The Republic* that it is morally permissible for "philosopher

kings" to tell "noble lies" to their subjects for the good of society. But according to King Robert, the opposite does not hold.

3. Strictly speaking, this *maegi* is not a citizen of Westeros. She resides across the narrow sea from the Sunset Kingdoms.

4. Bernard William, *Truth and Truthfulness* (Princeton, NJ: Princeton University Press, 2002), p. 96. I actually don't think that this definition is exactly right. See my essay "The Mendacity Bifurcation" in *The Big Bang Theory and Philosophy*, ed. Dean Kowalski (Hoboken, NJ: John Wiley & Sons, forthcoming). But my objections won't matter for our purposes here.

5. Martin, *A Game of Thrones*, p. 292.

6. Ibid., p. 175.

7. Ibid., p. 413.

8. Ibid., p. 331.

9. Ibid., p. 514.

10. Ibid., p. 529.

11. Ibid., p. 328.

12. Ibid., p. 310.

13. Ibid., p. 382.

14. Ibid., p. 428.

15. Ibid., p. 725.

16. Ibid., p. 413.

17. By contrast, when the Jedi master Obi-Wan Kenobi (from another fantasy world that you are probably familiar with) causes an Imperial Stormtrooper to utter the words "These aren't the droids we're looking for," the Stormtrooper really has no choice.

18. Of course, despite making different choices, Eddard and Sir Thomas both end up getting their heads chopped off.

19. Martin, *A Game of Thrones*, p. 504.

20. Mark Twain, "My First Lie, and How I Got Out of It," in *The Man That Corrupted Hadleyburg* (Oxford: Oxford University Press, 1996), p. 168.

21. Thomas Carson, *Lying and Deception* (Oxford: Oxford Univ. Press, 2010), pp. 53–54.

22. Ibid., p. 56.

23. Kant would never *lie* to his king because he thought that lying is always wrong. But interestingly, he did try to deceive his king on at least one occasion. See James Mahon's "Kant on Lies, Candour and Reticence," *Kantian Review* 7 (2003), 102–133.

24. Roderick Chisholm and Thomas Feehan, "The Intent to Deceive," *Journal of Philosophy* 74 (1977), pp. 143–159.

25. Martin, *A Game of Thrones*, p. 651.

26. Ibid., p. 710.

27. Ibid., p. 757.

28. Jennifer Saul, *Lying, Misleading, and What Is Said* (Oxford: Oxford University Press, forthcoming).

29. See Alan Strudler's "The Distinctive Wrong in Lying," in *Ethical Theory and Moral Practice* 13 (2010), pp. 171–179.

30. Martin, *A Game of Thrones*, p. 506.

31. Ibid., p. 506.

32. Hugo Grotius, *On the Law of War and Peace* (Whitefish, MT: Kessinger, 2010), p. 232.

33. Martin, *Game of Thrones*, p. 316.

34. Ibid., p. 802.

35. Ibid., p. 504.

36. It might also be better to lie to a king if one thinks that it will keep him from doing something very bad. Eddard seems to think that Robert might just kill the queen and her children if he found out the truth. So it might be better to deceive him even if he were not about to die.

37. Martin, *A Game of Thrones*, p. 527.

38. Ibid., p. 322.

39. Ibid., p. 421.

40. *Monty Python and the Holy Grail* (Python Pictures, 1975). For more on the doctrine of the divine right of kings in that medieval fantasy, see Patrick Croskery's "Monty Python and the Search for the Meaning of Life," in *Monty Python and Philosophy*, eds. Gary L. Hardcastle and George A. Reisch (Chicago: Open Court, 2006), pp. 166–167.

41. I would like to thank Andrew Cohen, Tony Doyle, Henry Jacoby, Laura Lenhart, Kay Mathiesen, Jennifer Saul, and Dan Zelinski for helpful suggestions on this chapter.

PLAYING THE GAME OF THRONES: SOME LESSONS FROM MACHIAVELLI

Marcus Schulzke

A Song of Ice and Fire is full of complex characters attempting to win the Iron Throne or at least to survive. Each employs his or her own strategy for reaching a particular goal, but over the course of the story it becomes clear that some of these strategies are far more successful than others. Some characters manage to escape even the most desperate circumstances, while others are outmaneuvered and killed. The philosophy of Niccolò Machiavelli (1469–1527) can help us understand why some characters succeed and others fail. Machiavelli was quite familiar with the struggle for power, and the word "Machiavellian" is still used to describe those who are adept at using force and cunning.

As Machiavelli explains, there are two different kinds of kingdoms, hereditary and new, which require two different kinds of rulers.[1] Hereditary rulers can maintain power by continuing the policies of their predecessors; they enjoy a secure position because they are part of an established dynasty that has built a secure power base. New rulers face a much greater challenge. By seizing control of a state from someone else, they not only make enemies, but in the process also show others how to capture the throne. Becoming a new ruler requires a great deal of skill and luck, and because only the former can be learned, it is important to emulate the skill of great rulers.

Machiavelli's most famous book, *The Prince*, is full of advice for those aspiring to establish themselves as new rulers. To illustrate timeless lessons about how to become a new ruler and how to protect one's self against challengers, Machiavelli tells stories of those who succeeded or failed in their quest for power. With its focus on the struggle to establish new kingdoms, *The Prince* is a perfect lens through which to view the events of A Song of Ice and Fire. As we'll see, the War of the Five Kings follows the logic of the Machiavellian struggle for power and illustrates many of Machiavelli's most important lessons.

Aerys Targaryen, the Mad King who ruled Westeros before Robert Baratheon, started from a position of strength, as he was part of a long line of Targaryen kings. He had all the advantages associated with a hereditary king, yet he squandered these by acting cruelly and irrationally. Once he was deposed, Westeros lost its ruling dynasty and the Iron Throne became an unstable seat of power controlled by new rulers who faced many of the difficulties Machiavelli describes. All surviving members of the Targaryen family, and all those who had supported the Targaryens, became Robert's enemies. Those who helped Robert reach the throne were eager to call in favors in return for their support and to work to gain power in the new court. With the Mad King's downfall, the contest to take firm control of the throne and to establish the next dynasty began.

Virtù and *Fortuna*

Machiavelli argues that two forces determine the battle for power: *virtù* and *fortuna*. Virtù is the skill one needs to take power and keep it, but what this skill actually consists of continually changes based on the circumstances. When going into battle against a rival, acting with virtù may be a matter of charging courageously forward to meet the threat, whereas in other circumstances, such as plotting an assassination, virtù may require caution and patience. Robb's skill in battle and Littlefinger's ability to manipulate others are very different ways of winning power, but each shows virtù.

Rather than giving a clear definition or a list of characteristics, Machiavelli illustrates the concept by telling a series of stories about those who had virtù and those who lacked it. The best way to learn it is by emulating great figures of the past, but one cannot follow their examples too rigidly, as this would make one predictable.[2] Instead of copying those with virtù, Machiavelli advises his readers to discover what general lessons can be learned from them and then to apply these lessons in novel ways to discover a unique path to the throne.

Despite his vagueness about the meaning of virtù, Machiavelli is very clear on one point: Virtù is not the same as virtue. Virtue is usually associated with moral qualities. A virtuous person is one who is honest, courageous, and loyal. A person with virtù can display each of these qualities, but only when they are useful. Those with virtù often *appear* to be virtuous only because this appearance makes it easier for them to take and hold power. Being morally virtuous can actually be a hindrance, as it may prevent one from doing what is necessary to gain an advantage over opponents.

A concern with morality makes strong characters like Ned Stark vulnerable, while those who know when to act immorally prevail. This point is made clear when Lysa accuses Bronn of not fighting with honor after he wins Tyrion's trial by combat.

Bronn points toward the hole his opponent fell into and tells her, "No . . . he did" ("A Golden Crown"). An aspiring king must therefore know when to be virtuous and when to be cruel. He must also know how to make his actions appear to be good or be able to blame others for misdeeds.[3] Machiavelli does not advise rulers to behave immorally, however. Rather, he advises them to avoid thinking in terms of morality at all. He says that actions are only good or bad to the extent that they increase or decrease one's power. Terrorizing others is often counterproductive because rulers who make themselves hated often provoke rebellions.

Fortuna can best be translated as luck. It encompasses whatever events are outside a person's control, whether they are good or bad. Fortuna includes everything from how other people act to natural disasters. When it is favorable, fortuna can help a person out of even the most desperate circumstances, as when Tyrion had the good fortune of finding Bronn to defend him in a trial by combat. Fortuna, though, is an unreliable ally that can defect in an instant. For this reason, Machiavelli argues that one should leave nothing to chance; those with virtù usually succeed because they make their own luck. As he puts it, "Fortune is a woman, and if you wish to master her, you must strike and beat her, and you will see that she allows herself to be more easily vanquished by the rash and the violent than by those who proceed more slowly and coldly."[4] Fortuna can be capricious, and thus it is essential to take precautions against it. In many of Machiavelli's historical examples, fortuna is the force that brings even the greatest generals and rulers to ruin.

The best one can hope for is to avoid fortuna's harmful consequences by planning for every contingency and adapting quickly to new events. Those who seek power must engage in a constant struggle to control fortuna by force and deception. They must have the virtù to control their circumstances, so that their circumstances cannot control them. Many of

Machiavelli's examples of virtù involve men who were successful partly because they were beneficiaries of good fortuna. As he points out, however, luck is rarely enough in itself. Many people have good luck, but greatness requires using it to one's advantage. As Machiavelli says, "Opportunities, therefore, made these men fortunate, and it was their lofty virtue [virtù] that enabled them to recognize the opportunities by which their countries were made illustrious and most happy."[5]

The Downfall of Kings

The struggle for the Iron Throne is, as Machiavelli would have predicted, shaped by the same forces of virtù and fortuna that shaped the struggle for power in Renaissance Italy. In the game of thrones, players constantly struggle against fortuna by extending the range of their power and eliminating rivals. Ironically, some of the most powerful figures in the story are those who are least able to win the struggle against fortuna. Viserys Targaryen, Robert Baratheon, Joffrey Baratheon, Ned Stark, and Robb Stark illustrate some of the most basic mistakes one can make when attempting to take or keep power.

Viserys Targaryen is prideful, arrogant, and violent. He perfectly fits Machiavelli's description of a deposed leader, as he thinks of nothing but claiming what he considers his place.[6] Viserys is willing to do anything, even sacrifice his own sister, in order to take the Iron Throne. However, he repeatedly makes serious mistakes that make him dependent on others. His decision to marry his sister to Khal Drogo is perhaps his greatest mistake, because it forces him to rely on both Drogo and his sister. His arrogance, of course, compounds this mistake.

Machiavelli argues that someone aspiring to power must either find support from average people or from the nobles.[7] The nobles may initially seem to be more attractive, as they have access to positions of power, the wealth needed to raise an army, and experience in politics. Machiavelli advises against aligning with the nobles, however, as they have one critical failing: they offer their support to a claimant to the throne only when it serves their purposes. Many lords, including Walder Frey and Roose Bolton, change their allegiances to gain an advantage. Had Viserys overcome his pride long enough to lead Khal Drogo's army into Westeros to reclaim the throne, he might have found that Drogo or his sister would expect favors in return. He would have been left completely dependent on them and would have been forced to give in to all of their demands. Yet, he never even had the opportunity to learn this lesson. Drogo and his sister realized the power they had over the arrogant man, and they lost their patience with him long before Viserys had an opportunity to invade Westeros.

The masses are much easier to please than the nobles, Machiavelli argues, because their only wish is not to be oppressed.[8] Anyone who can promise them security and freedom will win their lasting support. Had Viserys sought support from average people, he might have found them more willing to indulge his arrogant habits.

King Robert Baratheon is a stark contrast to Viserys, but he too suffers from serious failings that make him a poor leader. Robert's rise to power indicates that he was once a man of great virtù. He managed to seize control of Westeros, reorganize its government, and place loyal supporters in key positions. Even when he becomes lazy and incapable of managing the state's finances, he has widespread support and is too powerful for any challengers to attack directly. Nevertheless, Robert is similar to Viserys in one important respect. He often allows his emotions to dictate his actions. For example, Robert is quick to turn on Ned in a moment of anger and dismiss him as Hand of the King when Ned insists that Daenerys not be assassinated—only to reverse his decision when the anger has passed.[9] These strong emotions render Robert capricious and incapable of removing himself from the conflicts in which he is embroiled. Without this ability, fortuna is able to sway his emotions and dictate his actions. Ultimately, Robert's lack of control over his emotions leads him to be a poor judge of his advisers and friends. His anger drives away honorable men like Ned Stark, and his pride leads him to become dependent on duplicitous advisers who echo his opinions.

Robert's heir, Joffrey, takes the throne when he is too young and immature to understand the consequences of his actions. Excited by his new power and eager to exert his will, at first his harsh actions are understandable. He must act violently to eliminate his enemies in King's Landing and to mobilize an army to oppose rival kings. Joffrey acts mercilessly against friends and enemies alike, however, and commits the fatal mistake of making himself hated. Machiavelli admits that cruelty is often necessary, but says it must be used cautiously so that it does not create enemies. Advising that unpopular measures should be acted upon quickly, Machiavelli says, "Cruelties should be committed all at once, as in that way each separate one is less felt, and gives less offence; benefits, on the other hand, should be conferred one at a time, for in that way they will be more appreciated."[10] Unfortunately, Joffrey is cruel not only when it is necessary but also whenever he feels like controlling someone.

In one of *The Prince*'s most famous passages, Machiavelli discusses whether it is better to be loved or feared. Not surprisingly, it is most desirable to be *both* loved and feared. But if one must choose one or the other, fear is much better than love because it is a more reliable emotion.

> Men have less hesitation about offending one who makes himself loved than one who makes himself feared, for love is held together by a chain of obligation which, because men are sadly wicked, is broken at every opportunity to serve their self-interest, but fear is maintained by a dread of punishment which never abandons you.[11]

Machiavelli, however, cautions those who would make themselves feared through terror, saying that the worst thing one

can do is to be hated, as hatred can drive people to action even
when they are afraid. Joffrey strikes fear into his friends and
enemies, but by continually acting cruelly, he makes himself hated
by members of the court, the residents of King's Landing,
and even his own brother. Luck saves him from being murdered by angry crowds when he and his companions ride
through the streets of King's Landing in *A Clash of Kings*, but
the fact that luck alone preserves his life is evidence that Joffrey
is a poor model of how a king should behave.[12]

Morality and Dependency

Not all of the cautionary tales in A Song of Ice and Fire involve
cruel or capricious kings. Some of the most admirable characters also display a lack of virtù. Although he never became
a challenger to the Iron Throne, Ned Stark rose to a position
of great power. A much different kind of leader than Viserys,
Robert, or Joffrey, Ned always made decisions with justice
and fairness in mind. A great warrior, and one of the story's
most honorable characters, Ned was also a skilled administra-
tor, a good friend, and a virtuous person. Despite all of these
strengths, however, he is a prime example of how disastrous
morality can be to those who are involved in politics.

Ned is often the beneficiary of good fortune, which allows
him to advance far without compromising his values. Fortune
gave him the position of King's Hand and returned him to that
office after he resigned from it. Ned rarely takes full advantage of what luck has given him, however. Instead, he acts
with restraint and a clear, uncompromising sense of right and
wrong. Machiavelli insists, though, that a critical part of virtù
is knowing when not to be good:

> For the manner in which men live is so different
> from the way in which they ought to live, that he who
> leaves the common course for that which he ought to fol-
> low will find that it leads him to ruin rather than safety.

For a man who, in all respects, will carry out only his professions of good, will be apt to be ruined amongst so many who are evil. A prince therefore who desires to maintain himself must learn to be not always good, but to be so or not as necessity may require.[13]

Ned lacks the skill of knowing when not to be good. His honesty and loyalty make him a good friend to Robert and a good role model for his children, but such values are costly when one tries to compete against those who are not restrained by morals. Ned warns Cersei that he will tell Robert the truth about the illegitimate heir to the throne, and reveals his plans to Littlefinger, thus allowing them to respond well in advance. He trusts too easily, rigidly keeps his word, and refuses to hide his thoughts or deeds. Ned's moral virtue ultimately leads to his death when he makes the fatal mistake of trusting Littlefinger, a man whose cunning far exceeds his own. The trust is particularly ill advised since Littlefinger even warned Ned that he could not trust anyone and that his decision to support Stannis Baratheon as Robert's heir would lead to violence.

Ned's son, Robb, displays similar values, but is much better at adapting to his circumstances. Of all the kings in A Song of Ice and Fire, Robb Stark is perhaps the one who comes closest to meeting Machiavelli's conception of virtù. He is an excellent general, adept at winning the support of unaligned nobles and capable of making long-term plans that extend his control over fortuna. However, Robb makes one of the mistakes that Machiavelli says is usually fatal: he relies too much on others for military support. Although Robb has his own loyal followers, he secures his crossing at the Twins and fills his ranks with more men by earning Walder Frey's support with the promise of his marriage to one of Walder's daughters. Thus he becomes dependent on a crossing controlled by an untrustworthy lord and on men whose loyalty rests only on a marriage contract. Robb may have had no choice but to earn Frey's trust when crossing at the Twins, but he neglected to end his dependency once he was in a more powerful position.

Machiavelli warns against forming any kind of dependencies, especially when one must depend on someone powerful. One of the most dangerous dependencies is borrowing auxiliary soldiers. Machiavelli argues that auxiliaries are less willing to risk themselves in battle and that when they win, they have an interest in promoting someone else's interests.[14] For these reasons, Machiavelli says that it is essential to rely only on one's own soldiers, even if doing so means fielding a smaller army. Although the Freys help Robb in many of his battles, they are quick to change sides when he breaks his marriage arrangements with their family.[15] By putting his trust in soldiers with overriding loyalties to a capricious ally, Robb made himself vulnerable. Even worse, Robb did not learn from his mistake. He repeated it by going to the Freys and once again trying to win their loyalty through favors, rather than following Machiavelli's advice and relying only on his own soldiers.

Always Wear a Mask

Strangely, some of the exemplars of virtù in A Song of Ice and Fire tend to be characters not in the highest positions of authority. They are not the most popular, or the most skilled orators, or even the greatest warriors. The characters with the greatest virtù are those who are capable of manipulating others, disguising themselves, and acting independently. They manage to survive in a world torn apart by war, even when they are hunted, attacked, or imprisoned.

Lord Petyr "Littlefinger" Baelish is one of the story's most distinctly Machiavellian figures. He lacks any military power and is relatively poor compared to other lords, but as the Master of Coin and the operator of an extensive network of spies, he holds great influence over the court. Although he never attempts to seize the throne for himself, he knows how to manipulate others so that he always ends up in a strong position, regardless of who rules over Westeros. Instead of openly siding with any of the claimants to the throne, he offers his assistance to everyone, but never commits to assisting them more than he must to retain his position. When Littlefinger must do something that might make him an enemy, he often uses someone else to do it for him, which gives him the power to deny his involvement or to mask it with the appearance of good will.

When Littlefinger offers Ned his assistance in naming Stannis as Robert's heir, he is clearly upset at the possibility that Ned's support of Stannis might lead to civil war. Nevertheless, rather than fighting Ned, he aligns himself with Cersei and uses her to capture Ned. Even when Ned is being led away, Littlefinger presents himself as the victim of circumstances who could not have acted differently.[16] Because he never actually kills anyone and rarely makes a decisive move himself, Littlefinger never has to reveal his true intentions. He is so adept at playing all sides and hiding his true motives that it is difficult even for readers to judge where his alliances lie.

Although she is one of the story's smallest and most vulnerable characters, Arya Stark is also among those who best exemplify the quality of virtù. She is cursed with misfortune throughout the series. She is small, less attractive than Sansa, marginalized because she is a girl, and scorned because of her unconventional behavior. When her father is killed and she is forced to flee King's Landing, Arya loses the few advantages she had and must survive by herself. In other words, fortuna is very hard on Arya; it challenges her relentlessly. Nevertheless, Arya manages to survive by skill alone. Arya masks not only her intentions but also her identity. Fittingly, Arya earns the trust of one of the Faceless Men—the assassins who are able to change their appearance at will. Even before she meets them, she is faceless, able to disguise herself as a girl or a boy and able to act whatever part she chooses to play.

Virtù requires that one adapt to the circumstances, whether these call for force or for deception. To illustrate this, Machiavelli uses the metaphor of the lion and the fox.[17] The fox is cunning and able to escape traps. The lion is able to strike fear into others and to defeat them in a fight. One must be capable of acting as a lion and a fox and of knowing when each role is appropriate to the circumstances. Although Littlefinger and Arya demonstrate virtù, they are unlike many of Machiavelli's examples of this quality because they do not have military skill. As Machiavelli explains, skill at fighting is the fastest way to rise to power and one of the qualities those with virtù usually possess.[18] Littlefinger and Arya are excellent foxes and they can sometimes be lions, but they can never match the virtù of those who are capable of leading armies in the field and defeating powerful opponents in combat.

Jon Snow, on the other hand, shows how much can be accomplished by someone who can be both a lion and a fox. He starts the series as an unwanted bastard, but rises through the ranks of the Night's Watch to become the Lord Commander. Jon is a skilled warrior, capable of physically overpowering others, as he repeatedly demonstrates when dealing with his enemies on both sides of the wall. However, he also knows when he cannot win through force alone. When the wildlings overtake his scouting party, Jon reluctantly follows orders to defect and convinces them that his shift in allegiance is genuine. Although he is inwardly torn by this decision, he does not reveal his true feelings to anyone. Instead, he overcomes his reservations and helps the wildlings for as long as he must in order to survive and return to the Night's Watch.

Littlefinger, Arya, and Jon are able to make themselves appear the way they want to appear, and to convince others that this appearance is real. This is just as Machiavelli would advise. In *The Prince* he places such great weight on appearance that the person with virtù is characterized as someone who is so flexible that even carefully constructed appearances must be changed at a moment's notice.

A prince should seem to be merciful, faithful, humane, religious and upright, and should even be so in reality; but he should have his mind so trained that, when occasion requires it, he may know how to change to the opposite.[19]

As this passage reveals, "seeming" to be good or bad is what matters. Machiavelli thinks actually possessing one quality or another is inconsequential as long as the right appearance can be maintained. In fact, genuinely having these characteristics could be fatal, as moral qualities might interfere with one's ability to take on false appearances and mislead others.

Those Who Make Their Own Luck

The characters who best illustrate the qualities Machiavelli associates with virtù are Tyrion Lannister and Daenerys Targaryen. Both are able to make their own luck, adapt to new circumstances, and deceive others. They escape numerous life-threatening situations, raise their own armies, and form advantageous alliances.

Tyrion is small and physically weak, yet he is consistently able to make up for his size. Even though he is not an exceptional fighter, he is a good commander, capable of winning a battle even when badly outnumbered. When King's Landing is threatened by Stannis Baratheon, Tyrion responds in the way Machiavelli would advise. He spends his time planning the future battle, exploring all the possible courses of action and simulating the fight in his mind. By the time Stannis is in striking distance of the city, Tyrion has already won the naval battle with a carefully laid trap that destroyed most of the invading fleet.[20]

One of Tyrion's greatest strengths is his ability to make sudden, radical changes. In this respect he is much like Littlefinger, yet his challenges are far more extreme. Littlefinger is skilled at maneuvering in the world of King's Landing, but he rarely has to prove himself in more difficult contexts. Tyrion, by contrast, is capable of exerting mastery over his circumstances in dungeons, in hostile territory, and on the battlefield. Tyrion has only one critical weakness: he is easily distracted by women. Even worse, he continually pursues women who will damage his reputation and his relationship with his family. Machiavelli warns that "men who persist obstinately in their own ways will be successful only so long as those ways coincide with those of fortune; and whenever these differ, they will fail."[21] Tyrion is obstinate in his pursuit of women, and though this repeatedly threatens him with disgrace, he is so skilled at manipulation and dissimulation that he rarely has to rely on fortune or help.

Although Machiavelli is clear that one needs exceptional skill to succeed in politics, he also explains that those who wish to use their skill to seize control of a throne must have an army. Even such wise lawgivers as Moses, Cyrus, Theseus, and Romulus would have failed without military power.[22] Daenerys begins the story as a frail girl, first at the mercy of her brother and then of her husband. She survives only because she is protected by Khal Drogo and Ser Jorah. She reaches her position as khaleesi by luck, as her marriage is orchestrated by others. As the story progresses, however, she becomes more competent and begins acting like the khaleesi. When Khal Drogo dies, she learns to survive on her own. Daenerys follows Machiavelli's advice of building her own army and reducing her dependency on others. Even more important, she recruits her supporters from the most vulnerable groups of people.

Unlike her brother, who attempts to recruit nobles to his cause, Daenerys fills the ranks of her army with the slaves she freed—people who are completely loyal to her and who have no aspirations beyond protecting their freedom. Daenerys is capable of making herself both loved and feared by her followers. By freeing them and giving them the opportunity to join her willingly, she ensures that she will retain their lasting affection. This kind of support is far more valuable than the castle walls so many of the great men of Westeros hide behind. As Machiavelli says, "The best fortress which a prince can possess is the affection of his people."[23] Daenerys is loved and feared by thousands of followers, capable of deceiving or influencing others, and able to make dispassionate decisions. This makes her the story's highest example of virtù and puts her in the strongest position to win the game of thrones.

A Final Lesson

Much like Machiavelli's Renaissance Italy, the world of A Song of Ice and Fire is torn apart by constant warring and political maneuvering. Those with exceptional luck and virtù survive, while others become victims of the conflict. Even those who possess virtù or benefit from good fortune must constantly be on guard. Just as in the real world, everyone is vulnerable. Perhaps Machiavelli's greatest lesson is that power is fleeting and that even the most powerful people can be destroyed when they become lazy or when they are challenged by someone with even greater skill. There is no security, even for those like Tyrion Lannister and Daenerys Targaryen. There is only the constant struggle for power.

NOTES

1. Niccolò Machiavelli, *The Prince* (New York: Barnes and Noble, 2004), p. 5.

2. Ibid., p. 30.

3. Ibid., p. 49.

4. Ibid., p. 128.

5. Ibid., p. 32.

6. Ibid., p. 9.

7. Ibid., p. 51.

8. Ibid., p. 52.

9. George R. R. Martin, *A Game of Thrones* (New York: Bantam Dell, 2005), pp. 354–355.

10. Machiavelli, *The Prince*, p. 50.

11. Ibid., p. 72.

12. George R. R. Martin, *A Clash of Kings* (New York: Bantam Dell, 2005), pp. 592–595.

13. Machiavelli, *The Prince*, p. 79.

14. Ibid., p. 70.

15. George R. R. Martin, *A Storm of Swords* (New York: Bantam Dell, 2005), p. 189.

16. Martin, *A Game of Thrones*, p. 529.

17. Machiavelli, *The Prince*, p. 89.

18. Ibid., p. 75.

19. Ibid., p. 90.

20. Martin, *A Clash of Kings*.

21. Machiavelli, *The Prince*, p. 127.

22. Ibid., p. 33.

23. Ibid., p. 110.

THE WAR IN WESTEROS AND JUST WAR THEORY

Richard H. Corrigan

Following the death of King Robert Baratheon, Ned Stark of Winterfell is declared a traitor and imprisoned for plotting against the boy-king Joffrey. In response, Ned's son Robb calls his bannermen to march southward with the ultimate aim of freeing his father. In the process, Robb offers support to his mother's house, the Tullys, who are under siege from the forces of the Iron Throne—led by Jaime Lannister. At the battle of Whispering Wood, the Lannister forces are taken completely by surprise and decisively crushed.

After the execution of Eddard Stark by Joffrey Baratheon, any chance of a peaceful resolution to the conflict appears to be lost. At the instigation of the Greatjon, and with immediate support from the Tullys and Theon Greyjoy, Robb is installed by his supporters as the King in the North, an office that has not been held since Torrhen Stark bent his knee and surrendered to Aegon the Conqueror. The war that Robb wages against the Iron Throne, and the Lannisters who control it, appears just and honorable. After all, who would not be led to such action if placed in similar circumstances? Still, we must ask the questions: What constitutes a just war? And are Robb's actions as justified as they first appear?

Just war theory traditionally holds that a war can be considered just only if it brings about the greatest good for the greatest number, is fought for a just reason in a noble fashion, and is waged by a legitimate authority. The question of whether Robb Stark's taking arms and marching on those faithful to Joffrey and the Iron Throne constitutes a just war requires careful consideration.

The Justness of Resorting to War

The idea of "legitimate authority" is of central importance, as it defines who is in a position to determine whether a war should be fought, and who has the right to act on the basis of that judgment. Robb is extensively advised by his mother, Catelyn, on the wisdom of waging war and also by his bannermen, such as the Greatjon, Theon Greyjoy, and his blood kin the Tullys. Joffrey is advised (and one might say manipulated) by his mother, Cersei, and his grandfather Tywin. Still, it is the right and sole responsibility of Robb and Joffrey to declare war, call the troops, and actually begin armed conflict. Once the legitimate authority has waged war, it is then permissible for his soldiers to actively engage with the enemy. According to the rules of just war, however, they are still bound by a code of honor and must conduct themselves in a noble fashion. This restriction is supposed to ensure that the war does not degenerate into unnecessary savagery and evil. The possible excesses of war are illustrated by the Dothraki, who believe that in the wake of battle, rape, slaughter, and pillage are their natural rights.

The question of who is the legitimate authority in the Seven Kingdoms following the death of Robert Baratheon is of crucial importance for the political and military climate that emerges. There are numerous claimants to the throne, including his (alleged) son Joffrey (who is backed by the might of the realm's most powerful family, the Lannisters); his brother Stannis of the Dragon Isle (whose claim is backed by little support); his youngest brother, Renly of Storm's End; and those who refuse to accept the legitimacy of those claimants, such as the Starks of Winterfell. The division of a former state into smaller factions does not mean that those factions are not capable of legitimately waging a just war. Once their leaders are supported by their followers, they may be considered legitimate authorities. Thus, opposing sides in civil wars may conduct a just war.

Just Cause

According to just war theory, a state may wage war only for a just reason. The most common reasons for legitimately engaging in widespread armed conflict include self-defense, the defense of a weaker nation from the unprovoked aggression of a superior power, the defense of innocents suffering at the hands of tyrannical regimes, and prevention of the violation of basic human rights.

Following the revelation that Joffrey is the product of incest, Stannis believes that he is the rightful heir to the Iron Throne, and that therefore he is justified in laying claim to what is rightfully his. Renly wishes to gain power and prestige and has little confidence in his brother's abilities. Considering his motivations, it is difficult to fully justify his rationale for waging war. Across the Narrow Sea, Daenerys is motivated by a will to see her homeland and to reclaim a throne that was wrested from her family. While we can empathize with her plight, we can also question whether her desire truly warrants the death and destruction it will cause.

In the conflict between Joffrey and Robb, it is possible that they are both motivated (at least in part) by what they consider to be a just cause. Joffrey sees himself as the rightful heir to the Iron Throne, as he is not aware that he is the product of incestuous relations between his mother, Cersei, and her brother Jaime. Thus, it is possible that he perceives all threats to his rule as self-defense. Of course, Robb, on the other hand, believes that there can be no justice under the rule of Joffrey, and that the people of the North should not be subject to the whims of a tyrant king who violates the basic rights of those he would rule. For this reason, Robb, at the prompting of his bannermen (especially the Greatjon), decides to establish an independent state in the North ("Fire and Blood").

Right Intention

A just cause doesn't guarantee right intention. In any instance of warfare, there may be numerous motivations for the conflict, including the intention to personally benefit from increased power, geographic expansion, financial gain, ethnic extermination, and so forth. Robb is not only fighting a war to ensure that his fellow Northerners have a just king. He is also doing it to avenge his father, Ned, and to recover his sisters Arya and Sansa. In fact, it is the treatment of his father that prompts him to call his lords together for battle in the first place.

When Viserys trades his sister to Khal Drogo for the might of his Khalasar, he is not just looking to reestablish his family's throne. He is also looking to punish those who took it from them, and have his revenge on the people who ensured that he was exiled from his homeland ("Cripples, Bastards and Broken Things"). The self-proclaimed "Last Dragon" has little interest in ruling justly or in looking after the needs of his people.

In the case of Robb, he has many motivations for waging war, but the desire that actually leads him to action must be to see his just cause fulfilled. In theory, this should prevent the possibility of ulterior motives ultimately undermining the ethical standing of the war. For example, if he has accomplished the just cause, he should not further pursue the war in order to punish those who unjustly executed his father. However, there are difficulties in establishing whether any particular war has a right intention. There can be big differences between what a state declares as its intention when going to war and what its actual intention is. So what are Robb's true motivations for going to war? He may be suffering from cognitive dissonance, the discomfort of holding two conflicting motivations at the same time. Robb seems to want both vengeance *and* a free kingdom in the North.

Proper Authority

A state is justified in going to war only if the decision is made by the legitimate authority according to legal and political processes established in the state. The citizens of the state must then be notified by the authority, as must the citizens of the rival state. If the state is governed by a tyrannical leader who rules with impunity, then that state lacks the legitimacy to wage a just war. Thus Joffrey does not have the ability to wage a just war, given the nature of his reign and the atrocities that he has committed against his own people. As the leader of an emerging state, Robb has been elected to the position of king by his kinsmen, and this lends legitimacy to his authority. The established norm in the Seven Kingdoms is that when a rightful king declares war, it is the duty of his lords to field their armies in his support. Although there is no formal declaration of war at the beginning of the hostilities that lead to the War of the Five Kings, the effective intention is made obvious through the declarations of fealty by the lords on the opposing sides.

Last Resort

If a war is to be considered just, then all other reasonable and peaceful avenues of conflict resolution must be exhausted before the state resorts to military confrontation. Failure to engage in diplomatic negotiation in order to reach a satisfactory conclusion means that the state has not expended sufficient effort in attempting to preserve the peace. War is a devastating enterprise that wreaks havoc on the lives of ordinary people. For a war to be just, every attempt must be made to ensure that bloodshed is avoided and that physical aggression is an absolute last resort. Joffrey is an arrogant king who believes that it is his right as sovereign to do as he pleases. He views Robb Stark as a Northern rebel who deserves to be crushed by his armies. He does not enter into negotiation, as he believes that it is beneath him to do so, and he often pays little heed to his advisers—although he is reliant on the military strength of his grandfather Tywin. From the perspective of the Northern alliance, under the kingship of Robb, there appears to be little option but to use all necessary force to ensure that Joffrey renounces his claim to the North.

In *A Clash of Kings*, Robb does offer some terms for peace, which are rejected out of hand.[1] One might question, however, whether Robb has in fact done everything possible to avoid an armed conflict. Should he have sent further emissaries? Should he have offered better terms? Still, as a legitimate authority, Robb gets to decide when he has done all that is reasonable to preserve the peace.

Probability of Success

War must not result in the pointless waste of human life. If it is anticipated that there is little likelihood of success in the proposed war, then it is futile to engage in the process. This idea may appear intuitively correct, but one must then ask whether small states *ever* have the legitimate right to go to war with larger aggressors who have superior military resources. If one should begin a war campaign only if there is a high chance of success, then Daenerys should never have begun to raise an army following the desertion of the Khalasar after Khal Drogo could no longer ride.

All sides in the War of the Five Kings believe that they have a possibility of achieving success. However, it is the *probability* of success that matters. For example, approximately nine years before the start of *A Game of Thrones*, Balon Greyjoy announced himself king of the Iron Isles in a rebellion against King Robert. His forces, however, were outnumbered ten-to-one and were ultimately slaughtered ("Cripples, Bastards and Broken Things"). The probability of success in this endeavor would have been insufficient to justify it. By contrast, the initial successes of Robb's troops indicate that he does in fact have a good chance of victory.

Proportionality of Loss versus Gain

It is the responsibility of a state to consider objectively whether the good that is to be secured through waging a war is justified in terms of the costs that it will exact. This is a theoretical calculation that must take into account the *universal* (or complete) cost of the proposed armed conflict. When assessing the cost-versus-gain ratio, the state must consider not only its own potential losses and gains, but also those of the enemy. The good to be achieved will usually be considered in light of the just cause, and the cost or evils will include inevitable outcomes such as casualties, loss of property, and so forth. If, after careful consideration, the securing of the just cause is deemed to be worthwhile even in light of potential loss, then the war is justified and should proceed. We must wonder, then, whether Robb has truly considered the possible overall cost to both his own people and the rest of Westeros.

Justness in Conducting War

The next concern relates to justifiable conduct in the actual execution of battle. It is up to the state to ensure that its armed forces adhere to the principles of right conduct when engaging with the enemy. In order to do so, the state appoints military officials to oversee the strategic planning of its campaigns and to ensure that regular soldiers do not participate in inappropriate behavior. Under just war theory there is a moral limitation to what is permitted in battle, and this ultimately means that all soldiers should refrain from unnecessary or excessive uses of violence and should not inflict needless pain and suffering on innocents who are not actually fighting in the war. During military engagements between the forces of Robb and Joffrey, some forces act immorally. For example, Joffrey's knight Ser Gregor Clegane kills the Lord Darry, who is only eight years old, and after defeating Jonos Bracken at Stone Hedge, Ser Gregor burns the harvest and rapes Bracken's daughter.[2]

Discrimination between
Combatants and Noncombatants

Soldiers are permitted to attempt to kill only targets that are actively engaged in the military campaign. The function of war, so understood, is to kill enemy combatants and not to indiscriminately slaughter all members of the opposing state. The Dothraki openly reject anything akin to this idea in the rape and pillage that they think is their due after being victorious in battle. One such example involves the atrocities committed on the Lhazareen "Sheep People" when Khal Drogo sacks their town (even though this was not in fact a war—as it was an isolated battle) ("Baelor").

It is legitimate, however, to pursue any target that is intentionally engaged in inflicting harm, either directly or indirectly, on the state's forces. Therefore, one may legitimately attack military personnel, equipment and installations, political adversaries who promote the war, and individuals and industries that manufacture goods and items that will be employed with the purpose of producing harm. Civilians who are not actively engaged in harming one's combatants should be exempted from intentional attack. Once again, think of Gregor Clegane's campaign of murder and terror and that of the troops of Tywin Lannister ("Fire and Blood"). Of course, in any armed conflict there will be unavoidable civilian casualties as the indirect result of conflict. Such collateral damage may be excused, providing that such deaths are not deliberate. For example, when Robert Baratheon was in the process of gaining the throne and laid siege to Storm's End, it was not his primary intention to kill the civilians who had taken refuge there, but it is likely that many were killed in securing the castle.

Appropriate Treatment of Prisoners of War

According to just war theory, hostages and prisoners of war must be treated in a humane way. It is not permissible to torture them physically or mentally (even to extract vital information), to use them as human shields, or to deny them basic human rights. This is one of the most contentious of the just war conditions, as theoretically it applies to any of the enemy's personnel, irrespective of their rank or knowledge. When Robb's troops capture Jaime Lannister at the Battle of Whispering Wood, he is imprisoned in Riverrun, where he is treated in a humane fashion ("Fire and Blood"). The earlier capture of Tyrion Lannister and his incarceration in the Eyrie by Catelyn Stark and her sister Lysa Arren cannot be considered in light of the justness of the war that follows, as it predated the actual announcement of war. Sansa is effectively a prisoner of Joffrey, but she fares much worse than Jaime, and is subjected to continual beatings at the whim of the king. One can also garner an indication of how well prisoners fare in the dungeons of King's Landing by considering the treatment of Ned Stark while he is awaiting trial for treason.

No Reprisals

"Two wrongs don't make a right." So reprisals are not permissible. That is, one may not violate the principles of just war to punish an enemy for having previously violated those same principles. Reprisals do not serve to restore equilibrium, and they do not ensure that future engagements in the war will conform to the principles of justness. Rather, history has shown that such reprisals often escalate the level of violence and lead to indiscriminate carnage. The idea of the just war is to ensure that the greatest good is served and that the aggression used to achieve the just cause is tempered and appropriate. Rather than debasing the state by emulating the activities of the enemy, a just state should take the higher moral ground so that if they are victorious, they will know that they won in the best possible fashion. Thus, it is better for Robb to ensure that his men do not rape and pillage than to allow them to do so as a reprisal for the activities of some of the followers of Joffrey. A marked difference in the degree of the nobility of the two opposing sides is evident throughout the conflict. The Northerners are prepared to fight for their just cause, but they refuse to employ strategies that would call the honor of their houses into question. In contrast, many of the followers of Joffrey are motivated by self-promotion, greed, and fear, and are prepared to do whatever it takes to be victorious.

Respect the Rights of the State's Own Citizens

While engaging in a war, the state may be tempted to temporarily suspend the human rights of its own citizens in order to facilitate the war effort. This is contrary to just war theory, which holds that the rights of the individual must be upheld to the greatest degree possible, given the situation in which the state finds itself. The individual is still entitled to legal due process as established by the state in a time of peace. Such high ideals have not always been upheld in times of conflict, and civil liberties have been compromised under the banner of increasing national security.

Joffrey egregiously violates this principle, imposing punishments on a whim—often just to entertain himself. He has knights duel to the death, heads and hands cut off, all with no real concern for the justness of his actions. The authority of the state under his reign is cruel and capricious, and Joffrey is likened by the inhabitants of the Red Keep to the Mad King Aerys II.

A Just War?

So the question that we are ultimately left to answer is whether either side in the war between Robb Stark and Joffrey Baratheon conforms to the principles of just war theory. Joffrey, along with his representatives and his soldiers, is clearly guilty of many injustices in conducting their war effort—against both the enemy and their own people. Robb, by contrast, is a legitimate authority and conducts warfare in noble fashion— treating prisoners humanely, not engaging in excessive violence, showing consideration for civilians and for his own people. His intention, however, is suspect. Robb and his bannermen profess a just cause, freedom in the North—a Northern king for a Northern kingdom free from tyranny. But is this the ultimate reason that Robb goes to war? Indeed, would the idea of a war for a free North be something he would've seriously considered had his honorable father not been executed? One must wonder whether the greater motivating influence involves avenging his father and punishing those responsible for his death.

We want Robb to be victorious, we think of him as generally justified in his undertakings, and we desire an end to the corrupt, capricious, and spoiled Joffrey. We believe Robb would be a far better ruler and establish and govern a more equitable state that is dedicated to higher ideals. However, having a noble spirit and a concern for one's kinsmen and one's people does not necessarily mean that one is waging a just war—even if the reasons for going to war are very persuasive. The requirements of a just war are difficult to satisfy in totality, and unfortunately, Robb appears lacking in one area—his right intention is not pure enough; or perhaps we should say that his dominant intention was not the right one. Although he is devoted to commendable ideals, his prevailing motivation is vengeance for his father, especially in his earlier military engagements. Therefore, we must ultimately conclude that although we might support his war, we cannot truly call it just.

NOTES

1. George R. R. Martin, *A Clash of Kings* (New York: Bantam Dell, 2005), pp. 110–111.
2. Ibid., p. 118.

PART TWO

"THE THINGS
I DO FOR LOVE"

WINTER IS COMING!: THE BLEAK QUEST FOR HAPPINESS IN WESTEROS

Eric J. Silverman

A Game of Thrones raises an important philosophical question: Is a life of virtue and justice the way to achieve happiness, or does a willingness to reject traditional moral rules result in happiness? Plato (424–348 BCE) advocates the view that the life of virtue and justice is the happy life, claiming, "surely anyone who lives well [justly] is blessed and happy and anyone who doesn't is the opposite. . . . Therefore, a just person is happy, and an unjust one wretched."[1] This view identifying the virtuous life of justice as the happy life, and the vicious life of injustice as an unhappy life, underlies many of the epic stories in our culture, such as those written by J. R. R. Tolkien, Victor Hugo, J. K. Rowling, and C. S. Lewis. As we'll see, George R. R. Martin's epic presents things differently.

"Is the Honorable Person Happy?"

"You wear your honor like a suit of armor, Stark. You think it keeps you safe, but all it does is weigh you down and make it hard for you to move."

—Littlefinger[2]

A Game of Thrones initially seems like it will illustrate this traditional view connecting virtue and happiness. As in many epic stories, we are presented with a classic hero who is the epitome of virtue. Eddard Stark is fiercely loyal to his family, friends, and kingdom. He has a history of courage in battle. He has a deep sense of duty, which causes him to abandon his personal safety and comfort for the sake of the good of the kingdom and his friends, as he accepts the unenviable role of acting as the King's Hand. As Maester Aemon suggests, he appears to be an extraordinarily virtuous man; "Lord Eddard is one man in ten thousand."[3] However, while the traditional view leads us to believe he will ultimately overcome all barriers and live happily ever after, he is instead betrayed, slandered, and executed while trying to resolve the political intrigues at King's Landing. In what appears to be a repudiation of the Platonic view, virtue and justice do not bring happiness for Eddard.

Yet, perhaps, "living happily ever after" was not the kind of happiness Plato was referring to when he claimed that the just person is happy. Plato was well aware that virtuous people do not always live happily ever after in this earthly material world. An obvious example of how earthly happiness is independent of virtue would have been evident in the life of his mentor Socrates (469–399 BCE), who was unjustly condemned to death. So when Plato claims that the just man is happy, he cannot mean that the virtuous person is guaranteed a successful life in terms of material earthly happiness.

Instead, Plato argues for a sharp division between the material world and the immaterial world and claims that the real self and real happiness are immaterial. Accordingly, in the *Apology*, after Socrates is unjustly condemned to death he insists, "a good man cannot be harmed either in life or in death, and that his affairs are not neglected by the gods."[4] Therefore, when Plato claims that the just man is happy, it is clear that he does not mean that the just person is guaranteed to flourish in the material sense. He knows that tragedy in the physical world is common, and that virtuous men can be stricken by bad luck, disease, or treachery.

Plato claims that real happiness has to do with the immaterial self, not the material body. The virtuous person's immaterial soul functions ideally. Plato identifies three distinct parts of the soul: appetite, spirit, and intellect. "Appetite" consists of our desires for pleasure, bodily satisfaction, and other material wants. "Spirit" refers to our emotions and especially to our desire to be honored in the eyes of others. "Intellect" refers to the best part of the self, the rational capacities that desire wisdom and knowledge over physical desires or social fulfillment.

Plato claims the virtuous person's soul functions ideally in that it is ruled by its best parts: reason rules, spirit is trained to reinforce the wise judgments of reason, and appetite submits to reason and spirit. To see the advantages of Plato's view, reflect upon the question "How does one identify the ideal diet that would enable the longest, healthiest life?" A person driven by appetite would simply indulge himself, would tend to overeat, and would choose a diet based on tastiness rather than healthiness. A person controlled by spirit would choose a diet based upon emotion. In contrast, a person driven by intellect would carefully formulate a diet based on the actual needs of health rather than appetite or emotion.

Plato believes that all of well-being works according to the same principles. The just person ruled by reason lives a happy life in search of wisdom and in virtuous service to the community. Therefore, no one can harm a person with a virtuous soul, because the only real harm one can experience is to become a vicious, unjust person. Ultimately, Plato points toward the possibility of both an afterlife and divine intervention whereby the just may flourish in this life and perhaps even after this life.

A rough illustration of these principles can be seen in the life of Bran Stark. Although, his young body is broken when Jaime Lannister pushes him from the heights of Winterfell, Bran flourishes. His body would never recover from his injuries, "He could not walk, nor climb nor hunt nor fight with a wooden sword as he once had."[5] Yet he experiences a different kind of flourishing as he develops his psychic abilities as a skinchanger, who can enter the body of other animals, and a greenseer, who can see all that the ancient weirwood trees have ever seen. As Bran's tutor Brynden promises, "You will never walk again . . . but you will fly."[6] In a similar way, when Plato claims that the just man is happy, he does not mean that he is guaranteed to flourish in the conventional physical sense, but in some more important immaterial sense. Happiness is not simply pleasure.

"Is the Devious Person Happy?"

"How would you like to die?"

—Shagga

"In my own bed, with a belly full of wine . . . at the age of eighty."

—Tyrion[7]

Of course, not everyone accepts Plato's view of happiness. Many people think happiness has more to do with physical pleasure and associated goods, like health, long life, and wealth, than virtue. This hedonistic view of happiness, which views happiness as constituted solely by pleasure, is the philosophical assumption behind Tyrion Lannister's desire for a life full of pleasure followed by a comfortable death in old age. In any case, the wise person is not quick to accept happy clichés no matter how attractive they seem.

Accordingly, in *The Republic*, Socrates and his discussion partners examine the possibility that the unjust person might be happier than the just person. They acknowledge that it *seems* as if the truly clever unjust person can appear virtuous through deception while exploiting every unjust opportunity, thereby gaining the benefits of both justice and injustice. As they describe the successful unjust man:

> He rules his city because of his reputation for justice; he marries into any family he wishes; he gives his children in marriage to anyone he wishes; he has contracts and partnerships with anyone he wants; and besides benefiting himself in all these ways, he profits because he has no scruples about doing injustice. In any contest, public or private, he's the winner and outdoes his enemies. . . . He takes better care of the gods, therefore, (and indeed, of the human beings he's fond of) than a just person does. Hence it's likely that the gods, in turn, will take better care of him than of a just person.[8]

This strategy for pursuing happiness is embodied in the constant machinations of Cersei Lannister. While trying to maintain a virtuous reputation, she pursues her goals through whatever means necessary. She is willing to lie, seduce, manipulate, and even murder her own husband in her quest for power, pleasure, and happiness. And by many external measures of happiness, she is successful. She has risen to power as the queen. She secures a powerful place in the kingdom for her children. She lives a life of luxury. She carries on affairs with virtually whomever she wishes.

Yet her strategy is ultimately unreliable, as the external challenges to her happiness are obvious. Her vicious actions require constant deception, while discovery and the accompanying consequences seem inevitable. Success in today's machinations may grant pleasure for the day, but tomorrow will require even more difficult manipulation to maintain today's accomplishments. If she succeeds in killing Jon Arryn, she may need to silence Bran Stark tomorrow. If she silences Bran Stark tomorrow, she may need to kill Eddard Stark the next day. If she kills Eddard Stark, she may need to face Rob Stark's armies afterward, and so on. This constant cycle of lies, manipulation, and violence results in an uncertain fate for her happiness. Whatever goods she obtains through vice today may be lost tomorrow.

"I Do Not Know Which of You I Pity Most"[9]

An even more serious obstacle to Cersei's happiness makes her an object of pity to honorable people like Eddard. While external challenges to her happiness may ultimately be overcome, her own vicious character acts as an inescapable internal obstacle to happiness. Regardless of whatever goods her schemes enable her to obtain, she constantly wants more. She is never satisfied with the goods she possesses, thereby making herself unhappy. Why couldn't she live happily as the queen or be satisfied with a discreet affair or two? Why did she have to kill her husband and deny him any legitimate heirs? Wouldn't she have had almost as much power, luxury, and happiness, without risking life, limb, and constant turmoil if she chose to be content? Her own appetite and greed for more than she possesses guarantee an unhappy existence.

Furthermore, Cersei's personality is marked by paranoia, instability, impatience, and imprudence. Her paranoia is evident as she warns her son, "Everyone who is not us, is an enemy" ("You Win or You Die"). Paranoia is a natural outgrowth of her own devious personality. She can never trust anyone because others may be just as manipulative. Her unstable desires undermine her relationships as well as her own happiness. Tyrion suggests that her vicious personality makes the entire kingdom vulnerable. As he explains,

> Westeros is torn and bleeding, and I do not doubt that even now my sweet sister is binding up the wounds . . . with salt. Cersei is as gentle as King Maegor, as selfless as Aegon the Unworthy, as wise as Mad Aerys. She never

forgets a slight, real or imagined. She takes caution for cowardice and dissent for defiance. And she is greedy. Greedy for power, for honor, for love.[10]

Cersei is the epitome of what Plato warns us against: a vicious, inharmonious, unstable soul. She is ruled by her appetites rather than reason. Since she is imbalanced within herself, she is the sort of person whose psyche makes her incapable of happiness regardless of her circumstances. Furthermore, she imagines insults, undermines her relationships, and is driven by insatiable greed. Plato claims that the vicious tyrant's most serious problem is that his psyche is dominated by its worst parts. He claims that the tyrant's soul is ruled by

> the beastly and savage part. . . . You know that there is nothing it won't dare to do . . . free of all control by shame or reason. It doesn't shrink from trying to have sex with a mother, as it supposes, or with anyone else at all, whether man, god, or beast. It will commit any foul murder, and there is no food it refuses to eat. In a word, it omits no act of folly or shamelessness.[11]

Cersei fits Plato's description of the tyrant perfectly. She is driven by unrestrained lusts, commits incest with her brother Jaime Lannister, plots the murder of her husband, and frames her brother Tyrion for the murder of her son. Like Plato's tyrant, Cersei's continual greed ensures that her desires can never be satisfied. She is incapable of achieving happiness, since no set of external circumstances can ever satisfy her monstrous and unstable internal desires. Whatever advantages her life possesses, she is pitiable and deeply unhappy.

"Life Is Not a Song, Sweetling. You May Learn That One Day to Your Sorrow"[12]

While Plato gets much correct about the nature of happiness, many contemporary readers will be unsatisfied with his account. After all, Eddard certainly doesn't seem happy. His story ends with a coerced confession, public humiliation as a traitor, and an unjust execution in front of his daughters. And though Cersei is clearly unstable and unhappy, it still seems that pleasure, success, and status must have some important connection with happiness. Plato's account doesn't seem compatible with either of these observations.

One way to modify Plato's views in a more plausible direction was developed by his pupil Aristotle (384–322 BCE). Plato claims virtue is sufficient for happiness in itself and that nothing else can influence happiness. Aristotle's theory of happiness is more nuanced and complex. One common interpretation of his view is that virtue is necessary for happiness, but it is not sufficient by itself to guarantee a happy life. Virtue may be the central component of happiness, but it cannot ensure complete happiness on its own because someone might possess virtue while "undergoing the greatest suffering and misfortune. Nobody would call the life of such a man happy."[13] In other words, virtue is one important component of the happy life, but there are others as well, such as physical health, pleasure, friends, material resources, and so on. Virtue may be the most important component of happiness, but even so, Aristotle warns that "those who assert that a man is happy even on the rack and even when great misfortunes befall him, provided that he is good, are talking nonsense, whether they know it or not."[14]

Aristotle's view of happiness could explain why both Eddard and Cersei are unhappy. Eddard possesses remarkable virtue, but lacks the external goods needed for happiness. A life that ends in misfortune, treachery, shame, and suffering is far from happy. Cersei has the opposite problem. She has all the external goods required for happiness, but lacks the internal stability and character needed for true long-term happiness. She lacks the central and most important component of happiness: virtue.

"When You Play the Game of Thrones, You Win or You Die. There Is No Middle Ground"[15]

There is a final puzzle about happiness in Westeros. Despite the significant number of people who are willing to risk their very lives seeking control of the kingdom, this choice seems foolish or imprudent. Obviously, the power, status, and material advantages gained by having influence in such a kingdom can be useful tools in the pursuit of happiness. Yet—as any reader of the series can see—few of the characters seem genuinely happy, even those who have power. Furthermore, if Cersei is correct that in playing the game of thrones one may only win or die, it seems imprudent for anyone to get involved in the political intrigues of the monarchy. Playing the game of thrones involves risking a total loss of happiness for a potential reward of only limited gain.

One way of analyzing the prudence of major decisions involves comparing the risks of failure, the rewards of success, and the odds of success. A choice is prudent when it offers a positive expected outcome. Consider gambling on a coin toss. There is a 50 percent chance of correctly guessing which side of the coin will come up. If you risked a dollar for a 50 percent chance of winning a mere additional ten cents, that choice would be imprudent, since the risk is disproportionate to the reward. If one were to risk a dollar for a 50 percent chance of winning an additional dollar, it might be acceptable either to take the bet or to refrain from the wager, since the risk and reward are identical with an equal chance of either outcome. Neither choice is obviously prudent or imprudent. If one were to risk a dollar for a 50 percent chance of winning one hundred dollars, it would be wise to take the bet, since the potential reward far outweighs the risk. It would even be prudent to place the wager if there was only a 10 percent chance of winning a hundred dollars from a one-dollar bet since the reward is so disproportionate to the risk.

The most famous philosophical argument based on such prudential concerns is Pascal's Wager. A mathematician, scientist, philosopher, and devoted Christian, Blaise Pascal (1623–1662) argued that embracing faith in God offers a potential reward of infinite happiness for a negligible risk. He compares choosing belief in God to making a wise bet on a coin toss with a very favorable payoff structure. He argues, "Let us weigh up the gain and the loss by calling heads that God exists. Let us assess the two cases: if you win, you win everything; if you lose you lose nothing. Wager that he exists then, without hesitation!"[16] Pascal allows that the claims of faith may not be certain. He argues, however, that the potential rewards from success if faith in God turns out to be correct are the infinitely desirable gain of eternal happiness, while there is only a trivial negative consequence if one has faith incorrectly. Therefore, the potential rewards of success are radically disproportionate to the risk of failure. Even if there were only a relatively small chance of faith being correct, it seems to be prudent to believe, since the infinite potential gains from faith are vastly disproportionate to any negative consequences if one is wrong.

Playing the game of thrones has the opposite payoff structure, however. By playing the game of thrones, one risks the extraordinary negative consequences of the total and complete loss of happiness through torture, public humiliation, and death, for the possible reward of only a limited increase in happiness. Even if one was likely to win at the game of thrones, it would still be foolish to play. Just as it is imprudent to merge onto a busy highway if there is even a 1 percent chance of causing a fatal accident, the potential negative consequences from failure in the game of thrones are so extreme that it is wisest not to get involved. Catelyn Stark seems aware of this risk early in the story as she begs Eddard not to go to King's Landing as King Robert's Hand. Whatever gain or honor there might be in serving as the King's Hand, the risks were simply too great.

Furthermore, the potential reward from winning the game of thrones might not be as desirable as it seems. Robert Baratheon demonstrates that becoming a king can actually undermine your happiness. We can see this truth as he confides to Eddard, "I swear to you, I was never so alive as when I was winning this throne or so dead as now that I've won it."[17] His victorious ascent to the kingship undermined his health by giving gluttony a free hand. It undermined his relationships by surrounding him with insincere opportunistic admirers and treacherous plotters. Winning the throne ultimately results in death as his own wife arranges his fatal "hunting accident." In playing the game of thrones, one risks the possibility of total loss for the possibility of limited gain, but even winning the game of thrones can have an unhappy result. Imagine a coin toss where the stakes are heads you die in failure, tails you wither in victory. What rational person would play such a game? If it is true that in the game of thrones one can only win or die, only a fool would play it.

What *Game of Thrones* Teaches Us about Happiness

One reason readers find George R. R. Martin's novels so engaging is that they provide interesting and deep characters while avoiding clichés about happiness. The characters are complex individuals driven by plausible motivations and desires. Neither the virtuous nor the vicious are guaranteed to flourish in his unstable world, and short-term victories do not ensure long-term happiness. The characters of A Song of Ice and Fire are much like us in that they are all imperfect people trying to flourish in the unpredictable world around them. They all have desires, and they all face challenges. Throughout the books we can see the truth of Aristotle's observation that all men desire happiness, though not all men achieve it.

NOTES

1. Plato, *Republic*, trans. G. M. A. Grube (Indianapolis: Hackett, 1992), 354a.

2. George R. R. Martin, *A Game of Thrones* (New York: Bantam Dell, 2005), pp. 513–514.

3. Ibid., p. 662.

4. Plato, *Apology*, appearing in *Plato: Five Dialogues*, 2nd ed., trans. G. M. A. Grube (Indianapolis: Hackett, 2002), 41 c–d.

5. George R. R. Martin, *A Clash of Kings* (New York: Bantam Dell, 2005), p. 70.

6. George R. R. Martin, *A Dance with Dragons* (New York: Bantam Books, 2011), p. 448.

7. Martin, *A Game of Thrones*, p. 460.

8. Plato, *Republic*, 362 b–c.

9. Martin, *A Game of Thrones*, p. 487.

10. Martin, *A Dance with Dragons*, p. 281.

11. Plato, *Republic*, 571c–d.

12. Martin, *A Game of Thrones*, p. 473.

13. Aristotle, *Nicomachean Ethics*, trans. Martin Ostwald (Upper Saddle River, NJ: Prentice Hall, 1999), 1096a.

14. Aristotle, *Nicomachean Ethics*, 1153b.

15. Martin, *A Game of Thrones*, p. 488.

16. Blaise Pascal, *Pensées and Other Writings*, trans. Honor Levi (New York: Oxford Univ. Press, 2008), p. 154. Of course, as with most arguments, there are potential objections to Pascal's Wager. For example, some might object that Pascal couldn't know the truth of the potential outcomes without knowing the truth of the view he is advocating. For a thorough treatment of Pascal's Wager and related arguments, see Jeff Jordan, *Pascal's Wager: Pragmatic Arguments and Belief in God* (New York: Oxford Univ. Press, 2006).

17. Martin, *A Game of Thrones*, pp. 309–310.

THE DEATH OF LORD STARK: THE PERILS OF IDEALISM

David Hahn

"You are an honest and honorable man, Lord Eddard. Ofttimes I forget that. I have met so few of them in my life. . . . When I see what honesty and honor have won you, I understand why."

— Varys, *A Game of Thrones*[1]

"For a man who wishes to act entirely up to his professions of virtue soon meets with what destroys him among so much that is evil."

— Niccolò Machiavelli[2]

When Varys confronts Lord Stark in the dungeons of King's Landing, Ned's fate is sealed. But how did Ned get to this point when he did everything so right? He investigated the murder of the previous Hand with diligence, and he acted with honor in his roles as Hand and Lord of Winterfell. As we'll see, the English philosopher Thomas Hobbes (1588–1679) and the Italian philosopher and politician Niccolò Machiavelli (1469–1527) would likely say that it is not *despite* Ned's honor that he ended up in the dungeons but *because* of it.

"If the Wicked Do Not Fear the King's Justice Then You Have Put the Wrong Man in Office"[3]

The metaphor is rather obvious: the king of the Seven Kingdoms sits upon a throne made of the melted swords of the kings of the realms brought to heel under Aegon the Conqueror. The throne represents both the danger of the position and the monopoly over force that the king possesses. His is the ultimate authority in the kingdom, and the sole possessor of the ability to make war. That power defines the sovereign; and while there are other duties, such as "counting coppers," it is the authority over force that is of prime importance. Philosophically, the reason for this is found in the nature of a state and how it comes to be.

If we were to make Thomas Hobbes a character in A Song of Ice and Fire, he would undoubtedly be a maester.[4] A scholar by trade, he was the tutor to Charles II of England. Like Robert Baratheon, he saw a kingdom ripped apart by civil war, as Charles I waged war against the Parliamentarians led by Oliver Cromwell. This civil war shaped Hobbes's political thought as he witnessed what happens when the rule of law is suspended.

Hobbes believed that all men seek after their own desires. Not that we are all chasing wine and women like King Robert, but the point is rather that, for example, Arya does not get taught the Water Dance unless her instructor gets paid. Likewise Ned isn't taking the promotion to Hand of the King unless he sees something in it for him. The "Dance Master" needs his payment before he will teach; that much is obvious. Ned's case, however, is a little more complicated. While he desires to stay in Winterfell, his sense of honor and duty compel him to do otherwise. It is the fulfillment of honor and duty that Ned receives as his bonus for accepting the position as Hand of the King and relocating to a place where he clearly does not want to be. Hobbes believed that *every* action has an underlying selfish motivation. Even actions that seem altruistic—feeding the peasantry, for instance—are driven by selfish motivations. It may be the sense of satisfaction one gets from helping the less fortunate, or assuaging the guilt of watching them suffer on the King's Road.

As Hobbes sees it, this selfish motivation actually brings about both the state and the institution of justice. Hobbes asks us to imagine the "state of nature," a state without any rule of law or any government whatsoever. The danger to each individual in this state is obvious: people lack security and are at odds with one another. If I want the food the farmer harvests, I can just take it. Of course, he will want to keep it as well, which puts us at war, or as Hobbes explains, "if any two men desire the same thing, which nevertheless they cannot both enjoy, they become enemies; and in their way to their End, endeavour to destroy, or subdue one another."[5]

This war endures as long as the state of nature exists. People will fight one another for more than just food, though. They will fight to gain more valuable things. For example, Viserys Targaryen hopes to gain the Dothraki hordes in order to take the Iron Throne. People will also fight for reasons of defense, to protect what they already have. Just consider the acts of building the great Wall and then keeping constant vigil with the Night's Watch. Lastly, people will fight for reputation. A person (or family) with a solid reputation of being ruthless to enemies can usually forgo having to fight for other reasons. As Tywin Lannister explains to Jaime Lannister regarding the consequences of the kidnapping of Tyrion, "Every day that he remains a prisoner the less our name commands respect. . . . if another house can seize one of our own and hold him with impunity we are no longer a house to be feared" ("You Win or You Die").

In a constant state of war, society cannot develop, and progress grinds to a halt: "there is no place for Industry; because the fruit thereof is uncertain; and consequently no Culture of the Earth," which reduces men's life to one that is "solitary, poore, nasty, brutish, and short."[6] Because of this pathetic and miserable life, the people are willing to lay down their swords and submit to a single authority. They will generate a thing that will "keep them in awe, and tye them by feare of punishment of their Covenants, and observation of these Lawes of Nature set down."[7]

Hobbesian fear and logic led to the unification of the Seven Kingdoms. True, it was not a mutual disdain for war, but rather the threat of annihilation from the dragons of Aegon that motivated the people of Westeros. Still, the ultimate desire to end the war created (literally in this case) the throne of the king. Six of the kingdoms (the North being a special case) laid down their arms and created a leviathan in the person of the king. "Leviathan" is Hobbes's word for the sovereign power, named after a mythical sea monster of great power. The idea is that it is better to submit to the power of the king, the leviathan, than to be subject to the state of nature, a state in which we have a war of all against all.

The king's ability to physically exercise his authority is important because only through that authority can the state's security be guaranteed. The laws established are meaningless unless there is some force to back them. And this illustrates the first of Lord Stark's mistakes. When he confronted Queen Cersei with his knowledge of Joffrey's incestuous origin, he had no power to back up the accusations. It seems that he assumed that Cersei's allegiance to the Kingdom would be enough. This assumption was well founded as long as Robert lived; Cersei wasn't willing to cross him because of the force of Robert. But once it was apparent that Robert was going to die, there was no reason to believe that her allegiance would continue.

Her words of allegiance were supposed to be sufficient. Words, however, derive their strength not "from their own nature (for nothing is more easily broken than a man's word) but from feare of some evill consequence upon the rupture."[8] Cersei demonstrates this and highlights Ned's naiveté when she rips up the will, asking, "Is this meant to be your shield, Lord Stark?" ("You Win or You Die"). Ned's mistake was that he believed he could enforce the King's Justice (or the Regent's Justice, as it were) with words, and that Cersei would surrender to the exile that she calls a "bitter cup to drink from" without the express threat of violence.[9] Of course Ned thought he had the city guard on his side—but we can't blame him for how that turned out.

"The Day Will Come When You Need Them to Respect You, Even Fear You a Little"[10]

If we were to place Niccolò Machiavelli into A Song of Ice and Fire, he would probably be serving as a member of the king's advisory council. During his life, Machiavelli, unlike most political philosophers, actually served in politics. He held the position of secretary to the Ten of Florence, which in modern times would be something analogous to the U.S. secretary of state. Machiavelli also served as ambassador to both the king of France and the pope, and formed the Republic of Florence's first militia. Unlike Hobbes, Machiavelli limited his conclusions to what he observed. There are no thought experiments about the state of nature or anything else in Machiavelli. Like Tyrion Lannister, Machiavelli derived his knowledge from books and firsthand experience.

History has unfairly made Machiavelli's name into an eponym for a cynical view of politics in which the pursuit of power justifies whatever means are used to achieve that power. The unfair portrayal is based on certain conclusions in Machiavelli's famous book The Prince in which he remarks that fear is better than love for a ruler.[11] Machiavelli is not saying that fear is more desirable than love, but rather that it is easier to maintain, and, once lost, it is easier to reestablish. Love, on the other hand, is both more difficult to maintain and almost impossible to force. Therefore, a ruler ought not to worry so much about whether his subjects love him. Rather, he should inspire fear that he will punish them if they break the rules.

Power is not to be sought for its own sake. Rather, power is to be sought for the sake of the state. Indeed, the security of the state is the highest goal for a Machiavellian. While this is often missed, Machiavelli's writing across four major works shows an approach that balances the will of the rulers with the will of the people. In fact, it is only in *The Prince* that he writes in favor of monarchy, while he gives more attention to a republic-style rule in the much longer *Discourses*.[12] In either case, while the security of the Seven Kingdoms can rest upon Machiavelli's ideas, our problem regarding Lord Stark is that he acts, in several instances, specifically as Machiavelli advises not to do.

"Most Men Would Rather Deny a Hard Truth Than Face It"[13]

As Robert's Hand, Lord Stark is charged with running the state's day-to-day affairs. While Robert is off chasing wine and women, Ned has to settle disputes, count coppers, and manage affairs. While the king will have the final say, Ned's decisions are in fact the king's decisions. This presents the major difficulty with Ned Stark: he makes these decisions not as the king, but as Ned Stark, and Ned Stark is an idealist. *Idealism*, briefly, is adherence to a system of ideas or principles that make up the law and serve as a guide to forming a system of justice. Idealism can be based on a philosophy or a religion, but in either case there is a set of core rules that will not be broken. Idealism has its place in politics, as it can direct the formation of laws or give a government a sense of purpose. In the real world, though, political ideals must oftentimes be transgressed out of necessity, especially in cases where the security of the state and its citizens would be put in peril.

For example, nearly all political entities have the law that no person shall kill another or compel another person to do so. It's a rule that is necessary for any society if it wishes to exist. Now, if there's an uprising in one of the realms of a kingdom and the king sends in a troop of knights to quell it, technically he has broken the rule. He has ordered the deaths of those rebelling, but practically speaking, it is necessary, for the security of the state, to break the rule. The hard truth is that sometimes the Hand must get dirty in order to maintain the security of the Seven Kingdoms. Ned, though, is usually unwilling to do this.

Just think of what happens when the news arrives that Daenerys Targaryen has wed the most powerful of the Dothraki Khals, Drogo, and that (even worse) she is pregnant. The situation is dire, as the Targaryens, descended from Aegon the Conqueror, are the true heirs to the throne. If Daenerys were to have a son, the Dothraki hordes could sweep through the Seven Kingdoms and take the Iron Throne. Thus the council recommends Daenerys's assassination.

Ned balks at the advice. It is unimaginable to him that King Robert would consider having a teenage girl killed. Moreover, he reasons that the Dothraki fear the ocean, because their horses cannot drink from it. So they will never cross the "the black water." Robert and the council, not willing to rely on this reasoning, have already decided that Daenerys must die. Varys explains to Lord Stark, "I understand your qualms, Lord Eddard, truly I do. It gave me no joy to bring this news to council. It is a terrible thing we contemplate, a *vile* thing. Yet we who presume to rule must do vile things for the good of the realm however much it pains us."[14]

Machiavelli would tell Ned that "a blunder ought never to be perpetrated to avoid war, because it is not to be avoided, but is only deferred to your disadvantage."[15] Ned's second objection, the one of practicality, can't be relied upon. It requires that the Dothraki never change their customs, or that their desire for glory will never overcome their fear of the sea. Although the king could command a strengthening of naval defenses and begin an earnest preparation for a possible war, this would severely tax an already bankrupt kingdom. The king and his council are being practical. If war can be avoided with one action, no matter how vile, that action ought to be undertaken. The burden of war on the kingdom, the cost of life, and the security of the state all point to the necessity of assassinating the Dothraki queen.

Concerning Ned's ethical objection, Machiavelli would remark that "it is necessary for a prince wishing to hold his own to know how to do wrong, and to make use of it or not according to necessity."[16] Ned isn't stupid; he just doesn't see the necessity of the action. The threat is years down the line, but a strong kingdom does not make decisions with the king's head on the chopping block. A weak government, on the other hand, is one in which "all choices they make, they are forced to make: and if they should happen to do the right thing, it is force, not their own good sense that makes them do it."[17]

Ned's idealism shapes his worldview. He doesn't see Daenerys as the queen of a ruthless and warlike people; he sees her as a teenage girl. While she is that, she is not just that. She's the queen of an army that could take the Seven Kingdoms. Thus, Ned's idealism in this case is incredibly dangerous to the security of the realm.

Threats to the Realm

"Who do you truly serve?"
"The realm, my lord, someone must."

—Lord Stark and Varys ("The Pointy End")

The Dothraki are an external and long-term threat to the kingdom. But there is also an immediate internal threat in the form of a conspiracy by the Lannister family to take the throne. In order to achieve their goal, the family has already done a number of things. The first is that they have wedded Cersei to King Robert. While this on its own represents nothing, Cersei's contempt for Robert certainly poisons the well.[18] The second thing is that Jaime Lannister, the Kingslayer, is the chief of the Kingsguard in charge of his security. These first two were rewards for the Lannisters' assistance in rising up against the Mad King, and Jaime's assassination of him. The third is a matter of policy, as the king likes to party and has put the entire kingdom into the debt of one family. This danger, while not as obvious as an opposing army, places undue power into the hands of a family with questionable loyalty. All three together are not necessarily dangerous, but the evidence of the Lannisters' disloyalty is quite striking.

When Ned entered the throne room after the end of the civil war, he found Jaime sitting on the Iron Throne. Thus, the Lannisters' motives should be obvious. Machiavelli warns all princes (and kings) that "they can never live secure in their principality so long as those live who have been despoiled of it."[19] While it's not exactly clear that the Lannister family has been robbed of the throne, they clearly think they deserve it. Furthermore, it's explicitly clear that the Targaryens have been robbed of it. The Seven Kingdoms thus face two threats: the external threat of the Dothraki-Targaryen alliance, and the internal threat of the Lannister conspiracy.

Ned's adherence to his virtue is admirable, but it is a hindrance in his role as Hand of the King. Littlefinger makes this explicit. When he is called to advise Eddard on what to do with Cersei and the Lannisters, he says, "You wear your honor like a suit of armor, Stark. You think it keeps you safe, but all it does is weigh you down and make it hard for you to move."[20] Littlefinger knows what needs to be done. So does Stark, but "it's not honorable, so the words stick in your throat."[21] Lord Stark can't ask Littlefinger to help him overthrow the Lannister family; he also can't abide anyone but Stannis Baratheon as king, even though Renly is the better choice and Stannis's ascent will mean war with the Lannisters. Stannis is the true heir, being the next of kin to Robert. It's a poor choice, though, and civil war follows.

"The Madness of Mercy"[22]

What should Ned have done? "For when the safety of one's country wholly depends on the decision to be taken, no attention should be paid either to justice or injustice, kindness or cruelty, or to its being praiseworthy or ignominious," advises Machiavelli.[23] For the security of the state, Ned had a couple of options, both of which were presented to him by Littlefinger. The first option would be to keep quiet and serve the kingdom as regent until Joffrey comes of age. This course of action would preserve the unity of the state. It could also give Joffrey some positive guidance, maybe tempering that sociopathic side that we see evident in the few brief glimpses we have of him on the throne. Ned would be constrained, though, as the queen would undoubtedly not let him run the kingdom without her say-so.

The second option is the more treasonous route, but, as Littlefinger says, "only if we lose."[24] They could promote Renly to the throne while at the same time dealing with the Lannister family. According to Machiavelli, Ned would have three options for dealing with them: "either kill them as the [Roman] consuls did; or expel them from the city; or to force them to make peace with one another. Of these three methods the last is the most hurtful, least reliable, and the most futile."[25] The last method must be ruled out, as Machiavelli says, especially here, because Cersei isn't one to keep her word. So the only real options are to either exile or execute them. While both will guarantee that they are out of the kingdom, the first would only be temporary; the Lannisters are too rich and too powerful not to attempt a return. In order to effectively get rid of the Lannisters they all must go, everyone from Jaime to Joffrey to Tywin. Their property must be confiscated, along with any other assets.

The real difficulty in this course is how to promote Renly without having Stannis raise his sword. The danger of Stannis is that he has not forgotten the old enemies of his family that Robert had forgiven in exchange for oaths of fealty. Would the people care? Probably not; as Jorah comments, "It is no matter to them if the high lords play their game of thrones, so long as they are left in peace."[26] The people desire justice and peace, which they so rarely get. If a war could be prevented with one stroke, is it not the more virtuous decision to make that stroke despite the apparent injustice of the decision?

It would be unjust to promote Renly to the throne, and it would be cruel to have the Lannisters killed or imprisoned. But either would have prevented the state from falling into civil war, while also preserving Stark's life. Ultimately, Lord Eddard Stark of Winterfell died not *for* honor, but *because of* honor. His unwillingness to do what was necessary to preserve the Seven Kingdoms not only cost him his life, but plunged the entire nation into civil war.[27]

NOTES

1. George R. R. Martin, *A Game of Thrones* (New York: Bantam Dell, 2005), p. 634.

2. Niccolò Machiavelli, *The Prince*, trans. W. K. Marriott (New York: Everyman's Library, 1992).

3. Martin, *A Game of Thrones*, p. 146.

4. For more on this idea, see Greg Littmann, "Maester Hobbes Goes to King's Landing," in this volume.

5. Thomas Hobbes, *Leviathan*; Project Gutenberg e-book, p. 88, released May 1, 2002 (ePub edition), retrieved from www.gutenberg.org/ebooks/3207 (I have preserved the antiquated spelling from the original).

6. Hobbes, *Leviathan*, p. 89.

7. Ibid., p.114.

8. Ibid., pp. 93, 99.

9. Martin, *A Game of Thrones*, p. 488.

10. Ibid., p. 600.

11. Machiavelli, *The Prince*, chap. 17.

12. Niccolò Machiavelli, *The Discourses*, trans. Leslie J. Walker (Penguin Classics, 1983).

13. Martin, *A Game of Thrones*, p. 126.

14. Ibid., p. 352.

15. Machiavelli, *The Prince*, p. 15.

16. Ibid., p. 70.

17. Machiavelli, *The Discourses*, p. 206.

18. Her contempt is not exactly undeserved either; Robert's continued infatuation with Ned's deceased sister is what Cersei points to as the turning point in their relationship.

19. Machiavelli, *The Discourses*, book 3, chap. 4.

20. Martin, *A Game of Thrones*, pp. 513–514.

21. Ibid., p. 514.

22. Ibid., p. 634.

23. Machiavelli, *The Discourses*, book 3, chap. 41.

24. Martin, *A Game of Thrones*, p. 512.

25. Machiavelli, *The Discourses*, book 3, chap. 27.

26. Martin, *A Game of Thrones*, p. 233.

27. Special thanks to Laura Hahn and Adam Lall for helping out with some of the plot details.

LORD EDDARD STARK, QUEEN CERSEI LANNISTER: MORAL JUDGMENTS FROM DIFFERENT PERSPECTIVES

Albert J. J. Anglberger and Alexander Hieke

"Have you no shred of honor?"[1] That is how Eddard Stark replies to Littlefinger's suggestion that the Lord of Winterfell should support Prince Joffrey's claim to the throne. Eddard knows Joffrey is not King Robert Baratheon's rightful heir, and hence honor dictates that he not heed Littlefinger's recommendations. Unlike Lord Stark, who possesses firmly established virtues, Cersei Lannister, the king's wife, cares little about virtues. She cares only about what benefits her children and herself. Just consider her reaction when Arya's wolf, Nymeria, bit the queen's son, Joffrey: "'The girl is as wild as that filthy animal of hers,' Cersei said. 'Robert, I want her punished.' . . . The queen was furious. 'Joff will carry those scars for the rest of his life.'"[2] It does not matter to the queen whether Arya tells the truth about what happened when her direwolf attacked Prince Joffrey—harm has been done to one of Cersei's offspring, and *someone* has to be held responsible. *Someone, anyone,* has to be punished. When Eddard's captain of the household guard reports that Nymeria can't be found, Cersei demands that Sansa's direwolf, Lady, be killed instead.

There is a striking difference between the morals guiding Eddard's actions and the motivations underlying Cersei's actions. Whereas Eddard is virtuous, Cersei is egoistic. It's not surprising, then, that readers consider Eddard to be the "good guy" and Cersei to be his "evil antagonist."

"You Never Could Lie for Love nor Honor, Ned Stark"[3]

Robert Baratheon knows his old friend and comrade well. Eddard Stark is an honest man; he even tells the truth without being asked to do so. Eddard reveals to Cersei that he has discovered the truth about Joffrey's lineage—even though the queen is one of Lord Stark's fiercest opponents and the information provides her with a significant strategic advantage. The virtue of charity urges Eddard to tell Cersei what he knows so that she and her children can get out of harm's way. When Varys asks: "What strange fit of madness led you to tell the queen that you had learned the truth of Joffrey's birth?" Eddard replies: "The madness of mercy."[4] Obviously, honesty and charity are among the virtues Lord Stark possesses, and hence he acts mercifully.

According to virtue ethics, a truly virtuous person is a truly good person.[5] The kind of character trait that counts as a virtue is not easily determined, but virtues are often thought of as dispositions. As a disposition, a virtue not only influences its possessor's actions but also his "emotions . . . choices, values, desires, perceptions, attitudes, interests, expectations and sensibilities."[6] An honest person, for example, not only performs honest actions, but also considers nothing but honest actions as possible options. Being virtuous is usually not easy. Virtues—like many other character traits—are acquired through training, and there may be setbacks in training.

Virtue ethics is primarily concerned with an agent's good *character* rather than with the goodness of his actions. Nonetheless, by applying the principle "Good actions are those a virtuous person would do," virtue ethics may also offer an answer as to what ought to be done.[7] For example, Eddard, possessing the virtues of honesty and charity, performs morally good actions both when he reveals to Cersei that he knows about Joffrey's lineage, and when he subsequently warns her about what might happen if the truth becomes public. In addition, Eddard also is courageous, just, and honorable, which makes him a pretty virtuous guy.

The Madness of Mercy—The Price of Honesty

Being virtuous and acting accordingly may come at a price. Eddard's frankness results in his imprisonment. His honesty makes him blind to other people's deceit. Thus it is Lord Stark himself who is wrongly accused of treason. Not only is he arrested, but as we know, an even worse fate awaits him.

Virtues can conflict with one another. For example, honesty can conflict with love. When Varys visits Eddard in the dungeon, he tries to persuade him to admit his alleged treason: "Give me your word that you'll tell the queen what she wants to hear when she comes calling." Eddard replies: "If I did, my word would be as hollow as an empty suit of armor. My life is not so precious to me as that." Varys reminds him: "And your daughter's life, my lord? How precious is that? . . . The next visitor . . . could bring you Sansa's head. The choice, my dear lord Hand, is *entirely* yours."[8] This situation involves a conflict: on the one hand, Eddard is bound by honesty and cannot bend the knee to Joffrey and accept him as king; on the other hand, he loves his daughters dearly and must not forsake them.

As Aristotle said, we have to rely on *phronesis* (*practical wisdom*) in situations like these. *Phronesis* "enables an agent to recognize some features of a situation as more important than others."[9] That is exactly what Eddard does: he regards the well-being of his daughters as more important, and so here, love triumphs over honesty. He eventually bends the knee to Joffrey and confesses his "treason" so his daughters can be safe. Robert seems to be wrong: Eddard can lie after all—he can lie for love.

Cersei loves her children, too. So does that make her virtuous as well? No. According to virtue ethics, if a character trait is lived out too extremely, it is no longer a virtue. A person can, in a sense, be too honest, too brave, and even too caring. If someone is too honest, she may likely hurt someone's feelings; if a person is too brave, he will be foolhardy; if someone is too caring, she might be overprotective and overlook the well-being of third parties. The ultimate goal of a virtuous life is a state called *eudaimonia*, which means something like "flourishing," "happiness," or "well-being." *Eudaimonia* cannot be achieved accidentally, but only through living a virtuous life. Being virtuous means administering the right dose of virtue in every situation, thus achieving what Aristotle termed the *golden mean*.

Cersei's love for herself and her children is unbalanced. Thus she forgets about other virtues, like honesty, altogether. Eddard, on the other hand, balances virtues such as honesty and sensitivity. For example, when Robert reprimands his squires for not being able to dress Robert in his armor, Eddard tells the king: "The boys are not at fault. . . . You're too fat for your armor, Robert."[10] This comment leads to Eddard and Robert sharing a good laugh and the king no longer being angry at his squires. Moreover, it shows how Eddard is capable of hitting the mark when it comes to applying different (competing) virtues.

Eddard also tries to find the golden mean when confessing his alleged treason, which eventually leads to his execution. The ultimate result seems to be a good reason for calling his decision *wrong*. But, quite to the contrary, it shows even more how virtuous Eddard Stark is. He does not even consider that someone could be as ruthless and cruel as Joffrey in having him beheaded.

"When You Play the Game of Thrones, You Win or You Die": The Rewards of Egoism[11]

Cersei didn't want Eddard to be executed. No, she did not virtuously feel mercy. Rather, she understood the grave consequences that killing Lord Stark could have. Cersei's decisions are always based on the well-being of her children and herself. She knows that Lord Stark's death will result in the Starks being the Lannisters' fiercest enemy. Moreover, while he is alive and prisoner, Stark can be used to bargain for peace. Cersei seems to base her choices on the likely outcomes of her actions, which makes her a *consequentialist*.[12] There are different versions of consequentialism, but the most common is *utilitarianism*, which holds that *all* affected subjects should be taken into account, and the moral status of an action is thereby determined by its positive and negative effects on all of them. Actions are assessed by the amount of happiness or harm caused to all those involved. Cersei clearly is no utilitarian. She certainly does *not* take into account *all subjects involved*. It may well be that for her, only *four* subjects are ultimately relevant: herself, and her children Joffrey, Tommen, and Myrcella. (Though Cersei needs Jaime for comfort and protection, we think that in the end she considers him to be just another means to her ends.) She is therefore a "minimally extended" *egoistic* consequentialist, and a very successful one at that. Cersei is among those who prevail in the first novel. Joffrey is king, her children are safe, her opponent Lord Stark is dead, and the fatal secret of her brother's having fathered her offspring remains undisclosed. The ruthlessness of her egoistic line of action seems to be paying off, at least so far.

Cersei's success does not mean that this kind of egoism is morally acceptable, however. If our goal is a functional society where people can live together peacefully, then a universal application of egoistic consequentialism should be avoided. Imagine a Westeros where all Seven Kingdoms are ruled by people like Cersei!

It's not just the egoistic variant of consequentialism that leads to problems; utilitarianism has to cope with severe difficulties as well. Since, according to utilitarianism, actions are evaluated only according to the amount of overall good they produce for society, the rights of individuals can easily be neglected. If, for example, the lords of the cities of Slaver's Bay keep a small number of slaves under relatively good conditions, then the overall good of their society may be increased—even though this would infringe upon fundamental rights of the individual slaves. From an enlightened and intuitive point of view, situations like these have to be avoided.

Virtue ethics might seem like a viable solution, but it runs into some problems of its own. Because it is primarily concerned with an agent's *character*, virtue ethics does not provide specific rules of conduct in many cases. Consequentialism focuses on *acts* (rather than agents) and therefore usually offers such rules. Since *the* central question of moral philosophy traditionally is "What ought to be done?" this is a pretty serious defect of virtue ethics. Moreover, it is not clear which character traits are to be considered virtues. Although Aristotle and others would disagree, some philosophers would argue that virtues are culture-dependent.[13] At any rate, there is certainly disagreement among cultures as to what counts as a virtue. Charity, for example, is not considered to be a virtue in Dothraki society, whereas it is clearly considered a virtue in Winterfell.

"And Pray That He Is the Man I Think He Is"[14]

George R. R. Martin's narrative mode in the novels is one reason why we tend to judge Eddard more favorably than we do Cersei. He chose a special version of the third-person perspective for his A Song of Ice and Fire series. In each chapter, a different point-of-view character takes the lead. Martin describes the events from a third-person point of view, but he applies the following constraints: (1) he restricts the description of all events to what the point-of-view character (POV character) can perceive, including the character's own actions and behavior; (2) in many cases he describes the mental states of the POV character in the current situation from a third-person point of view; (3) and sometimes he even lets us know parts of the "inner world" of the POV character by quoting his or her thoughts in the first-person point of view (indicated by italics in the books).

Eddard Stark is one of these POV characters, thus (1), (2), and (3) apply to him. Recall the scene where Eddard sits at the king's deathbed and lays down Robert's last will:

> "Robert . . . *Joffrey is not your son* [(3)]," he wanted to say, but the words would not come [(2)]. The agony was written too plainly across Robert's face [(1)]; he could not hurt him more [(2)]. So Ned bent his head and wrote, but where the king had said "my son Joffrey," he scrawled "my heir" instead [(1)]. The deceit made him feel soiled [(2)]. *The lies we tell for love*, he thought. *May the gods forgive me* [(3)].[15]

These particular features of Martin's narrative mode grant us special access to the POV characters: we know their thoughts, feelings, intentions, and motives; we know their beliefs and how they reason. (Of course, introspection does not guarantee certainty: people sometimes misjudge themselves.) Since we know Eddard Stark as a POV character, it is comparatively easy to say what kind of a man he is. In particular, we know the moral principles he accepts and obeys, what his character traits are, and what his particular motives in certain situations are. Consider the previous quotation, which also shows Eddard Stark's virtuous character: he does not have the heart to tell his king and friend the painful truth about Joffrey, but he has qualms about deceiving Robert.

If we restrict our observations to the first novel, *A Game of Thrones*, Cersei is presented in a way quite different from Eddard: we know her only through other POV characters' chapters. Sometimes she is characterized in a more or less neutral or intersubjective way, as perceived by the POV character, or described by the POV character's thoughts, especially by the results of their reasoning. She is also sometimes presented through reports by other characters. This may pose various problems for well-founded judgments. Consider the following quotes:

> "The Lannister woman is our queen, and her pride is said to grow with every passing year."[16] (Catelyn to Eddard)
>
> "My sweet sister Cersei lusts for power with every waking breath."[17] (Tyrion to Catelyn)
>
> "She *forbade* him to fight, in front of his brother, his knights, and half the court. Tell me truly, do you know any surer way to force King Robert into the melee?"[18] (Varys to Eddard, insinuating that Cersei might have already planned the king's death on an earlier occasion.)
>
> "Cersei had the babes killed, and sold the mother to a passing slaver. Too much an affront to Lannister pride, that close to home."[19] (Littlefinger to Eddard)

In these statements, two character traits are attributed to Cersei by Catelyn and Tyrion: pride and lust for power, respectively. Moreover, she is said to have plotted against her husband and arranged for the death of infants. Of course, we know as readers that it is risky to trust Varys and Littlefinger in their statements about Cersei, because they have strong interests of their own and thus want Eddard to believe certain "facts." Like Eddard, we readers get a picture of Cersei shaped by various reports. We judge Cersei not only on the basis of her words and actions but also, and sometimes even primarily or exclusively, on the basis of accounts by third parties. For example, we learn from a third-party report that Cersei might have commissioned Jon Arryn's death. In reading *A Storm of Swords*, however, we discover that this is not true.[20] So, obviously some important reports about her motives and actions are unreliable, which makes a well-justified moral judgment very difficult.

"How Are You Any Different from Robert, or Me, or Jaime?"[21]

Indeed, the *most reliable* ways of confirming our moral judgments about other people involve observing their actions directly, and being informed by trustworthy third-party agents. This may be another problem for the applicability of virtue ethics, as we may not be able to attribute virtues to people by simply observing the actions they perform. Not even a sequence of morally good actions enables us to infer that the agent possesses a certain virtue. For example, if a merchant acts honestly all the time just because this is the most profitable strategy, he still would not have the virtue of honesty. Virtuous people do good actions, but sometimes nonvirtuous people do as well. However, if someone performs morally bad actions most of the time, that would provide a good reason to assume that she is not a virtuous person.

If it is true that Cersei tends to get rid of people "inconvenient" to her plans by having them killed, then she is obviously not a virtuous person. But we always have to take a closer look at the information on which we base our moral judgments. If the informants are not that trustworthy, or if the chain of communication is very long, then the reliability of information may suffer, and, therefore, our judgments might not be well confirmed. Both factors may influence our moral judgments of Cersei. For reasons already mentioned, many informants may either tell outright lies or they may present only part of the truth. Further, the chain of communication may be very long, involving mere speculations from people with "strong interests." Imagine, for example, one of Varys's "little birds" conveying some vital information to his master. Neither is aware that one of Littlefinger's eavesdroppers is spying on them and in turn is reporting all this to Lord Baelish—who eventually reveals a "digested" version of the message to Lord Stark. Obviously, the message Stark receives may not be reliable.

Reasoning may be unreliable, too, as we are not logically infallible. That means we sometimes draw false conclusions by faulty reasoning—conclusions that are not backed up by our previous (maybe even true) assumptions. Additionally, our reasoning may involve false assumptions leading to false conclusions. We find instances of both types of unreliable reasoning in *A Game of Thrones*. Eddard draws the false conclusion that he will survive by confessing his alleged treason. He clearly underestimated Joffrey's ruthlessness and independence. When Petyr Baelish tells Catelyn Stark that it is Tyrion Lannister's dagger that was used in the attempted murder of her son Bran (false assumption), she concludes that it was Tyrion who hired the assassin. This leads to Catelyn arresting Tyrion and bringing him to the Eyrie (thus initiating a whole series of important events).

Does all this mean that Cersei is a *good* person after all? Well, no! It just means that a moral judgment about Cersei is not as easily established as it looks at first sight. Eddard, being a POV character, is easily judged as being the good and virtuous person who is, of course, not perfect, but tries to be. George R. R. Martin provides the information needed for a well-justified moral judgment about Eddard's character. In the case of Cersei, we lack this kind of information, just as we do in our moral judgments in real life.

Even though intentions are highly relevant to our moral (as well as legal) judgments, we still have to base our judgments on observations and reports. The attributions of beliefs and intentions are educated guesses, based on our personal experience with the agents and on third-party accounts about them.

Martin's novels keep us guessing about the real intentions of Cersei, though they give us direct access to the intentions of POV characters like Eddard. In real life, though, we have direct access to the intentions of only one person, ourselves. Everyone else's intentions involve guesswork based on observations and reports.[22] So the characters in A Song of Ice and Fire can be puzzling, but characters in real life can be even more puzzling.

NOTES

1. George R. R. Martin, *A Game of Thrones* (New York: Bantam Dell, 2005), p. 511. This novel was originally published in 1996.

2. Ibid., p. 156.

3. Ibid., p. 310.

4. Ibid., p. 634.

5. For this thesis, see Rosalind Hurtshouse, "Virtue Ethics," in *Stanford Encyclopedia of Philosophy*, ed. Edward N. Zalta, plato.stanford.edu/archives/win2010/entries/ethics-virtue/; Philippa Foot, *Virtues and Vices and Other Essays in Moral Philosophy* (Oxford: Blackwell Publishing, 1978). In Western philosophy, virtue ethics goes all the way back to Aristotle (384–322 BCE). His *Nicomachean Ethics* (Aristotle, *The Nicomachean Ethics* [Oxford: Oxford Univ. Press, 1998]) is widely considered to have laid the foundations of this field. In the aftermath of the Age of Enlightenment, virtue ethics was largely neglected. It was only in the 1950s that it had its big comeback, with a paper by G. E. M. Anscombe, "Modern Moral Philosophy," in *Philosophy* 33 (1958), pp. 1–19. In the last fifty-odd years, a few classic papers have been published; some of them have been reprinted in Roger Crisp and Michael Slote, eds., *Virtue Ethics* (Oxford: Oxford Univ. Press, 1997); Stephen Darwall, ed., *Virtue Ethics* (Oxford: Blackwell Publishing, 2003).

6. Hurtshouse, "Virtue Ethics," section 2.

7. For a more rigorous account of this principle, see Rosalind Hurtshouse, "Virtue Theory and Abortion," in *Philosophy and Public Affairs* 20 (1991), pp. 223–246. For some problems with this thesis, see Robert B. Louden, "On Some Vices of Virtue Ethics," in *American Philosophical Quarterly* 21 (1984), pp. 227–236.

8. Martin, *A Game of Thrones*, pp. 636–637.

9. Hurtshouse, "Virtue Ethics," section 2.

10. Martin, *A Game of Thrones*, p. 307.

11. Ibid., p. 488.

12. Among the most prominent proponents of consequentialism (in its most common form, utilitarianism) are Jeremy Bentham (1748–1832) and John Stuart Mill (1806–1873). See, for example, Jeremy Bentham, *Introduction to the Principles of Morals and Legislation* (Mineola, NY: Dover Publications, 2009) (originally published in 1789); John Stuart Mill, *Utilitarianism* (New York: Oxford Univ. Press, 1998) (originally published in 1861). For further reading, see Stephen Darwall, ed., *Consequentialism* (Oxford: Blackwell Publishing, 2003).

13. For the culture dependency of virtues, see Martha Nussbaum, "Non-relative Virtues: An Aristotelian Approach," in *Midwest Studies in Philosophy Vol. 13, Ethical Theory: Character and Virtue*, Peter A. French, Theodore Uehling, Jr., and Howard Wettstein, eds. (Notre Dame, IN: Univ. of Notre Dame Press, 1988), pp. 32–53.

14. Martin, *A Game of Thrones*, p. 202.

15. Ibid., pp. 504–505.

16. Ibid., p. 27.

17. Ibid., p. 368.

18. Ibid., p. 320.

19. Ibid., p. 381.

20. George R. R. Martin, *A Storm of Swords* (New York: Bantam Dell, 2005). This novel was originally published in 2000.

21. Martin, *A Game of Thrones*, p. 487.

22. This part of our chapter has to do with an old problem in philosophy, the problem of *evidence*. See Thomas Kelly, "Evidence," in *Stanford Encyclopedia of Philosophy*, ed. Edward N. Zalta, plato.stanford.edu/archives/fall2008/entries/evidence/, for further reading and relevant references.

IT WOULD BE A MERCY: CHOOSING LIFE OR DEATH IN WESTEROS AND BEYOND THE NARROW SEA

Matthew Tedesco

On each side of the Narrow Sea, a character pivotal to events in *A Game of Thrones* faces a medical crisis. At Winterfell, young Bran Stark is climbing the walls of the great castle when he peers through a high window and witnesses the Lannister twins Jaime and Cersei engaged in a secret act of incest. To protect this secret, Jaime shoves Bran from the window, leaving Bran crippled, comatose, and fighting for his life. Later in the same book, on the vast grasslands of the Dothraki Sea, the mighty and undefeated Khal Drogo takes a wound in battle that initially seems inconsequential, but soon festers. Drogo rapidly weakens and falls from his horse. Like Bran Stark, his life sits precariously on the edge of an arakh. Befitting genuine medical crises, both Bran and Drogo are placed in the care of people with expertise in treating the injured and sick.

Bran is treated by Maester Luwin, a Citadel-trained learned man long in the service of House Stark. In contrast, Drogo's wife Daenerys Targaryen seeks out the more controversial dark magic of the maegi Mirri Maz Duur in order to save her beloved sun and stars.

The best works of fantasy use places, persons, and powers sprung from the imagination in order to connect with the parts of us and our lives that are most real. These two medical crises in *A Game of Thrones* are gripping and philosophically interesting, not for the medical details themselves, but rather for the hard moral issues that surround the decisions made both during and after the treatment of both Bran and Drogo. These issues are of special interest to philosophers working in biomedical ethics—the area of philosophy that concerns moral issues and problems surrounding biological research, medical research, and the practice of medicine. These are no esoteric, armchair exercises. Rather, they are the issues we face when we are forced to make the most profound and difficult choices for ourselves, our families, and our loved ones. At the core of biomedical ethics are matters of life and death, of mortality and personhood, of the choices we may make, and the choices we must not. The medical crises of Bran and Drogo are windows into some of these important philosophical matters.

"Give Me a Good Clean Death"[1]

"It would be a mercy."[2]

—Jaime

Jaime Lannister utters these words to his brother Tyrion as Bran lies in his coma. Ever the knight and most at home with a sword in his hands, Jaime opines that it would be better to end the boy's life cleanly and quickly than allow him to go on living as a "cripple" and a "grotesque." As readers, we are privy to Jaime's private motives: his crime against Bran has not been discovered, nor has his incestuous relationship with his sister that has spawned three children, including Prince Joffrey. Presumably Jaime would prefer to keep it that way, so Bran's death would be a very convenient thing.

We as readers may be outraged by more than Jaime's private agenda here. Even if someone else, someone entirely disinterested in Bran's life or death, had made the comment, we would still reject the suggestion that a quick death for Bran would be a mercy. Should Bran awaken, he will have a serious handicap, as he will no longer have the use of his legs. But this would not prohibit Bran from leading a good life, filled with interesting pursuits and meaningful relationships, even if some of those pursuits (like his love of climbing) have now been foreclosed. In light of this, we as readers believe it would certainly *not* be a mercy to end Bran's life. On the contrary, it would be a seriously immoral thing to do to him.

Even if he is wrong (and with sinister motives to boot) regarding Bran, Jaime's suggestion is worth considering more generally. It is certainly true that the concept of mercy—understood as acting with compassion and care for someone else's well-being—is important when we are faced with life-and-death decisions, and in the end it may be morally decisive. On the grounds of appealing to mercy, there certainly seem to be dire medical decisions where Jaime's reasoning here—the choice of death—is morally defensible. In the late stages of a terminal illness, with death certain and every conscious moment filled with unmanageable pain, many choose to end whatever course of treatment is prolonging life in order to hasten death. We choose this course of action for ourselves, we choose it for our loved ones, and in the most tragic of situations, we choose it on behalf of our newborn children when their afflictions are hopeless. In all of these cases, our concern is for the well-being of the seriously ill person, and it is this concern for well-being that is at the heart of mercy.

Jaime Lannister's notion of mercy, however, is a bit different. When Jaime suggests that Bran's father "end his torment," and when he speaks of a preference for "a good clean death" over life as a cripple, he is probably not imagining Lord Eddard Stark asking Maester Luwin to stop caring for Bran so that his son may die gradually. Jaime is instead recommending something much quicker—a decisive stroke of Valyrian steel, delivered by House Stark's greatsword Ice, to bring an immediate end to Bran's life. This distinction among different acts of mercy maps closely onto an important conceptual distinction in biomedical ethics: the distinction between passive and active euthanasia. When needed life-sustaining treatment is withdrawn from a terminally ill patient, this constitutes passive euthanasia. In virtually every case we can imagine, passive euthanasia is a slower act of mercy than actively providing the patient with "a good clean death" by taking some definite action to end the patient's life (such as, for example, administering a lethal dose of a drug). When I remove some needed life-sustaining intervention from you—such as your ventilator or feeding tube—your death will occur only when you suffocate or starve to death. From the standpoint of mercy, once the decision has been made that death is preferable to life, avoiding the suffering that accompanies a slow, painful death certainly seems like the merciful thing to do. In this respect, perhaps we ought to follow Jaime's lead, and allow terminally ill patients to choose active euthanasia over passive euthanasia. This is, after all, the choice we make for our pets when they are deathly ill and we seek the most humane, merciful end.

Yet, while passive euthanasia is widely practiced and widely considered to be a morally permissible (and often morally praiseworthy) act, active euthanasia is far more controversial. The American Medical Association has consistently drawn a sharp distinction between the two practices. Its policy statement "Decisions Near the End of Life,"[3] initially adopted in 1991, affirms this distinction, explicitly permitting the withdrawal and withholding of life-sustaining treatment in respecting the autonomous choices of patients, while forbidding both active euthanasia and physician-assisted suicide. This prohibition is sometimes justified on the grounds that there is an important moral distinction between killing and letting die. The idea is that while there can be cases where it is permissible to let someone die, killing is a morally different category.

Many philosophers have challenged this alleged moral distinction between killing and letting die. In his paper "Active and Passive Euthanasia," James Rachels (1941–2003) argues, like Jaime Lannister, that active euthanasia can be a merciful choice, and forbidding active euthanasia while permitting passive euthanasia is endorsing the course of action that causes more suffering once the choice of death has already been made.[4] And to those who recoil at the notion of allowing killing, Rachels argues that killing and letting die are in themselves morally equivalent acts. We fail to see this because killing is so often accompanied by other morally troubling factors (such as bad intentions, or a viciousness of character). But when we hold all of those other factors fixed, we find no moral distinction between killing and letting die; both are actions subject to moral evaluation given the details of the particular circumstances in question. Other contemporary philosophers, such as Dan Brock, have argued that the mistake is found in categorizing withdrawing medical treatment as merely letting die.[5] According to Brock, to kill is to intentionally cause death, however it may occur. Because passive euthanasia is intentional, and because it causes death, it is an act of killing, no more or no less than active euthanasia.

"You Love Your Children, Do You Not?"[6]

Beyond this controversial distinction between active and passive euthanasia, other facts surrounding Bran's medical crisis also highlight important issues for biomedical ethicists.

One complicating feature of Bran's crisis is that he is, as we meet him in the first book, just seven years old. Imagine for a moment that Bran's medical condition were very different: instead of being crippled from a fall, imagine instead that Bran is afflicted with an aggressive metastatic cancer. His death is certain and soon, but some recurring treatment is prolonging his pain-filled life. When an adult is in such a state and chooses to terminate treatment, the moral justification for affirming that wish is respect for the patient's autonomy. Young children, though, are almost certainly not autonomous, or at least are not fully autonomous if we imagine autonomy as something that is attained gradually over time. So if respect for autonomy is paramount in justifying passive euthanasia, but children lack the capacity for autonomy, it might seem like the option of passive euthanasia is foreclosed for children.

This, though, is not the case. On the contrary, the choice of passive euthanasia is sometimes made on behalf of children by their parents. On reflection, this is not very surprising. After all, parents choose for their children in important matters, including medical decisions, all the time. Parents generally are charged with shepherding their children into adulthood, and prior to their children being regarded as autonomous decision makers, parents are responsible for safeguarding the well-being of their children. When children cannot decide for themselves, parents are empowered to decide for them, under the presumption that the decision is made with only the child's well-being in mind. In the tragic cases of deciding on death for their children, however, some of those choices are bound to be controversial. Consider the following two real-world cases of parents choosing death for their children:

1. In 1963 at Johns Hopkins Hospital in Maryland, a child is born prematurely, with both Down's Syndrome and an intestinal blockage easily corrected by surgery. Upon learning that the child was born with a mental handicap, the parents refused the surgery for the child,

who was then allowed to starve to death over eleven days.[7]

2. In 1980 at Derby City Hospital in England, a child named John Pearson, also born with Down's Syndrome, is also rejected by the parents because of this handicap and is therefore prescribed by the presiding doctor, Leonard Arthur, "nursing care only"— no nourishment, but water and a regular narcotic. John died three days later of bronchopneumonia. Dr. Arthur is charged with the baby's murder but found not guilty.[8]

It's not surprising that many have been upset by these cases. In all three cases—Bran Stark, John Pearson, and the Johns Hopkins case—a child is afflicted with a serious handicap, where the handicap forecloses a range of possibilities in life and makes a range of other actions and choices more difficult. But unlike, for example, the most severe forms of spina bifida, the handicaps in question are not so brutal and all-encompassing that they make life not worth living. There are handicaps that are so severe that they make any sort of decent life simply impossible; crippled legs and Down's Syndrome do not fall into that category.

Yet something else is true about these handicaps, something morally important that makes these kinds of life-and-death decisions far more controversial. In all three cases, the handicap in question places a significant burden on those charged with the care of the child, ordinarily the child's parents. (Bran's situation is a little bit more complicated.) Generally speaking, the act of burdening someone is not morally irrelevant, particularly when the burden is not desired. If I decorate my yard in a way that causes you to regularly have to clear debris from your yard, I have burdened you, and this is a morally important fact. You have a legitimate complaint against me, and if I fail to help relieve that burden, I have wronged you. Bran now lacks the use of his legs, and this imposes a burden on others, a burden vividly illustrated by the way in which he is borne on Hodor's back in a kind of saddle devised by Maester Luwin. (The fact that a mentally handicapped servant is conscripted in order to be a kind of human beast of burden raises a range of interesting moral questions too!) While children with Down's Syndrome can certainly live a good long life, there is no question that caring for such a child is difficult, and so a burden on the child's parents.

The mere fact that these handicaps impose special burdens is not itself controversial, nor is the general fact that burdens matter morally. What *is* controversial, however, is the question of whether or not this fact of burdensomeness, particularly in the case of newborn children with serious handicaps, can ever legitimately be factored into the life-and-death decisions that parents make regarding their children. Bran has the good fortune of being born into a powerful family, descendants of the Kings of the North prior to the rise of the Targaryens. But we are reminded at various points in A Song of Ice and Fire that the game of thrones played by the powerful is a remote consideration for the average citizens of Westeros, who may live their entire lives without ever setting foot in a great city or laying eyes on royalty. What if Bran had been born into such a family? What if there were no maester to rig a riding device, no simple servant descended from giants for Bran to ride? What if the burden of his ruined legs on his parents was very high? Would the choice of "a good clean death" be morally permissible, even if it would, strictly speaking, *not* be a mercy?

The standard view regarding decisions made by parents on behalf of their children is that the only morally relevant consideration is the welfare of the child; all other considerations, including how burdened the parents may be by the child's condition, must be put aside. But in practice, depending on the details of the particular family situation into which the child is born, the burden may seem a difficult thing to simply disregard. Beginning with Duff and Campbell's "Moral and Ethical

Dilemmas in the Special-Care Nursery" in 1973, some have argued that given the great variability in prognoses, the capacity of families to manage the care of handicapped children, and the availability of social support, we ought to acknowledge the moral importance of burdensomeness and allow it to factor into life-and-death decisions made by parents for their children.[9] Critics of this view worry that there is a kind of slippery slope created by legitimizing this consideration. Once we allow children to be euthanized for being burdens on their parents, it becomes hard to avoid the fact that, in a certain sense, *all* children are burdens, and distinguishing among burdens is a perilous business.

"When Will He Be as He Was?"[10]

Throughout this discussion of the various moral issues surrounding Bran's medical crisis, it has remained the case that his handicap, though serious, does not rise to the level of justifying a mercy killing. As readers, we are outraged by Jaime Lannister's suggestion, and it serves to reinforce the early impression we have of the villainy of the Kingslayer. Later in *A Game of Thrones*, we witness a mercy killing, carried out by Daenerys Stormborn, the soon-to-be the Unburnt, Mother of Dragons, against her husband, Khal Drogo. Yet as readers, this act does not lead us to condemn Dany. If anything, we admire her for making the hard choice, and we accept it as a legitimate (and perhaps the morally best) course of action. Setting her act against the proposed mercy killing of Bran Stark may help us sort out our moral intuitions regarding hard life-and-death decisions, but it will also raise a new set of tricky moral issues for us to confront.

Here's what we know of Khal Drogo's medical crisis: The once-fearsome Khal, whose hair has never been cut because he's undefeated in battle, has taken a wound that has festered. The seriousness of his condition is illustrated in his fall from his horse, because a khal who cannot ride cannot lead. As he edges toward death, his wife, Dany, desperately seeks the help of the maegi Mirri Maz Duur over the warnings of Khal Drogo's bloodriders. The maegi saves Drogo, but her dark magic costs Dany the life of her unborn son, Rhaego, the prophesied "Stallion Who Mounts the World." Furthermore, the Drogo that survives Dany's bargain with the maegi is utterly diminished. He is entirely uncommunicative, and his once-piercing stare is now blank. Yet we are left with this provocative observation from Ser Jorah Mormont as Drogo lies vacantly in the sun under buzzing bloodflies: "He seems to like the warmth."[11] Even in his severely compromised state, Drogo can seemingly still experience the pleasure of the sun, and he is in no apparent pain. Given the presumed permanence of Drogo's condition, Dany kills him, smothering him with a cushion.

Most readers are not horrified by Dany's act, or even bothered by it in the slightest. Yet, at first glance, she has just engaged in the premeditated killing of a defenseless human being. This sounds a lot like the worst sort of murder, and we regard murder as among the worst of crimes. So how does Dany remain a hero of our story? Well, Drogo's condition is not unlike a range of serious cases—from traumatic brain injuries to degenerative conditions that radically impair cognitive functioning—where someone is left utterly diminished from the person they once were. So our moral evaluation of Dany's mercy killing is bound up with much more than just this story.

One important feature of Drogo's crisis becomes clear when compared with that of Bran Stark's. When we are outraged by Jaime Lannister's suggestion that Ned Stark kill his son out of mercy, at least a part of our outrage has to do with the life that we expect Bran to be able to lead once he recovers. No, he will never again climb the walls of Winterfell or run across its grounds. But there is still every reason to believe that he will engage in meaningful relationships, pursue sophisticated projects, and generally enjoy the range of goods that characterize lives that are, one might say, distinctively *human*. But this phrase is deceptive, for there are a range of beings who remain in all respects biologically human, yet can never again (and perhaps never could in the first place) enjoy those pursuits in the way that beings like you and I can.

"This Is Not Life"[12]

Consider the distinction between being a *human* and being a *person*. The former is a biological category, describing the biological makeup of a thing; the latter is a moral category, describing what kind of moral standing a thing has. In virtually all cases, those two categories overlap, but not always. We can, for instance, imagine beings who are not biologically human, but who are plausibly enough persons, given their cognitive sophistication and ability to engage in the kinds of projects and life plans that we recognize as distinctive in ourselves. Perhaps the race of giants beyond the Wall or the legendary Children of the Forest fall into this category. And following this reasoning one step further, we might imagine beings who are biologically human but not persons, unable to fulfill the criteria (whatever they are) for personhood. Drogo is drawn to the sun, but so are plants, reptiles, and a range of other nonpersons. If there is nothing more to say about the life he can lead, then perhaps he is not a person any longer, and Dany's mercy killing is not an act of murder. Murder is the premeditated killing of an innocent person, and there is a great moral difference between intentionally killing my neighbor and intentionally killing the mosquito that has landed on my arm. Whatever else is true about my neighbor and the mosquito, one is a person, the other is not, and this distinction is of paramount moral importance.

The question of what it is to be a person has been pursued, perhaps most deeply, in the literature on abortion. Insofar as fetuses are, without question, biologically human, some philosophers have defended the moral permissibility of abortion by attempting to show that fetuses are not persons, and so the killing of a fetus fails to take on the moral importance of the killing of a person. Michael Tooley, for example, identifies self-consciousness—having a conception of oneself as a continuing subject of experiences—as the fundamental criterion of personhood.[13] Similarly, Mary Anne Warren identifies a list of five criteria (consciousness, reasoning, self-motivated activity, the capacity to communicate, and the presence of self-concepts), and argues that some unspecified number of these amounts to personhood. Importantly, whatever entity lacks all five is not a person.[14] Critics of the moral permissibility of abortion have responded with different accounts of our moral specialness. Don Marquis, for example, has argued that the serious wrongness of killing beings like you, me, and fetuses has to do with the way it deprives something of a "Future like ours," a deliberately vague concept meant to broadly capture the range of projects, pursuits, and relationships that make our lives distinctive.[15]

Without presently taking a stand on the moral status of abortion, it is interesting to note that on all of these accounts, both defending and rejecting the permissibility of abortion, Dany's killing of Khal Drogo is certainly *not* the killing of a person, and so, not murder. On the flip side, if Ned Stark had heard and taken Jaime Lannister's advice to kill Bran, that would have been the killing of a person. So this distinction regarding the nature of personhood is helpful in making sense of the different moral responses we have to the prospect of a mercy killing in the medical crises of Khal Drogo and Bran Stark. But where does this reasoning take us?

Contemporary philosopher Peter Singer has famously and controversially argued that the killing of a significantly disabled infant is not the killing of a person. While these infants are clearly biologically human, they lack the qualities that make something count as a person.[16] For Singer, such killings would clearly fail to count as murders, and in many cases, these killings would not be wrong at all. If the disability in question is one that leads to a life of significant pain and discomfort, then as radical as Singer's claim might seem, the case he describes is actually less controversial than Drogo's killing, assuming that the mental states of Drogo and the infant are roughly equivalent. Drogo is in no pain, and while Drogo may not now be a person, he has the possible advantage of having been one once (though whether and how much of an advantage this might be is also controversial).

If we still recoil at Singer's position, what are we to make of our response? Is it, in the end, the residue of an irrational taboo that we ought to bring to light and reject? Or should we look further into the moral features of these cases—questions of quality of life, of burdensomeness, of personhood—and perhaps beyond them, into other morally important considerations? In philosophy, as in these profound and life-altering decisions that we sometimes face, answers are rarely easy. But cases like the medical crises of Bran Stark and Khal Drogo allow us to plumb the depths of these difficult matters.

NOTES

1. George R. R. Martin, *A Game of Thrones* (New York: Bantam Dell, 2005), p. 91.

2. Ibid.

3. Council on Ethical and Judicial Affairs, American Medical Association, "Decisions Near the End of Life," *Journal of the American Medical Association* 276 (1992), pp. 2229–2233.

4. James Rachels, "Active and Passive Euthanasia," *New England Journal of Medicine* 292 (Jan. 1975), pp. 78–80.

5. Dan Brock, "Voluntary Active Euthanasia," *Hastings Center Report* 22 (Mar./Apr. 1992), pp. 10–22.

6. Martin, *A Game of Thrones*, p. 486.

7. J. M. Gustafson, "Mongolism, Parental Desires, and the Right to Life," *Perspectives in Biology and Medicine* 16 (Summer 1973), pp. 529–533.

8. Helga Kuhse, "A Modern Myth: That Letting Die Is Not the Intentional Causation of Death," *Journal of Applied Philosophy* 1, no. 1 (1984), pp. 21–38.

9. Raymond S. Duff and A. G. M. Campbell, "Moral and Ethical Dilemmas in the Special-Care Nursery," *New England Journal of Medicine* 289 (Oct. 1973), pp. 890–894.

10. Martin, *A Game of Thrones*, p. 759.

11. Ibid.

12. Ibid.

13. Michael Tooley, "Abortion and Infanticide," *Philosophy and Public Affairs* 2 (Autumn 1972), pp. 37–65.

14. Mary Anne Warren, "On the Moral and Legal Status of Abortion," *The Monist* 57 (Jan. 1973), pp. 43–61.

15. Don Marquis, "Why Abortion Is Immoral," *Journal of Philosophy* 86 (April 1989), pp. 183–202.

16. Peter Singer, *Practical Ethics*, 2nd ed. (Cambridge: Cambridge Univ. Press, 1993), pp. 175–217.

PART THREE

"WINTER IS COMING"

WARGS, WIGHTS, AND WOLVES THAT ARE DIRE: MIND AND METAPHYSICS, WESTEROS STYLE

Henry Jacoby

Long, elegant hands brushed his cheek, then tightened around his throat. They were gloved in the finest moleskin and sticky with blood, yet the touch was icy cold.[1]

Wary, he circled the smooth white trunk until he came to the face. Red eyes looked at him. Fierce eyes they were, yet glad to see him. The weirwood had his brother's face. Had his brother always had three eyes?[2]

In A Song of Ice and Fire, as George R. R. Martin's wonderful characters play their game of thrones, we can wonder about the value of Machiavellian virtues, the rights of kings and who shall rule, as well as moral issues about virtue and honor, incest and betrayal. But though they are often in the background, we should not forget about the strange creatures and supernatural happenings in Westeros either. These afford us the opportunity to wax philosophical about mind and metaphysics, as you will see.

What Is It Like to Be a Direwolf?

> She could outrun horses and outfight lions. When
> she bared her teeth even men would run from her,
> her belly was never empty long, and her fur kept her
> warm even when the wind was blowing cold.[3]

Metaphysics is the branch of philosophy that investigates the ultimate nature of reality. What is real? What is the fundamental nature of the universe? These sorts of questions take on a different meaning when asked about the world of Westeros and beyond. Whereas we might ask whether God exists, the maesters and other thinkers surely speculate about the existence of *their* gods—the old gods, the seven-faced god, the god of light, and the drowned god. Whereas we wonder about space, time, and the laws of nature, it gets a lot more complicated when you have seasons that can last for years—not to mention all the other supernatural violations of the natural order that occur.

What is the nature and place of persons in the universe? The main metaphysical question about *persons* no doubt concerns the mind. Persons have physical bodies—some tall and strong like Jaime the Kingslayer's, even outrageously huge like Ser Gregor, the Mountain That Rides; others not so much, like Tyrion the Imp or skinny little Arya Stark. No matter what size, our bodies, like other physical things, take up space, have mass and energy, and obey the laws of nature. But unlike swords and cups of wine, we can think and reason, experience and feel. These activities are the province of the mind. But what are minds? Are they just functioning brains? The view known as *materialism* (or *physicalism*) indeed claims that this is true, and that persons are nothing more than extremely complex physical objects. Is this view correct, or does it leave something out?

In addressing this question, the contemporary American philosopher Thomas Nagel said that there wouldn't be much of a problem to this so-called *mind-body problem* if it weren't for one very big obstacle: *consciousness*.[4] The problem, he said, is this. Physical things are *objective*, which basically means that they can be described completely in third-person terms. So, for example, I could describe to you my hardcover copy of *A Dance with Dragons*, and nothing would be left out. But consciousness has a *subjective* element to it; indeed, consciousness seems to be essentially subjective. As Nagel put it, *there is something it is like to be conscious.* And this "what it's like" can't be described in objective, third-person terms. If this is true, then it's hard to see how consciousness could be a physical process, hard to see how the mind could just be the functioning brain.

Sometimes when we talk about what something is like, we use phrases such as "This tastes like cardboard" or "I felt like a kid again." When Nagel, however, says it's "like" something to have a conscious experience, he isn't making a comparative statement at all. He's saying that experiences feel a certain way to the experiencer; and how that experience feels—"what it's like"—can be known only by one who has had the experience in question. For example, unlike Daenerys, we can't truly imagine what raw horse heart tastes like. At least not unless we ate one ourselves!

Take a more familiar example: pain. When Arya stabbed and killed the stable boy in order to facilitate her escape from King's Landing after Lord Eddard's beheading, the boy felt a pain sensation. There was something it was like for him to have that experience, and someone who had never experienced that sort of sensation couldn't know what it's like. In fact, we can't even know that the pain sensations, colors, sounds, and so on that we experience are the same as what these experiences are like for others. To make this point more vividly, Nagel asked us to think about creatures that experience the world in a way that's very different from the way we do. Using bats as his example, Nagel claimed that we could *never* know what it's like to be a bat. Looking to Westeros, let's forget about bats, and ask instead, "What is it like to be a direwolf?"

If direwolves are conscious—and maybe they're not, more on this in a minute—they embody a point of view. The world seems a certain way to a direwolf. When we try to imagine how that would be, how it would feel, we end up at best imagining *ourselves* in the beast's body, which is not at all what it is to actually *be* a direwolf. So while one could come to know what a raw horse's heart tastes like—though I never will—we can never know what it's like to be another creature. We can never embody that creature's point of view; only our own.

Wargs and Consciousness

I am him, and he is me. He feels what I feel.[5]

This may sound pretty convincing, but just like who's betraying whom, and the crooked paths where our favorite characters find themselves, things are always more complicated in Westeros. The extra complication is that in this world, certain individuals known as *wargs* can actually transfer their consciousness into the bodies of direwolves and other animals. Orell, one of the wildlings, transferred his consciousness into an eagle, and this eagle went on to try to rip out one of Jon Snow's eyes after the wildling was dead. Well, at least his body was dead. And Bran can put his consciousness not only into his direwolf Summer, but into Hodor as well. Hodor!

So does Bran know what it's like to be a direwolf? Or does he know only what it's like for him (Bran) to be "inside" of the animal with access to its sense organs? It's hard to come up with a definitive answer here. Sometimes it seems like Bran and Summer share their consciousness. Other times, either Bran is just *there*, silently noting what his direwolf is sensing, or Bran's consciousness alone is operating "inside" of Summer's body. The first option *could* be the case, so it looks as though in the world of A Song of Ice and Fire, it *is* possible to embody more than one point of view, and therefore to be able to know what it is like to be something as strange as a direwolf. Does this tell us anything about the nature of consciousness?

Descartes and Direwolves

> . . . if they thought as we do, they would have an
> immortal soul like us. This is unlikely, because there
> is no reason to believe it of some animals without
> believing it of all, and many of them such as oysters
> and sponges are too imperfect for this to be credible.[6]

The great French philosopher and mathematician René Descartes (1596–1650) would have dismissed all of this "what it's like" talk when it comes to direwolves, or any other animal for that matter, because he believed that animals were not conscious at all. He thought they were more like complex machines. Descartes thought this was true for two main reasons. First, he believed that consciousness required the existence of a soul—a nonphysical substance—and only persons had souls. Actually, saying that persons "have" souls is not quite correct; Descartes thought persons *were* souls. In other words, for Descartes, you are not your body, but rather you are an immaterial substance that is causally connected to your body. So when Sansa looks at Sandor Clegane and sees this very large dangerous man with half of his face burned off, she is seeing the Hound's body only, and not the Hound himself. What makes this *his* body is the fact that when he, the Sandor

Clegane soul, if you will, decided to slash Mycah, the butcher's boy, with a sword, the Hound's body is the one that did the slashing. And the same is true in the other direction. When Gregor held his brother's face to the burning coals when they were children, it was the soul that was Sandor that felt the pain, and not some other soul.

So persons have souls, and consciousness takes place only in souls. Since animals don't have souls, they're not conscious. The second reason Descartes denied the existence of animal consciousness was that he thought that animal behavior could be completely explained in physical terms. This points to a difference between us and the other animals, because our behavior, Descartes thought, could not be explained in purely physical terms.

To illustrate this difference, Descartes focused on language. When Lord Commander Mormont's raven says "Corn!" or "Snow!" Descartes would have said that this was a mechanical happening without any understanding on the bird's part. But when the commander himself makes those same sounds, they have meaning *for the commander*. Further, the process by which we take our thoughts, which have meaning, and turn them into words that convey those meanings could not be explained in any mechanistic way. At least that's what Descartes claimed.

Whether or not Descartes was right about this, the strategy of his argument was instructive. To argue for the existence of something that can't be perceived, like the soul or the gods of Westeros, you might argue that without it, something is left unexplained. When it came to animals, Descartes thought the physical explanations were enough, so there was no need to postulate anything further. With persons, the physical explanations were not sufficient to account for language, meaning, and thought. So something further was needed. And according to Descartes, that something must be a nonphysical conscious thing: a soul.

There are many difficulties with Descartes' position. First, many animals have sophisticated languages—the higher primates as well as dolphins and whales come to mind—so do they have souls as well? Perhaps their language has no meaning for them and is not being used to convey thought. If so, Descartes could accept the fact that these animals have a form of language, while maintaining that the important difference between them and us still holds. But there are still major problems with his view.

The cognitive and neurosciences have proposed various accounts of language and its relation to thought. Descartes was right that no simple mechanistic model could explain language. But the physical explanations available to us are much more complex than what was available in the first half of the seventeenth century, when Descartes was writing. So if physical explanations fail to fully explain human behavior, it's probably not because of the relationship between thought and language. We would need another reason to divide persons from other animals, to deny the latter consciousness based on this type of argument.

A second, and much worse, problem for Descartes is that, given what we know about animals (the primates and higher mammals at least, which in Westeros would certainly include direwolves) in terms of anatomy, physiology, and biological origin, denying animal consciousness seems dubious at best. In fact, the reasons we have for thinking that other people are conscious are pretty much the same reasons applied to animals. To illustrate, think of Jon Snow and Ghost. Jon knows that he is conscious, as each individual similarly does. He assumes that his friends and not-so-friends on the Night's Watch are also conscious, but this is something he infers and does not know directly as he does in his own case. Why does he make this inference? Why do each of us make similar inferences every day?

Well, first, there is the behavioral evidence, both verbal and nonverbal. The brothers of the Night's Watch behave pretty much just as Jon does. You talk to them, they seem to understand, and they respond accordingly. They say they are cold, and move toward the fire. When stabbed, they cry out in pain. Ghost behaves in similar fashion, responding to Jon's commands, trying to stay warm, and so forth. When attacked by Orell's eagle, Ghost exhibited pain behavior similar to Jon's as well. So if the behavioral evidence convinces us that other persons are conscious, the same sort of evidence ought to be convincing when applied to animals.

Second, animal physiology is quite similar to our own. It would be absurd to think that brains and nervous systems, designed (either by the gods or in a biologically natural way) to register pain, would do so in us but not in biologically similar creatures.[7] Imagine thinking this of a fellow human: "Well, I know her brain and nervous system are like mine, and I know she shares a biological history with me in terms of evolution and human reproduction, but I bet she has no conscious experiences." Why is this any less absurd when considering a seemingly aware, perceptive animal, like a direwolf?

Direwolves and animals in general can perceive their surrounding environment. They can smell food and hear predators; they can utilize their other senses as well. How is any of this possible without consciousness? Descartes (I know, I'm piling on here; were he alive, next I'd be asking to cut off some of his fingers) did have an answer to this. He thought that perception had three levels. The first, and lowest level, was a purely mechanical affair in which the information in the environment physically pressed upon the sense organs. At the next level, there was conscious awareness of the experience. And at the highest level, there was the ability to reason and make judgments about the experience. Descartes thought that animals functioned entirely at the first level, devoid of consciousness. The two higher levels were missing entirely in them since they lacked souls.

Sometimes we too perceive our surroundings without consciousness. In the classroom where I lecture, I often pace back and forth in the front of the room near the desk. And although I'm not paying attention to the desk—I'm not consciously aware of it—I navigate around it easily enough. My senses are detecting it, but there's no conscious awareness attached. A more familiar example that philosophers like to discuss is *the long-distance driver*. This happens to everyone: You're driving along on a highway for hours; you look up and see that you're already near your destination, and you have no awareness of having gone past many familiar sights. Maybe you were listening to music or to *House and Philosophy* on audio, but you weren't paying attention to the road at all. (Contrast this with the driving experience you have in heavy traffic in a rainstorm, when your awareness is totally present and focused.) Yet you don't hit anyone or drive off the road; you still perceive the environment.

Wargs Again

"When I touched Summer, I felt you in him. Just as you are in him now."[8]

Much of the time, our perception isn't so lacking in consciousness, but it might be possible that animal perception is *always* like this. That's what Descartes thought. In our world, it's possible, but extremely unlikely. Again, given all we know about animals biologically, and the similarity of their brains and sense organs to ours, we have every scientific reason to think that most higher animals have conscious sensory experiences very similar to our own.

That's in our world; but what about Westeros and beyond? If we revisit wargs, there are some very interesting possibilities. Consider a case where Bran's consciousness is "inside" Summer, so that Bran is experiencing what is happening where Summer's direwolf body is located, perhaps very far away. Summer could be operating just as Descartes suggested, at sensation level one, while Bran's consciousness provides the two higher levels—the awareness of the sensations and the ability to make judgments about them.

At first, the possibility of wargs looks bad for materialism. If one can transfer one's consciousness somewhere else, then it appears that consciousness must be separate from brain function. In a world with wargs, must materialism then be false? Does this mean, in other words, that consciousness must be some sort of nonphysical phenomenon? No. There are several possibilities.

Perhaps consciousness is some sort of energy field generated by brains—pure speculation here—and wargs' brains can send this energy field into other brains. Now, there are two ways to think about this. If we say that physical things obey physical laws, and warg brains violate these laws, then the existence of wargs would mean that materialism is false. That's one possibility. The other possibility is *magic*. Wargs are supernatural creatures, after all. The fact that they can do what they do requires only that physical laws get violated, not that anything nonphysical occurs. This, to me, seems to be the more plausible explanation in this strange world.[9]

What about in our world? Remember, we started talking about wargs as a way of exploring Nagel's "what it's like" problem—the problem of *subjectivity*. If there are subjective facts about what it's like to have a given experience, and if such facts can be known only from the point of view of the experiencer, does that show that the physical facts aren't *all* the facts? I don't see that it does at all. The great British philosopher Bertrand Russell (1872–1970) argued that our experiences, which he thought were identical with brain events, were different from other physical facts only in how they are known (not in what they're made of). We know our experiences *directly* because they occur in us (in our brains); other physical events that occur outside of our brains (in a different space-time region, Russell would say), we know *indirectly*, by inference. If Russell is right (he is; trust me on this), then subjectivity poses no problem for materialism in our world either.

What about the Wights?

A shard from his sword transfixed the blind white pupil of his left eye.

The right eye was open. The pupil burned blue. It saw.[10]

Another way that philosophers try to argue against materialism is by the supposed possibility of zombies. Now you might be thinking that what they have in mind—the philosophers, not the zombies who lack consciousness and have nothing in mind—sounds a lot like those terrible creatures created by the Others: the wights.[11] But you would be mistaken. The zombies that philosophers are talking about, I like to call *phenomenal zombies*. A zombie of this type would be some physical duplicate of a conscious being but would lack conscious experience altogether.

So imagine a creature physically just like Sansa, who lacks consciousness. It's all dark on the inside. Some of you might think that I'm describing the real Sansa here, but that would be mean. Anyway, "Zombie Sansa" is a physical duplicate of the real Sansa who behaves, both verbally and nonverbally, exactly like her counterpart. But Zombie Sansa has no conscious experiences of any sort taking place. If this is possible, then it seems like materialism must be false; there is more to a person than just their physical being.

Many philosophers think that phenomenal zombies are possible, but I believe they are not. If materialism is true, then we know that when your brain is in the right state, you are conscious. Even if materialism is not true and consciousness is nonphysical, it's connected to the appropriate brain states in a lawlike way (even Descartes granted this). What this means is that whether or not materialism is true, given that your brain is in the right state, and given that the laws of nature are the way they are, there must be consciousness. So when someone thinks they can conceive of Zombie Sansa—remember, a being that's an exact physical duplicate of Sansa but without consciousness—what they are conceiving is a case where the laws of nature are operating differently. But a brain state that operated according to different laws of nature would be a different brain state. This is true because which brain state one is in is relative to some theoretical description of the brain. If brains operated according to different laws, then a different theoretical description would be in order. The phrase "same brain state" in part means "operates according to the same laws in the same way."[12]

Thus, in our "thought experiment" where we try to imagine a physical duplicate of Ned Stark's oldest daughter who lacks consciousness, we're actually imagining a being that has a different sort of brain operating according to different laws of nature. A materialist would not be troubled by this; such a being would after all *not* be a physical duplicate of our Sansa. Because of magic, however, in Westeros I think we would have to say that Zombie Sansa *is* possible to imagine. There it might be that sometimes the lawlike functioning of our brains can go awry. Different metaphysics, different conclusion.

Back to the Wights

> Then he saw it, a shadow in the shadows, sliding toward the inner door that led to Mormont's sleeping cell, a man-shape all in black, cloaked and hooded . . . but beneath the hood, its eyes shone with an icy blue radiance.[13]

When we return to thinking about the wights—the real zombies like those we see in monster movies as opposed to the philosophers' phenomenal zombies—we can again wonder whether they are possible, and if so, what that tells us about ourselves.

First, is there an analogous thought experiment in which we imagine a physical duplicate of a living person, but the duplicate is not alive? Well, there used to be a popular view known as *vitalism*, which claimed that living things differed from nonliving things by having an additional substance, a vital fluid or life force. In other words, living things were made of different stuff. Vitalism has been thoroughly discredited by the biological sciences. We now understand life pretty well. We know that living things aren't made of different stuff, and that being alive is a matter of your physical stuff having a certain structure and function.

As a consequence, imagining a functioning physical duplicate of a person who is not alive doesn't seem possible. The wights coming from beyond the Wall, however, is a real and terrifying scenario; but their existence, just like the Zombie Sansa of my earlier thought experiment, is possible only because the supernatural is at work. The normal laws of nature don't always apply in this world.

Moreover, a closer examination of the wights reveals that they're not entirely without life anyway—and the same is true of familiar movie zombies as well. The Others, who seem to be a demon race we know very little about (as of *A Dance with Dragons* at least), somehow are able to reanimate certain corpses, thus creating the wights. They have some signs of life—they can move, for example, and appear to have limited brain function—but they don't show evidence of most normal metabolic processes. They don't eat, eliminate waste, or reproduce, and they can't be killed in common ways. So what we have here is perhaps best described as partly dead and partly alive. This changes little, however, when it comes to their conceivability.

Neither wights nor phenomenal zombies pose any threat if one wants to defend a materialist view. Neither is possible in our world; both are possible in Westeros and beyond because of supernatural forces at work, rather than nonphysical ones.

In our world, we think we can imagine phenomenal zombies because we don't as yet have a fully worked-out theory of consciousness. Our theories about life, on the other hand, are pretty much settled, and this is an important difference. What we know, as well as what we don't know, impacts what we can and can't conceive. When you throw some supernatural elements into the mix, mind and metaphysics become as tangled as the roots of a weirwood tree, and as mysterious as the messages in Melisandre's fires.

NOTES

1. George R. R. Martin, *A Game of Thrones* (New York: Bantam Dell, 2005), p. 11.

2. George R. R. Martin, *A Clash of Kings* (New York: Bantam Dell, 2005), p. 766.

3. George R. R. Martin, *A Storm of Swords* (New York: Bantam Dell, 2005), pp. 883–884.

4. Thomas Nagel, "What Is It Like to Be a Bat?" *Philosophical Review* 83 (1974), pp. 435–450.

5. George R. R. Martin, *A Dance with Dragons* (New York: Bantam Books, 2011), p. 61.

6. René Descartes, *Letter to the Marquess of Newcastle*, Nov. 23, 1643. Reprinted in Tom Regan and Peter Singer, *Animal Rights and Human Obligations*, 2nd ed. (Englewood Cliffs, NJ: Prentice Hall, 1989), p. 17.

7. Voltaire remarked, "Do not suppose this impertinent contradiction in nature." In his *Philosophical Dictionary*, "Animals," reprinted in Regan and Singer, p. 21.

8. Martin, *A Clash of Kings*, p. 438.

9. Some might question this distinction at first, but saying that physical laws got violated is *not* the same as saying that something nonphysical occurred. If there was real magic and someone could, for example, actually make cards disappear and then reappear, no nonphysical cards would be involved. But maybe the laws of physics holding the atoms of the cards together could temporarily be suspended, so the disappearing could occur.

10. Martin, *A Game of Thrones*, p. 11.

11. Keep in mind that the Others and the wights are not the same. The Others are a demon race who can reanimate corpses; the animated corpses are the wights. The Others can be killed by *dragonglass*, but not by fire, while the opposite is true of the wights. Adding to the confusion is that the wildlings often refer to the Others as "White Walkers."

12. Think of it this way: The laws of nature aren't "added on" after the fact to objects, like, say, the laws of chess (or I could've said *cyvasse*). You can take a chess piece and use it in some other way (as a paperweight, for example) where it's no longer obeying the laws of chess. But you can't do the same for water, or for a particular brain state.

13. Martin, *A Game of Thrones*, p. 565.

MAGIC, SCIENCE, AND METAPHYSICS IN A GAME OF THRONES

Edward Cox

In Westeros and beyond, before the beginning of *A Game of Thrones*, magic has been disappearing.[1] The dragons, the children of the forest, and the Others are gone. They live only in tales told to the young. In this way Westeros is like our world. There seems to be little place for magic or the supernatural in our world, and even the long-held belief in immaterial souls is threatened by the advance of physical science. Yet magic returns to Westeros. Part of the appeal of fantasy in general, and *A Game of Thrones* in particular, is the idea that there might be room left in the world for a sense of wonder, for things that escape the net of explanation in terms of the physical sciences. There is room in our world for the wonders of science. But is there room for the wonder of magic, or at least for nonphysical things?

Let's Get Physical

Physicalism is the philosophical view that there are only physical things. Is physicalism true, or are there ghosts, immaterial souls, or other nonphysical things? These are questions of *metaphysics*—questions about the fundamental nature of reality. Science can help us answer such questions. A fantasy novel can't give us answers, but it can help us imagine ways in which the world might differ if physicalism were to be false.

So let us reason like maesters and begin by getting clear on our concepts. A more precise definition of physicalism includes two ideas. First, everything that exists is physical. That means there are no immaterial souls, minds, or vital forces. Second, everything about the world depends on arrangements of this physical stuff. It may not be obvious why this second claim is necessary for a statement of physicalism, so consider this example: Imagine that there are two people who are completely physically identical. When speaking of duplicates, I do not mean twins, but physical duplicates down to the exact arrangement of the molecules making up their bodies. According to the first of the two statements of physicalism, these two bodies won't be made up of any nonphysical parts, but it is still possible that they could differ in other ways. For example, one exact duplicate might be happy while the other is sad, or one could be conscious and the other asleep. If only the first part of the statement of physicalism were true, some features, or *properties*, as philosophers call them, of the world might differ without there being any difference in the physical stuff that makes them up. The second claim, that everything about the world is determined by the arrangement of physical stuff in it, emphasizes the dependence of everything on the physical world. For one identical person to be happy and the other sad, there would have to be a corresponding difference in their brain chemistry; they could not have identical atoms in all the same locations while being in a different mental state.

Now that we have a definition of physicalism, we can try to decide whether it is true in our world or in Westeros. One way of trying to show that physicalism is true is by arguing that only physical things could have any effect. Consider, therefore, these two statements:

1. For something to exist, it must have an effect of some kind.
2. Every physical effect has only a physical cause.

Before trying to decide whether these claims are true, we should show how they support physicalism. Let's start by considering what must be the case for something to be a cause, to have any effect at all. For something to have an effect, it must either have a physical effect or a nonphysical effect. So, when Jaime Lannister pushes Bran out the window of the First Keep in Winterfell, perhaps ironically, he attributes his action to his love for Cersei.[2] According to our statement 2, if Jaime's love causes the physical damage to Bran's body, by means of his physical pushing and Bran's physical body falling, then Jaime's love must be a physical state, presumably some brain state. So, if the first alternative is true, that Jaime's love causes a physical effect, then that emotion must itself be physical as well.

On the other hand, we might think that Jaime's brain state causes the physical pushing, the physical falling, and ultimately the physical damage to Bran's body, but Jaime's love is something else, something nonphysical. Then, we might ask, if Jaime's love is not a physical state of his brain, what is there for it to do? The only remaining possibility appears to be that it has some nonphysical effect. For instance, it might affect some nonphysical state of Bran's. But how this would work is a mystery.

It seems more likely that, given what we know through empirical studies, anything that affected Bran's nonphysical mind—assuming for the moment that there are such things—would have to do it by affecting his brain. We know that our conscious experiences, for example, are affected by drugs, alcohol, and blows to the head; our mental states are altered by the chemical changes that occur in our brains. So in our example, assuming that Bran's mind is nonphysical, if Jaime's love is to have an effect on it, we can best explain this by describing how it affects Bran's brain. We would then be left to conclude either that Jaime's love did nothing (which is ruled out by statement 1), or that it somehow affected Bran's brain. But, by statement 2, for Jaime's love to have that physical effect, it must be physical. Therefore, love, and everything else, has to be physical.

Philosophers are a contentious bunch, and not all of them agree with every assertion from the previous paragraph, but we can use some illustrations from *A Game of Thrones* to see why those assertions are nonetheless likely to be true. Let's start with the idea that everything that exists has to have an effect. The reason to think this claim is true is that if something existed and had no effect, we would have no reason to believe in it. For example, one of the reasons Maester Luwin believes the Children of the Forest no longer exist is that they never seem to do anything. No one in the Seven Kingdoms has seen the Children of the Forest or been affected by them in any way for thousands of years. It is the fact that they don't do anything that leads people to doubt whether they are real. Admittedly, we are assuming that to know something or to have reason to believe in something, it would have to have an effect. While there might be other ways of knowing, if we tried to imagine something that not only did not do anything but *could* not do anything at all, we would have to wonder why anyone would believe in it. We could never *disprove* the existence of something that never does anything, but its existence would be completely unknowable. So statement 1 looks like a reasonable thing to believe.

The main reason to believe statement 2 has to do with the success of science in explaining the world in physical terms. And we also have reason to believe the second part of our definition of physicalism—that everything that happens in the world depends on the arrangement of the underlying physical stuff that makes it up—based on the perceived authority of the physical sciences. That means we should talk a little about what science is and how it can tell us about reality.

Science, in the actual world, can tell us a lot about what sorts of things exist and what sorts of things do not exist. In fantasy novels such as *A Game of Thrones*, magic limits the possibility of comprehensively explaining everything in terms of physical things and forces, and the laws governing them. Fantasy novels show different ways things could be, and the happenings in Westeros can serve to expand our view of the way things are, and the ways in which these things relate to one another.

Science in *A Game of Thrones*

There is an organized system of knowledge of the natural world in *A Game of Thrones*, but it is not a topic much discussed in the books. The maesters, the closest equivalent to scientists in Westeros, are highly respected as knowledgeable advisers to rulers. Each maester is a generalist, with knowledge of medicine, politics, engineering, and warfare. The maesters' expertise is practical, but to have such applied knowledge, they must have theoretical knowledge underlying it.

Although not all of the science in George R. R. Martin's world resembles that of our world, the maesters' knowledge shows that some of it does. For example, the maesters know to boil wine to clean wounds, and so it is likely that there are microorganisms that cause infections in Martin's world.[3] In addition, the maesters' understanding of physical forces allows them to construct the Wall and the elaborate pulley system that brings people and goods into the Eyrie.[4] So there are likely to be laws of motion and physical force much like our own.

There also appear to be biological units, perhaps genes, that explain the heritability of physical characteristics. For example, by reading *The Lineages and Histories of the Great Houses of the Seven Kingdoms, With Descriptions of Many High Lords and Noble Ladies and Their Children*,[5] and following up on Robert Baratheon's bastard children, Eddard Stark discovers that the Baratheons always give birth to black-haired children. "Always [Stark] found the gold yielding before the coal."[6] This indicates that something at least similar to actual-world genetics operates in Westeros.[7] In a similar vein, we see that children of the Starks and Tullys inherit coloration and facial structure from one side of the family or the other. Indeed, we discover that some of the Starks—for example, Arya Stark, Jon Snow, and Lyanna Stark, Eddard's sister—have longer faces than other members of the family.[8] These facts suggest there are units of inheritance that offspring take from their parents and that these units explain how traits are passed down from one generation to the next.

It is even possible that some of what the inhabitants believe to be sorcery might simply be advanced technology. The folded steel of Valyrian blades, reputed to be the product of sorcery, may be simply the result of advanced sword-making techniques such as those practiced by medieval Japanese swordsmiths.[9] These scientific and technological facts suggest a world operating in many respects according to the same principles and made up of the same constituents as our own. If this evidence were all that was available, we might conclude that physicalism was true in Westeros.

Magic and Causation

These examples show that there is some reason to think that all the features of Westeros are determined by arrangements of physical stuff. The more complete scientific explanations in terms of physics, chemistry, and biology become, the more likely it is that the world depends on these physical things. However, magic might limit these scientific explanations and show how things could have different effects even if all the arrangements of physical stuff were the same.

We now come to the evidence for the principle that everything depends on the constituents of the physical world. What would it mean for some of the features of the world *not* to depend on the arrangements of physical stuff underlying them? It would mean that a change could occur without any change occurring in the physical stuff. That does not seem plausible, and one illustration from *A Game of Thrones* can help show this.

When Jafer Flowers and Othor are reanimated and attack the Night's Watch, their bodies appear to undergo some sort of physical transformation in order for them to be animate. It is very unlikely that something could be physically exactly the same as a corpse and act as Dead Othor did. Put simply, corpses cannot walk, see, or be cut into pieces and continue to fight. Given the ordinary physical, chemical composition of a human body, there does not seem any way that it could do these things while in the same physical state as ordinary dead matter. We do indeed find this to be the case given the physical differences between their bodies and other, more normal corpses. As Samwell Tarly notes, the bodies of Dead Othor and Flowers do not smell like other bodies and have not decayed as ordinary flesh would.[10] In order for them to be reanimated, it appears there must be some change in the underlying material structure or organization of their physical bodies. Another way of putting this idea is that Dead Othor and Flowers cannot be wights, or the walking dead, without some change in their physical bodies. If you recall, this is the second part of our definition of physicalism, that every feature of the world depends on arrangements of physical stuff.[11]

Let's now see what support there is for our statement 2, that every physical effect has a physical cause. If statement 2 is true, then given what's been argued so far, physicalism seems to be true as well. So, what reason is there to think that this principle is true?

In our world, statement 2 is supported by achievements in the physical sciences. As scientists discovered laws of physics, chemistry, biology, and the neurosciences that appeared to explain events independent of immaterial minds, souls, or life forces, it suggested that nothing outside the physical could have any effect on the physical world. The physical sciences seem to provide complete explanations for the events in our world. But what would a world in which the physical sciences were *not* complete in this way be like?

Science and Magic in Westeros

In Westeros, magic limits the methods of science in discovering the truth. Maester Luwin, the maester of Winterfell, believes there is no magic, and that the children of the forest, and the Others, no longer exist.[12] The science of the maesters is actually quite useful, and the maesters themselves, given the evidence available to them, might reasonably believe that by following scientific principles, they will eventually discover all the facts about the world around them. But in Westeros, science fails to perceive certain important aspects of reality in that world, in particular, the existence of magic. Magic is based on apparently unrepeatable events or phenomena and would thus forever escape discovery by the maesters' science.

For example, Daenerys's perception of warmth in her dragon eggs is not available to others. She feels them as warm, nearly hot, and comes to believe that they are ready to hatch if they can be placed in a hot enough fire; but Ser Jorah Mormont attests that the eggs feel cool to the touch.[13] In another case, Bran's mystical perception, his ability to see things far distant in his dreams, is not available to anyone else. Yet we know these are not mere dreams because he sees his mother on a ship in the Bite, Sansa crying herself to sleep, and other things that he could not have otherwise known.[14] The fact that both Bran and Rickon Stark dream that their father has returned suggests that some real knowledge has been given to them, magically.[15] Their knowledge is real, but until the raven arrives with news of Eddard Stark's death, not everyone could know it. Although the effects of magic sometimes become public knowledge, some aspects of magical occurrences remain private.

The elusive nature of these magical events raises the question of whether supernatural events could occur in our world. Given the inability of science to discover phenomena that are perceivable by only one individual, there might be magic in our world that cannot be discovered by scientific means. Evidence can never *disprove* the existence of this kind of magical occurrence. But until someone can demonstrate the reality of such events, it would not be wise to believe in them until they have publicly discernible effects.

It is not necessary that magic be unpredictable or incomprehensible. In some fantasy worlds, supernatural entities are discoverable and explainable using scientific methods. Magic in such a world consists of perfectly comprehensible forces or supernatural agencies that operate according to general principles and laws. In Robert Jordan's Wheel of Time series,[16] the One Power operates in predictable ways according to principles that can be used to explain and predict events in the world; in Patrick Rothfuss's *The Name of the Wind*,[17] at least some magic follows rules that one can learn and apply in a laboratory. The most extreme form of a scientifically comprehensible system of magic is the world Lyndon Hardy, a physicist, depicted in his novel *Master of the Five Magics*.[18] These fantasy worlds differ from ours not so much because they cannot be understood scientifically, but because they reveal different fundamental forces at play in those universes. Science may reveal a reality in our world that is purely physical, but the reality that science discovers in other worlds might be quite different.

Magic and Metaphysics

What, then, does magic have to do with the nature of reality? There are only a few explanations for how magic works. It might be that magic simply alters the laws of physics without adding nonphysical forces or things. However, I think that if magic is a force or feature of the world, then it has to be a nonphysical one. If magic were physical, then it would have to follow the laws of physics. One possibility is that magic is governed by a *different* set of physical laws without additional forces, and thus there would be no need for anything nonphysical. But a world with different physical laws would not necessarily be a world with magic. Magic, I think, involves some violation of physical laws, and some kind of nonphysical thing.[19]

Just as people once thought that there were vital forces—basic life forces that could not be explained in terms of anything physical—magic might involve nonphysical forces that operate directly on the physical world. Or, magical principles might change some basic physical principles or laws of nature. Thus magic would produce a change in the physical world by something not fully explainable in physical terms.

Magic in Westeros often involves exceptions to usually reliable generalizations. For example, under normal circumstances, it would be exceedingly unlikely that untutored children would be capable of training large and dangerous wild animals to respond to complex voice commands; yet the Starks' direwolves are capable of following complicated commands quickly. And Bran's connection to his direwolf Summer is far stronger than could be explained by any ordinary training or bonding.[20] The exceptional bond between the Stark children and their direwolves is not the sort of thing one would find in a purely natural world.

In other cases, there are no regularities. The length and timing of summers and winters follow no regular, predictable pattern, and although there apparently is "a hundred-year-old discourse" on the subject by "a long-dead maester," no scientific or natural explanation is ever suggested for this fact.[21] The only pattern appears to be that long winters follow long summers. A particularly long winter, however, is related to the activity of the Others. Either something about the onset of a long winter awakens them, or they bring on the long winter by their presence or by their activity. Whichever it is, the seasons illustrate another way in which magic, presuming the Others are supernatural and their relation to the seasons is supernatural, does not follow regular patterns.

These irregularities appear to be violations of physical laws. The strongest argument that these are violations involves Daenerys hatching her dragons in the funeral pyre of her husband, Khal Drogo.[22] Her willpower, along with an enormous number of perfectly aligned circumstances, such as her heritage as "the blood of the dragon," the sacrifice of the maegi Mirri Maz Duur, and the appearance of the blood-red comet, appear essential to her body's not burning in the conflagration. When Drogo's funeral pyre starts, Daenerys and everyone else step back from the intense heat of the flames. Daenerys's steeling herself, reminding herself of her decision before stepping into the fire, suggests that her immunity is not somehow a purely physical aspect of her body; she does not ordinarily have an inhuman body chemistry that prevents burning or feeling heat. So in order for her mental resolve to protect her from the flames, there must be a change in the chemical process of combustion that would ordinarily cause a human body to burn in that intense heat. This example suggests that when magic affects the world, it does so by disrupting physical, chemical, or biological processes.

What follows from these examples is that *all* causation requires physical causation. Daenerys's belief and determination alone cannot cause a change in her overall state without influencing the chemical process of combustion. The corollary of this conclusion is that in our world, nonphysical things, such as immaterial souls, could not have an effect on the world without having a physical effect. The more scientists are able to explain events in our world through physics, chemistry, and biology, the less likely it is that there are nonphysical influences that exist. And the more we think that everything else depends on the physical, the less likely it is that any nonphysical thing can have any causal influence at all. Given this argument, the only way for there to be souls, or nonphysical minds, is for there to be violations of the laws of physics.

Are souls and vital forces magic? Would there have to be magic for physicalism to be false? Souls and vital forces might be perfectly natural phenomena—predictable and verifiable by the methods of science—but not explainable in physical terms. But for them to be real, according to the argument I have presented, they would have to affect the physical world in violation of the laws of physics, chemistry, or biology. Advances in science make such violations increasingly unlikely. So in our world, immaterial stuff may turn out to be just as improbable as magic.

NOTES

1. George R. R. Martin, *A Game of Thrones* (New York: Bantam Dell, 2005). I speak only of Westeros, but strictly speaking, some of the events I describe occur beyond the Narrow Sea.

2. Ibid., p. 85.

3. Ibid., p. 384.

4. Ibid., p. 374.

5. Ibid., p. 274.

6. Ibid., p. 486.

7. It is tempting to describe the black-hair gene as dominant since all Baratheon are black-haired and they always have only black-haired children. This, however, would not fit what we know of genetics, even with the oversimplifying assumption that there are only two hair-color genes that are either recessive or dominant. Assuming that the gene for black hair is dominant, and for fair-hair recessive, the Baratheons would be black-haired even if they had one dominant black-hair gene and one recessive fair-hair gene. In that case, a Baratheon child could be fair-haired if both parents had at least one recessive fair-hair gene. Thus, a black-haired Baratheon could have a fair-haired child if the Baratheon parent had a recessive fair-hair gene that was not expressed because he or she also had the dominant black-hair gene. Since the genes of both parents, at least one of

whom must have the recessive fair-hair gene, given the case in which one parent has fair hair, are randomly inherited by the children, there is no way to guarantee that Baratheon children always have two dominant black-hair genes and never get a recessive fair-hair gene from the other parent. In this sense, the universal black hair of the Baratheon family cannot be explained in terms of simple genetics. Either Martin did not understand how genetics works or it works slightly differently in Westeros. But there do seem to be units of inheritance, since children seem to receive the characteristics of one parent or the other.

8. These facts about the inheritance of features are, I think, important clues to Jon Snow's true parentage.

9. Martin, *A Game of Thrones*, p. 235.

10. Ibid., pp. 556–557.

11. Some philosophers believe that consciousness is an exception to this principle, since we can imagine there being changes in conscious states without a change in the physical state. This is not the place to investigate such an argument in detail, but see Henry Jacoby, "Wargs, Wights, and Wolves That Are Dire," in this volume, for a discussion of consciousness.

12. Martin, *A Game of Thrones*, p. 736.

13. Ibid., p. 756.

14. Ibid., pp. 162–163.

15. Ibid., p. 736.

16. Citing all thirteen volumes of the Wheel of Time series would take more space than I have available, but the first volume is *The Eye of the World* (New York: Tor Fantasy, 1990).

17. Patrick Rothfuss, *The Name of the Wind* (Kingkiller Chronicles, Day 1) (New York: Daw Books, 2009).

18. Lyndon Hardy, *Master of the Five Magics* (New York: Del Rey Books, 1984).

19. For a different view, see Jacoby, "Wargs, Wights, and Wolves That Are Dire."

20. This bond is especially noticeable when Summer saves Bran from attempted murder. Martin, *A Game of Thrones*, p. 133.

21. No author or title is listed for the book that Tyrion is reading in the library at Winterfell in ibid., p. 86.

22. Ibid., pp. 805–807.

"YOU KNOW NOTHING, JON SNOW": EPISTEMIC HUMILITY BEYOND THE WALL

Abraham P. Schwab

The world beyond the Wall serves as a constant reminder to the Black Brothers of their vast expanses of ignorance. The first pages of *A Game of Thrones* alert us to this ignorance— Gared, Will, and Ser Waymar Royce do not know what has happened to the wildlings they were chasing, or why the bodies have disappeared. They understand neither why it is so cold, nor the nature of the enemies that are about to kill Will and Ser Waymar. If only Royce had not assumed that the enemies were mere wildlings, he might have saved Will's life and his own. This kind of ignorance comes up again and again as the men of the Night's Watch encounter Others, wildlings, and everything else beyond the Wall.

We should not be surprised that the men of the Night's Watch are ignorant in some areas. *Epistemology*, a major branch of philosophical inquiry, is the study of what we know, how we know it, and what it means to know something. Understood in a certain way, it's an exploration of our ignorance and has led to the views that there is no truth (nihilism), that you already know what you will know (recollection), and that there is truth, but we can't know it (skepticism).

The study of epistemology is valuable for lots of reasons; done right, it can help us make informed decisions. While many chapters in this volume deal with philosophical questions of how one should behave, answering those questions depends first on determining what one knows. Think, for example, of Stannis's offer to Jon to take control of Winterfell. What Jon should do takes on a different cast depending on whether he knows, or even believes, that Bran and Rickon are dead.[1]

Not Knowing That You Know Nothing

Ygritte's refrain "You know nothing, Jon Snow" marks spaces of ignorance. In some cases, it marks a disagreement, as when Jon and Ygritte argue about whether Mance can defeat the Night's Watch. In others, it's an expression of pleasure, as when Jon and Ygritte flirt and fool around. In most of the twenty or so times that Ygritte utters these words, it implies that Jon misunderstands something about wildlings. They mark Jon's failure to be epistemically humble.

Take, for example, the exchange between Ygritte and Jon about the courting rituals between a man and a woman.[2] Jon cannot abide the physical taking of women by wildling raids. Ygritte argues that the man who could take her would be strong and smart, and she asks, "What's bad about that?" Jon retorts that the man may never bathe—Ygritte says she would throw him in the river or dump water on him. What if he were brutal and beat her? Ygritte says she would kill him in his sleep. Though Jon recognizes wildlings are different, he fails to grasp the extent to which "he knows nothing." He doesn't know or understand the norms that govern wildlings' social interactions, and fails to apply this ignorance to particular judgments. He still assumes that the norms that govern wildlings should be commensurate with the norms that govern people in the Seven Kingdoms. Aware of his ignorance in the abstract, he still assumes too much in the particular.

Jon is far from alone in this problem. Samwell Tarly also assumes too much. When Small Paul comes back as a wight and attacks, Sam assumes that the dragonglass dagger will be effective. And why wouldn't it? He killed one of the Others with the dagger, and the Others turned Small Paul into a wight, so the dagger should work on wights as well. Right? And yet the dagger shatters on the armor of Small Paul, laying bare Sam's epistemic overreach.[3]

This comparison is a little unfair to Sam, though. Sam's decision is constrained by time, whereas Jon's decisions are not (or at least not as much). Sam wasn't expecting the wights to show up right then and so must make a decision *right now*. Jon's judgments, however, aren't needed immediately for his survival. We might excuse Sam for failing to be epistemically humble—he simply doesn't have the time to evaluate whether dragonglass will harm wights. Jon, however, has the time to invoke the cool calm of reflection.

Consider now how Lord Commander Mormont and others view Mance Raydar as King-beyond-the-Wall. Along with Jon, and later on, Stannis Baratheon, Mormont takes Mance to be king in the way Robert Baratheon was king. Beyond the Wall, Jon soon finds out about the dangers of homonyms. Mance Raydar may be a "king," but he is a king of "free men," and so the term "king" has a different meaning beyond the Wall. There are no worries about speaking one's mind beyond the Wall, even if the king should find it offensive. There is also little pomp, and the infrastructure of authority is not so rigid. Because Lord Commander Mormont failed to understand that Mance was a different kind of king entirely, he failed to recognize that *warfare* could be entirely different as well. As we can see from the Old Bear's orders and actions, he "knew" that the force that Mance was gathering was like a force that the king of the Seven Kingdoms would gather. He "knew" that the best way to attack and defend was in the same manner as one attacks and defends south of the Wall: direct violent confrontation. For contrast, think of how Dany deals with the sellswords as she is preparing to take Yunkai. She recognizes the fault lines in the relationships between the sellswords and the city. This allows her to defeat the sellswords more easily and take Yunkai.[4] If only Lord Mormont had doubted that the wildlings were a force like his own, a group of similarly committed individuals who follow a common disciplinary structure, he might have considered alternatives to violent confrontation, which may have kept him from waiting on the Fist of First Men.

What Even a Blind Man Can See

Epistemic humility requires the ability to recognize what we don't know, but often think we do. Epistemic humility also requires us to recognize what we *should* know. It requires that we believe those things for which we have seen robust evidence. Maester Aemon Targaryen, and not Sam, can tell that Gilly no longer has her own baby but is caring for Mance's. Sam "knows" that Gilly is upset because she has to travel by boat and go far south of the Wall. But Maester Aemon knows that her cries are the cries of a mother in mourning. Sam fails to recognize what he should know—that Gilly is upset because she left her baby at the Wall.

Jon never seems to fully accept his special connection with Ghost. I'm not talking here about his fellow-feeling, his love, or his compassion for the animal, but rather of his ability to literally feel what Ghost is feeling, to see what Ghost is seeing, to hear what Ghost is hearing. He is told by many friends and foes that he is a warg, and yet he persists in his doubts. As a result, he fails to take advantage of the possibilities of his connection to Ghost, as Bran does with Summer. Sam has similarly unfounded doubts about himself. Sam doesn't know he's brave, yet he attacks and kills an Other. He doesn't know he's brave, but he attacks the wight Small Paul in the hopes that Gilly and her baby can escape.[5] Because he believes he is not brave, Sam's brave actions are random and poorly planned.

In one way or another, both Sam and Jon are stymied by their failure to know themselves. Compare these two with Arya, who redefines herself at every turn and in significant ways (she is a boy, then a mouse, then a ghost, and so on). Arya, in contrast to Sam and Jon, recognizes the nature of her current role (as a mouse she hides, as a ghost she uses her unseen influence) because what she knows is accurate (she is powerless, but she has unseen power). If she, like Sam and Jon, had failed to understand the uniqueness of her situation, it's unlikely she would have survived. Look also to Bran. Like Jon, he has a special connection to his direwolf, Summer, but for him there is no gnawing doubt. This recognition makes it possible for him, through Summer, to help Jon escape from the wildlings. Jon's and Sam's failures to believe are illustrations of lacking appropriate confidence. They fail to be epistemically humble because they fail to recognize when a claim to ignorance has been undermined by robust evidence.

What we have, then, is a view of epistemic humility as a governor of beliefs, similar to some mechanized device like a piston. At one extreme, it keeps the piston from aiming too high, from claiming too much. On the other extreme, it keeps the piston from dropping too low, from claiming too little. As a governor, epistemic humility keeps us from claiming to know that which we should not, and keeps us from ignoring that which we should claim to know.

Calibrating Confidence in What We (Don't) Know

Up to now we've been talking about epistemic humility in two extreme cases—when we've reached the limits of what we know (and so must recognize our ignorance beyond that point), and when we have robust support for something we know (and so must recognize that we do in fact know something). Most of what we know, though, falls somewhere between those two extremes. Take, for example, when Jon takes his vows in a weirwood grove outside the Wall.[6] In doing so, he becomes a member of the Night's Watch. At this point, does he *know* that this will require him to kill a wildling? No, but he should have a great deal of confidence that this will be the case. Epistemic humility, then, also requires an attempt to calibrate the confidence we have in things we claim to know.

In calibrating our confidence, we must distinguish between times when we know something and when we do not, and we must distinguish between different levels of support for the things we know. In contemporary epistemology, the strongest candidate for such a standard is the three-pronged requirement of justified true belief (also known as JTB).

Justified True Belief

To know something, you have to believe it. If you don't believe that George R. R. Martin will finish A Song of Ice and Fire, you don't know it. Or, for example, take the fact that Jon refuses to believe that Benjen Stark is dead. Because he does not believe that Benjen Stark is dead, he could not possibly know it. To know something, one has to believe it.

To know something, it must also be true. Even if I believe Martin will finish the series, to know that he will requires that it be true. I can't know that he will finish the series if, in fact, he will not. I may believe it (and so satisfy the first condition), but if it's not true, it can't be known.

Finally, to know something, the belief not only has to be true, but it has to be justified. When Samwell Tarly and the rest of the Night's Watch are retreating from the Fist of First Men, he, Grenn, and Small Paul are attacked by an Other. Small Paul disarms the Other as he dies and Sam attacks. He thrusts at the Other with his dragonglass dagger even though he has no reason to believe it will be more effective than Small Paul's axe.[7] And yet, it turns out the dragonglass kills the Other. Still, Sam could not *know* that the dragonglass would be effective because he lacked a justification. Guessing correctly does not constitute knowledge.

At the same time, some justified beliefs may turn out not to be true. Remember the Night's Watch's first encounter with wights? They found two members of Benjen Stark's party (Othor and Jafer Flowers) lying cold and still, not far from the Wall.[8] They have good reason to believe these men, as dead men, will not lead to any harm. They show no signs of life and none of the men of the Night's Watch has ever encountered a dead man who comes back to kill them. But we know how that turns out.

A Trip to King's Landing

I don't know about you, but for me it was quite a shock when I found out that Littlefinger and Lysa Arryn conspired to kill Jon Arryn and intentionally misled Catelyn Stark.[9] Ned Stark's motivation to go to King's Landing was predicated upon a lie. Informed by the note that Lysa sent Catelyn, Ned believed that the Lannisters killed Jon Arryn, and so would try to kill Robert Baratheon. Why do I bring this up? Because it points to a prickly problem for JTB: what counts as justification? Ned and Catelyn appear to have a good reason for believing the Lannisters had killed Jon Arryn—the word of Lysa Arryn. And yet, this justification leads directly to a false belief. So what should count as justification?

Everyone who has taken an introductory philosophy class has likely encountered the most stringent of justification requirements: absolute certainty. René Descartes (1596–1650) poured the acid of doubt on everything to see what remained. It turns out not much can withstand the acid of doubt. I mean, what *can't* you doubt? The only thing Descartes was left with (at least at first) was the certainty of his own existence (otherwise how could he do the doubting?). Descartes extrapolates from this single piece of knowledge to add all sorts of other knowledge claims. Without delving into the details of his justifications or their problems, we may still recognize the implications of adopting his standards for justification. The advantage of this view is that if we know something, we really know it. If we wait until we have absolute certainty, we'll never claim to have justification for a belief that doesn't turn out to be true. The disadvantage, however, is that we would have very few beliefs for which we could claim justification.

There is an alternative that's worth a brief mention: reliabilism. Consider an epistemological refrain from the Seven Kingdoms: "dark wings, dark words." The reasons for this saying, often repeated as news is brought by raven, are never explained. Nonetheless, as a process for predicting the kind of news that has arrived, this little mantra is quite accurate. That is, the vast majority of the time that messages are brought by raven, they carry bad news. This process (did the news come by raven?) for determining the kind of news that has come is fairly reliable. A reliabilist epistemology aims to identify reliable processes for producing beliefs. The more reliable the process, the more valuable (in epistemic terms) it is. Take, for example, the difference between a belief based on rigorous scientific inquiry and a belief based on astrology. Scientific inquiry has a much stronger track record for producing true beliefs, though one could possibly get a true belief from astrology. So reliabilism would favor the rigorous inquiry.

Reliabilism, though, is not a panacea. Just because a process is reliable doesn't make it infallible—dark wings could, after all, bring bright words. Using absolute certainty, we would be justified in believing very little, but those things we were justified in believing would always turn out to be true. Reliabilism allows for a larger set of justified beliefs, but some of our justified beliefs may turn out to be false.

Getting back to Lysa Arryn's deception, let's ask again, should Catelyn and Ned take Lysa's word as justification? Should the word of other people *ever* count as justification? Given how easy it is to be misled by others, it may be tempting to say no and to claim that the only good justifications can come from an individual's personal experiences and thoughts. If we adopted absolute certainty as our criterion for justification, we would obviously have to conclude that the testimony of others cannot justify our beliefs. If, however, we adopted something close to reliabilism, it's at least possible for testimony to justify belief.

One reason to allow testimony is that exclusively relying on personal experiences or reasoning would define most of what we believe as unjustified. For example, think of Ned Stark's ultimate demise on the steps of Baelor's Sept.[10] If testimony cannot count as justification, who, among Ned Stark's family, could claim to know that Ned's head was separated from his shoulders by Ser Ilyn Payne? Only Sansa. Yoren kept Arya from looking, and no one else from the Stark clan was at King's Landing. If we restrict justification to personal observations or thoughts, we must conclude that Rob, Catelyn, Jon, Bran, Rickon, and Arya could never know that Ned Stark was beheaded by Ser Ilyn Payne, even if every member of the crowd in front of Baelor's Sept told them.

To avoid such a preposterous conclusion, it is generally accepted that the testimony of others can provide justification. In technical terms, we call this "epistemic trust." As a justification, epistemic trust grows stronger as the number of individuals who provide independent verification increases.

Back to the Wall

As we find out when Jon Snow says his vows, the men of the Night's Watch are an ecumenical bunch. They do not demand that any member of the Night's Watch say his vows before any particular gods—just the gods of that man's choosing. In this way, the men of the Night's Watch avoid (at least in the area of to whom one swears their vows) a particularly poor epistemic perspective—dogma.

In adhering to dogma, the reliability of knowledge resides in its ability to match up with a set of precepts or principles that are swallowed whole. These principles or precepts, often handed down from an authority, are not to be questioned. There are a number of dogmatic characters in A Song of Ice and Fire, from Aeron Damphair to His High Holiness, the High Septon. At the Wall, we see this in Melisandre's beliefs about Stannis Baratheon as the messianic figure of Azor Ahai come to battle the Others, as well as the comet indicating the rightness of her cause. Despite the fact that Stannis's sword fails to give off heat (as Aemon Targaryen notes), Melisandre does not consider the possibility that she is mistaken about Stannis's role.[11] And I doubt that telling Melisandre that not everyone takes the comet as proof of the rightness of her cause would dissuade her. She has reached a conclusion she is no longer willing to reconsider—her beliefs, like all dogmatic beliefs, suffer from a problem of circularity. Dogma claims that certain beliefs are true and justified. How do we know that these beliefs are true and justified? Because the dogma informs us. And why does the dogma tell us to believe these things? Because they are true and justified. And it goes on like that. As you may have inferred, dogma is an enemy to epistemic humility. It knows, just because.

A perspective that, in a moderate form, is key for epistemic humility is skepticism. In its most extreme form, skepticism doubts everything. Everything. As skeptics, then, we could never know anything. An intellectually provocative perspective, skepticism unfortunately lacks tractable application. It would literally keep us from claiming to know anything. In a sense, extreme skepticism is at the opposite extreme from dogma. While dogma just knows, skepticism never knows.

That said, a moderate version of skepticism is far better than dogma. This form of skepticism casts doubt on particular conclusions rather than knowledge in general. An easy example of this moderate skepticism is the way that Harma Dogshead and Rattleshirt view Jon Snow after his "betrayal" of Qhorin Halfhand.[12] Despite the evidence (killing Qhorin Halfhand, wearing a different cloak, sleeping with Ygritte, providing information about the Night's Watch garrisons and movements), they doubt that he has really turned his cloak. As you know, their skepticism turns out to lead to the true belief.

And yet, skepticism about particular conclusions doesn't always help us. When Janos Slynt and Alliser Thorne claim that Jon is a traitor, they are skeptical of his claim that he was only pretending to join the wildlings. When Jon doubts that he saw the wildlings on the Milkwater through Ghost's eyes, he is being skeptical of that fact.[13] In both of these cases, though, it turns out that the skepticism keeps them from the true belief. Jon was looking through Ghost's eyes and Jon was not a traitor, or at least not the kind of traitor that Slynt and Thorne paint him to be. And so skepticism about particular conclusions will not always help us avoid false beliefs or keep us from epistemic arrogance.

The Horn of Winter

One of Jon's false beliefs is that Mance never found the Horn of Winter. One blow from the Horn of Winter was said to bring down the Wall. He, the Old Bear, Stannis, and, it seems, everyone south of the Wall, "knew" that the wildlings' goal was to bring down the Wall. They "knew" that if the wildlings had the Horn of Winter, they would blow it. Only when Jon sees the horn in Mance's tent[14] does he learn of yet another failure to be epistemically humble. As it turns out, the wildlings goal was not to bring down the Wall, but to leave the Wall intact and get south of it. If only the people of the Seven Kingdoms had been humble enough to see this possibility, they might have been able to work with the wildlings to discuss their common enemy—the Others. Because, after all, winter is coming.[15]

NOTES

1. George R. R. Martin, *A Storm of Swords* (New York: Bantam Dell, 2005), pp. 1057–1059.

2. Ibid., pp. 558–559.

3. Ibid., p. 645.

4. Ibid., p. 581.

5. Ibid., pp. 644–646.

6. George R. R. Martin, *A Game of Thrones* (New York: Bantam Dell, 2005), pp. 520–522.

7. Martin, *A Storm of Swords*, p. 252.

8. Martin, *A Game of Thrones*, p. 552.

9. Martin, *A Storm of Swords*, pp. 1114–1115.

10. Martin, *A Game of Thrones*, pp. 725–727.

11. George R. R. Martin, *A Clash of Kings* (New York: Bantam Dell, 2005), p. 149.

12. Ibid., pp. 952–954.

13. Ibid., pp. 766–767.

14. Martin, *A Storm of Swords*, p. 1018.

15. Thanks to Darin McGinnis for his insights and help with the chapter.

"WHY IS THE WORLD SO FULL OF INJUSTICE?": GODS AND THE PROBLEM OF EVIL

Jaron Daniël Schoone

The grief on Lady Catelyn Stark's face was clearly visible when she hit Ser Jaime Lannister with a large rock in the final episode of *Game of Thrones'* season one. She had just received word that her husband, Lord Eddard Stark, had been beheaded by order of King Joffrey. Catelyn tells Jaime Lannister that he will be "going to the deepest of the seven hells if the gods are just." Jaime, still recovering from the head trauma, replies with a question: "If the gods are real and they are just, then why is the world so full of injustice?" ("Fire and Blood").

This question is the essence of what philosophers call *the problem of evil*. The problem centers around the apparent contradiction between the existence of a good and just God on the one hand, and the evil that is clearly visible in the world on the other hand. For why would a good being with the power to stop evil allow it to exist? Many philosophers and theologians have attempted to answer this question. We know the world that George R. R. Martin has created in A Song of Ice and Fire contains many different gods and beliefs. Does the problem of evil challenge belief in these gods as well?

Is the Problem of Evil Really a Problem?

The Greek philosopher Epicurus (341–270 BCE) was one of the first to state the problem. His version, quoted by the eighteenth-century British philosopher David Hume (1711–1776) in his *Dialogues Concerning Natural Religion*, asks: "Is he [God] willing to prevent evil, but not able? Then he is impotent. Is he able, but not willing? Then he is malevolent. Is he both able and willing? Whence then is evil?"[1]

In other words, according to Hume and Epicurus, the existences of God and evil are logically incompatible. Suppose one believes in the existence of a god who is:

1. Omniscient, meaning that this god knows everything, including exactly when and where evil will happen;
2. Omnipotent, meaning that this god has the power to prevent evil (or anything else, for that matter) from happening;
3. Perfectly good, meaning that this god wants to prevent evil from happening.

If such a god exists, then there should be no evil at all in the world. However:

4. There *is* evil in the world.

Therefore, the conclusion must be that such a god does not exist.

Omniscience, omnipotence, and perfect goodness are three important attributes of the God of the major Western religions. For those religions the problem of evil presents a real danger; if left unsolved it would make belief in such a God irrational. Jaime makes a similar point when he presents the problem of evil to Catelyn: because of evil, believing in the gods of Westeros is irrational as well. And Jaime is certainly not the only one who draws that conclusion. Consider the Hound, Sandor Clegane, who is confronted by Sansa Stark in *A Clash of Kings* with all his evil deeds:

> "Aren't you afraid? The gods might send you down to some terrible hell for all the evil you've done."
>
> "What evil?" He laughed. "What gods?"
>
> "The gods who made us all."
>
> "All?" he mocked. "Tell me, little bird, what kind of god makes a monster like the Imp, or a halfwit like Lady Tanda's daughter? If there are gods, they made sheep so wolves could eat mutton, and they made the weak for the strong to play with."
>
> "True knights protect the weak."
>
> He snorted. "There are no true knights, no more than there are gods. If you can't protect yourself, die and get out of the way of those who can. Sharp steel and strong arms rule this world, don't ever believe any different."
>
> Sansa backed away from him. "You're awful."
>
> "I'm honest. It's the world that's awful. Now fly away, little bird. I'm sick of you peeping at me."[2]

But What Is Evil?

In order to deal with the problem of evil, we must first be clear on what counts as evil. There appear to be two very distinct types of evil in the world: *moral* evil and *natural* evil. Moral evil is the kind of evil that humankind causes by its free decisions. Ordering the beheading of Eddard Stark, or the Hound's murder of Mycah, the butcher's boy, would be examples of this type of evil. Natural evil, on the other hand, refers to pain and suffering caused by the occurrences of nature and not by human beings; shipwrecks in a storm would be an example here.

Unfortunately, not everyone believes the same things to be morally good or evil. The Dothraki Horse God, for instance, appears to have no moral issue with raping and killing. And according to Theon Greyjoy, describing the Drowned God of the Ironmen living on the Iron Islands: "The Drowned God had made them to reave and rape, to carve out kingdoms and write their names in fire and blood and song."[3] Thus, what some might count as evil, others might count as normal or even appropriate behavior. If morality is relative, then objective evil doesn't exist. And if there's no objective evil—if nothing is *really* evil—then the logical contradiction alluded to earlier might be avoided.

This then is the first solution that we will encounter: the problem of evil doesn't appear to affect those who believe that there is no real evil in the world, only subjective judgments on our part. On second glance, however, it seems that most of the inhabitants of the Seven Kingdoms and beyond do believe many things to be really evil, and not just subjectively so. Even someone like Theon Greyjoy would agree that injustice has been done to him when he is taken as a hostage by Eddard Stark. Thus, although one possible solution is to refuse to believe that there actually exists any evil, this appears to be a very weak position. Even in a relativist view, why the gods allow what the inhabitants consider to be evil must still be addressed.

Augustine and Catelyn Defend the Faith of the Seven

The most widespread faith in the Seven Kingdoms is the so-called Faith of the Seven, which has similarities to Roman Catholicism. These include the sudden and fast conversion of Westeros to the Faith, and the hierarchical structure of the religion, with the High Septon as head of the church. Most important, the Faith has only one god, which has seven faces. This is similar to the Christian dogma of the Trinity: one God but three persons. It appears that this god of the Faith has the necessary attributes that give rise to the problem of evil: it is a potent (perhaps even omnipotent) and just god. Thus the god of the Faith should be able and willing to prevent evil from happening. Yet, as we know, there is evil in Westeros.

The philosopher and church father Augustine of Hippo (354–430) presented two important arguments for why God is not responsible for the existence of evil. First, Augustine submits that evil is not something that exists of its own right. Evil is merely the *deprivation* of goodness. This is similar to blindness being the deprivation of eyesight. Blindness is not a positive or definite entity. It is simply the lack of a definite entity, sight. We call someone blind when his eyes are not working. Similarly, according to Augustine, evil is what we call something that is not good. Therefore, God has never *created* evil, for evil is not something that can be created at all.[4]

Augustine's second argument concerns the cause of evil, namely our own *free will*: our ability to choose our own actions. God has deemed it a moral virtue that man has free will and is not simply a puppet that acts only by means of preprogrammed instincts. Thus, although God has created a world that is good and just, human beings can choose to ignore the rules set out by God, and that, according to Augustine, is the cause of evil. Put these two arguments together, and it becomes clear, says Augustine, that God is not the cause of evil; nor can God prevent this type of evil, for preventing evil would mean that individuals would have no free will.[5]

This is called the *free will defense*. So in Westeros, the cause of evil does not lie with the seven-faced god, but with people who act according to their own free will. Remember that Jaime Lannister asked Catelyn Stark: "If the gods are real and they are just, then why is the world so full of injustice?"

To this question, Catelyn replied: "Because of men like you."
Even when Jaime told her to "blame those precious gods
of yours, who brought the boy to our window and gave him
a glimpse of something he was never meant to see," Catelyn
simply answered: "Blame the *gods*?" she said, incredulous.
"Yours was the hand that threw him. You meant for him
to die."[6]

It appears that Catelyn has a point. It was indeed because of
the actions of men like Jaime and his nephew Joffrey that her
husband was murdered.

Problems with the Solutions

Do Augustine's arguments succeed in explaining why moral
evil exists? Well, it seems that things are a bit more complicated than Augustine realized. Take, for instance, his definition of evil as the deprivation of good. This would be a
proper definition of evil only if good and evil were *polar
concepts*. Polar concepts are things that are defined in terms
of one another. For instance, there can be no *mountain* unless
there is also a *valley*. Just try to imagine a world with only
mountains and no valleys. That would be a logical contradiction, for mountains require valleys to count as mountains,
just like there can be tall men only if there are also short
men, and there can be counterfeit coins only if there are also
genuine coins.[7]

Can the same be said about good and evil? Are good and evil
like mountains and valleys? Well, I am perfectly able to imagine
a world with only goodness (such as an endless summer), or a
world with only evil happening (one long, nightmarish winter
with the Others coming from everywhere). Thus they do not
appear to be polar concepts. And that casts doubt on Augustine's
assertion that evil is the deprivation of good. Moreover, the evil
acts that men do—rapes, murders, and the like—seem better
characterized as actual occurrences, rather than deprivations.

But even if we consider these acts to be deprivations, we can still ask why God allows them: why would he allow there to be "less good" when he could bring about more?

The free will defense is also subject to counterarguments. Some philosophers and neuroscientists question whether we actually have free will.[8] But even supposing that we do, there is one very important assumption underlying the free will defense: namely that having free will is, overall, so very important that it *justifies* the occurrence of all the evil in the world. In other words, it must be the case that having free will and the possibility of evil is somehow *better* than to have no free will and no evil.[9]

It is very hard to defend this assumption, however, due to the sheer amount of evil in the world. Although Eddard Stark's death was tragic, at least he was a grown man who had a full life behind him. But think of all those poor innocent children killed during wars. Even unborn children are not spared; think of Daenerys Targaryen's baby. Is free will such a valuable good that it somehow *makes up* for all these, often very horrible, deaths? And further, it seems reasonable to assume that one should try to stop or prevent an evil that someone had freely chosen to bring about, even if doing so would interfere with that person's free will. Why is it then not also reasonable to assume that God should likewise stop or prevent the evil that results from our free decisions? It's not easy to answer these questions.

David Hume and the Impotence of the Old Gods

Having considered the Faith of the Seven, let us turn our analysis to the old gods, the nature spirits that were worshipped by the Children of the Forest and are still worshipped by the Northerners. They must have had at least *some* power, for why would anyone worship and pray to gods who have no power at all and hence exert no influence on the daily lives of human beings? Such gods would be *impotent*, in Hume's sense of the word. But does it follow from the fact that they have *some* power, that they would have *enough* power to prevent all kinds of evil entirely? This seems very unlikely. Faith in the old gods meant faith in a polytheistic religion, a religion with multiple gods. And in such polytheistic religions, there is usually no omnipotent God.

Think of the Greek gods. Even Zeus, who was more powerful than the other Olympian gods, could not prevent evil from happening. Nor did he have power to control events in the domains of his brothers Hades (the underworld) and Poseidon (the sea).

Thus, if the old gods are anything like the Greek gods, then they cannot prevent all evil. They are, in one sense of the word, impotent. The old gods are also powerless in certain areas, especially those where the weirwoods have been cut down. Osha explains this to Bran when she tells him that his brother Robb should have taken an army north instead of south. And when Arya stayed in Harrenhal and tried to pray to the old gods, she wondered whether she perhaps should "pray aloud if she wanted the old gods to hear. Maybe she should pray longer. Sometimes her father had prayed a long time, she remembered. But the old gods had never helped him. Remembering that made her angry. 'You should have saved him,' she scolded the tree. 'He prayed to you all the time. I don't care if you help me or not. I don't think you could even if you wanted to.'"[10]

The old gods might even be a tiny bit malevolent; they are often unwilling to help those who request their help. As King Robert Baratheon told Eddard Stark: "The gods mock the prayers of kings and cowherds alike."[11] So it seems that the problem of evil does not apply to the old gods; since they appear not to be powerful enough or willing enough to prevent evil from happening, you can't wonder why they don't do so.

Blaming the Gods for Natural Evil

Natural evil is the harm caused by natural events, such as earthquakes and hurricanes. For instance, Steffon Baratheon, the father of Robert, Stannis, and Renly Baratheon, was killed along with his wife and one hundred men on his ship the *Windproud* during a storm. Stannis Baratheon, recounting this event, explains that "I stopped believing in gods the day I saw the *Windproud* break up across the bay. Any gods so monstrous as to drown my mother and father would never have *my* worship."[12]

At first glance, the existence of natural evil cannot be explained in the same way as the existence of moral evils such as murder and rape. For it appears that no one's free will has directly caused these natural evils, nor can anyone, except the gods, stop such evils from happening. And as Stannis rightfully concluded, it seems that the gods, old and new, were not willing or able to prevent this type of evil.

However, Augustine and other proponents of the free will defense, such as the contemporary philosopher Richard Swinburne, would still blame humans for this type of evil. They argue that natural evil *is necessary for* moral evil to exist. To illustrate this, consider the prologue to *A Clash of Kings*. Master Cressen decides to poison Melisandre by using the *strangler*, a dissolvable crystal that in fact is a deadly poison.[13] But how did Cressen know that this crystal is poisonous? Well, he probably was taught that this crystal had the appropriate deadly effect by maesters of his Order. But how did these maesters know? There must have been a *first* murder using this crystal at some point in time. But how did the first murderer *know* that this crystal would have a deadly effect? Presumably, this person would have noticed that the crystal or its contents were deadly because someone had digested it by accident, dying in the process. But this latter event just *is* a natural evil. Thus, according to this line of reasoning, there must be naturally occurring evils if men are to know how to cause moral evils. Natural evils are thus a prerequisite for the occurrence of moral evils.[14]

This reply seems very weak. The idea that moral evil requires the existence of natural evil doesn't seem true. God—or in this case the gods—could've created human beings with an innate knowledge of how to harm or kill others. Or one might simply learn from trial and error. Further, even if one grants that poisons are needed for some reason, the existence of hurricanes, floods, and earthquakes, which lay waste without reservation or bias, remain unexplained. No one has figured out how to use such natural disasters to create moral evil.

A second explanation of natural evil is offered by the German philosopher Gottfried Leibniz (1646–1716). Leibniz argued that the world we live in is the *best possible world*. God could not have created the world any better than it currently is. And natural evil just is a necessary part of the best possible world. To take a modern example, plate tectonics—which Leibniz of course knew nothing about—cause earthquakes, but they also refresh the element carbon in the so-called carbon cycle. Without this carbon cycle, carbon-based life forms (such as us) could not exist on this planet. Good and evil go hand in hand, and we simply live in the world with the most optimal combination of both.[15]

This argument, as well as the previous one, has a flaw that we have noticed earlier. The sheer amount of suffering and evil around us makes us wonder whether God or the gods have actually done a good thing in creating this world if it has to include all these evil things as well. And in reply to Leibniz, it certainly seems possible to imagine a world that's better than ours.

R'hllor and Natural Evil

Although humans cannot cause natural evils such as storms, floods, and earthquakes themselves, gods could. These would have to be malevolent and evil gods, of course. But does the existence of evil gods mean that there are no good gods around?

According to the religion of the R'hllor followers, there are two gods: R'hllor, the Lord of Light, who is the good god, and his enemy the Great Other, the god of darkness, cold, and death. These two gods are at war with one another, and the world is their battlefield. The R'hllorian faith displays many commonalities with Zoroastrianism, an old Persian faith in which the good god and evil gods are also at war, and humans are either on the side of the good god or else on the side of the evil god.

The faith of the R'hllor followers can explain why there are natural evils: they are caused by the evil god. Examples include cold winters and the fearsome Others.

Although this type of faith can account for natural evil while still including a good and just god, it suffers from two problems that we have seen before. The first is that R'hllor and the Great Other appear to be equal in power: neither of them is omnipotent. If R'hllor was omnipotent, then he could have simply destroyed the Great Other. That R'hllor has not done so suggests that he *can't* do so, and the same goes for the Great Other. So neither is omnipotent, and Hume has taught us that without omnipotence the logical problem of evil doesn't arise. Only an omnipotent god is capable of preventing all evil from happening. And, of course, the Christian God is omnipotent; so if you are concerned about defending his existence, you will have to look elsewhere.

The second problem is that the followers of R'hllor are not innocent little kittens. Melisandre, the priestess of R'hllor, has caused many deaths. Think of poor Cressen, who drank the *strangler* poison that was meant for Melisandre.[16] And think of Renly Baratheon, killed by the shadow of Stannis, which was created by Melisandre.[17] If we can infer the will of the god by the actions of his followers, then it is doubtful that R'hllor can be counted as a good god, despite his colorful titles.

Gods Don't Care about Men

The problem of evil poses some interesting questions for the gods of Westeros, but it doesn't establish their nonexistence. At least in Westeros, the *logical* problem of evil, which says that the problem of evil leads to a *logical contradiction*, fails. However, there is a second type of the problem of evil, which is called the *evidential* problem of evil. The evidential problem of evil is less stringent, concluding simply that evil provides *evidence* against the existence of gods. As we have seen in this chapter, although there are possible explanations for why there is, or must be, *some* evil, philosophers sympathetic to these explanations are hard-pressed to show why there is so much cruelty, evil, and injustice in the world. It therefore seems that the sheer amount of evil in the world of A Song of Ice and Fire, and perhaps also in our own world, provides evidence, though not absolute proof, for the nonexistence of the gods.

Notice again, though, that these arguments concern only just, good, and powerful gods. The problem of evil, whether logical or evidential, does not argue against uncaring gods. And many of the inhabitants of Westeros would agree that the gods lack such charming characteristics. Thus when Catelyn Stark told Brienne:

> I was taught that good men must fight evil in this world, and Renly's death was evil beyond all doubts. Yet I was also taught that the gods make kings, not the swords of men. If Stannis is our rightful king . . .

Brienne replied:

> Robert was never the rightful king either, even Renly said as much. Jaime Lannister *murdered* the rightful king, after Robert killed his lawful heir on the Trident. *Where were the gods then?* The gods don't care about men, no more than kings care about peasants.[18]

NOTES

1. David Hume, *Dialogues Concerning Natural Religion* (part 10, 1779), ed. Richard Popkin (Indianapolis: Hackett Publishing, 1980), p. 63.

2. George R. R. Martin, *A Clash of Kings* (New York: Bantam Dell, 2005), p. 757.

3. Ibid., p. 169.

4. St. Augustine, *The City of God*, ed. R. W. Dyson (Cambridge: Cambridge University Press, 1998), book XI, Chapter IX, p. 461.

5. St. Augustine, *Confessions*, ed. M. Boulding (New York: New City Press, 1997), book VII, chapter 3, verse 5.

6. Martin, *A Clash of Kings*, p. 793.

7. G. Ryle, *Dilemmas* (Cambridge: Cambridge Univ. Press, 1960).

8. Richard Double, *The Non-Reality of Free Will* (New York: Oxford Univ. Press, 1991); and more recently from scientists, Daniel M. Wegner, *The Illusion of Conscious Will* (Cambridge: MIT Press, 2002); and Benjamin Libet, "Do We Have Free Will?," *Oxford Handbook on Free Will*, ed. Robert Kane (New York: Oxford Univ. Press, 2002), pp. 551–564.

9. H. J. McCloskey, "God and Evil," *Philosophical Quarterly* 10, no. 39 (1960), p. 111.

10. Martin, *A Clash of Kings*, p. 683.

11. George R. R. Martin, *A Game of Thrones* (New York: Bantam Dell, 2005), p. 116.

12. Martin, *A Clash of Kings*, p. 162.

13. Ibid., p. 21.

14. T. J. Mawson, "The possibility of a free-will defence for the problem of natural evil," *Religious Studies* 40 (2004), p. 27. See also R. Swinburne, *The Existence of God* (Oxford: Oxford Univ. Press, 2004).

15. Gottfried Wilhelm Leibniz, *Theodicy: Essays on the Goodness of God, the Freedom of Man and the Origin of Evil* (New York: Cosimo Books, 2009), p. 198.

16. Martin, *A Clash of Kings*, p. 29.

17. Ibid., p. 502.

18. Ibid., p. 561.

PART FOUR

"THE MAN WHO PASSES THE SENTENCE SHOULD SWING THE SWORD"

WHY SHOULD JOFFREY BE MORAL IF HE HAS ALREADY WON THE GAME OF THRONES?

Daniel Haas

The first season of *Game of Thrones* ends with a cruel and immoral boy seated on the Iron Throne. Joffrey Baratheon, thanks to the Machiavellian maneuvering of his mother and the death of his "father," becomes king over all of Westeros. He is an absolute monarch who answers to no one, as Eddard Stark dramatically discovered.

Joffrey's newly acquired power bodes ill for all of Westeros. As king, he is above rebuke and immune from punishment for his actions. While his subjects cower in fear, surely they must hope that Joffrey will change his ways and become a just and moral ruler.

But why should Joffrey be moral if he doesn't have to face any negative consequences for his actions? Although the people of his kingdom might prefer him to be a moral ruler, why should that motivate him? If he has the power to do whatever he wants, isn't it reasonable for him to do exactly that? In fact, what reason do any of us have to be moral in the absence of negative consequences?

The World Will Be Exactly As You Want It to Be ("Lord Snow")

King Joffrey doesn't see any reason why he should behave morally. He's born to privilege and power and is well aware that few people have the power to overtly question his behavior. Even before his "father's" unfortunate "accident," Joffrey is well aware that he can get away with pretty much whatever he wants. And that's exactly what he does.

When Joffrey decides to pick on Arya and her friend Mycah, the butcher's son, it's not Joffrey who is punished for being a bully. Sure, Arya disarms the prince, her direwolf bites his hand, and Joffrey's sword is thrown in the river, but Joffrey is not called to account for picking a fight with Arya in the first place. Instead, Arya is punished, her direwolf is chased off, and both Mycah and Sansa's innocent direwolf, Lady, are killed. Joffrey literally gets away with murder. He treats others poorly, and they get punished for calling him out on his misbehavior.

Not surprisingly, when Joffrey becomes king, he continues to act as if he can do whatever he wants. Cersei says of her son, "Now that he's king, he believes he should do as he pleases, not as he's bid."[1] What changes when Joffrey is king, however, is that he believes he really is accountable to no one for his actions. Before his coronation, he at least knew he answered to his parents and, to a lesser extent, to the rest of his family, but once the Iron Throne is his, Joffrey believes he is above rebuke. This perceived privilege gives him license to engage in all sorts of horrible actions, not least of which is the merciless beheading of Eddard Stark.

Joffrey's self-indulgent, sadistic behavior leaves most fans of A Song of Ice and Fire with a visceral distaste for him.

Even George R. R. Martin has admitted that he took a certain guilty pleasure writing the scenes in which Joffrey finally gets his comeuppance.[2] We can all agree that Joffrey ought to be a better person. Even though he has the political power to do whatever he wants, there are some things you just don't do. No matter how much your future in-laws upset you, you don't cut off their heads in front of your fiancée.

But does Joffrey have reason to behave differently, given that there's no external negative consequence for his actions? Isn't he rational to do exactly what he wants to do, given that he need not fear punishment? What reason does Joffrey have to behave morally if nothing outwardly bad will happen to him as a response to his actions? Wouldn't we all do the same (maybe we wouldn't beat up our fiancées)? If you can get away with it, why not smite your enemies, cheat on your college entrance exams, or download a couple of movies without paying? If you're guaranteed not to get caught and guaranteed not to suffer any negative repercussions for your misbehavior, why care about what morality dictates? Wouldn't it be rational to behave like Joffrey and do whatever you want when you know you can get away with it? Or is there some self-interested reason that Joffrey and the rest of us should behave morally, even in the absence of external negative consequences for our actions?

A Man with Great Ambition and No Morals, I Wouldn't Bet against Him ("Fire and Blood")

Why be moral? This question dates back to Plato's (428–348 BCE) *Republic*, in which the characters Socrates and Glaucon discuss the nature of justice.[3] Playing devil's advocate, Glaucon makes the case that we behave justly (or morally) only because we're afraid of getting caught and punished. Socrates (speaking for Plato) disagrees and suggests that the just man is always better off than the unjust man. As a counterexample to

Socrates' claim that the just man is always better off, Glaucon recounts the myth of the ring of Gyges.[4]

In Glaucon's story, Gyges, a simple shepherd, discovers a magic ring that turns whoever wears it invisible. Once learning of the ring's magical properties, Gyges realizes he can fulfill his wildest ambitions. He uses the ring to fulfill his lust for power. He seduces the queen, kills the king, and seizes the throne for himself. Gyges has the ability to satisfy his every desire, and so he does.

Glaucon then asks Socrates to consider a scenario in which there are two magic rings, one given to a just man and the other given to an unjust man. Glaucon proposes that both the men will behave poorly. Not even the just man could resist the temptation to fulfill his every desire. After all, why should he resist? With the ring of Gyges, the just man has no reason to fear reprisal. His immoral acts will go unseen. With this kind of power, wouldn't it be rational for him simply to do what is in his best interest, to do whatever he feels like? Wouldn't he be kind of silly not to take advantage of the opportunity? Glaucon maintains that not only would most people use the ring, but that it would be irrational not to use the ring.

If Glaucon is right that only a fool would act morally in the absence of sanction, perhaps Joffrey is on to something. The ring-of-Gyges scenario is very similar to the way in which Joffrey conceives of the privilege of sitting on the Iron Throne. As king, Joffrey believes he will be immune from sanction. After all, justice in Westeros is the "king's justice." What the king says and does goes. If someone doesn't like it or, even worse, questions his behavior, then Joffrey, as king, can simply dish out one of his many ingenious punishments, such as when he has a traveling minstrel's tongue cut out for singing a song that mocks the death of Robert Baratheon and not so subtly accuses the Lannisters of killing the king. From Joffrey's perspective, the privilege of sitting on the Iron Throne is just as good as having your own magic ring.

Being king might come with nearly limitless power, but unfortunately for Joffrey, not even a king can hide his actions from his subjects. The ring of Gyges is so enticing precisely because its wearer gets to behave immorally without gaining the bad reputation that Joffrey and other despicable people earn for themselves. And as much as Joffrey would like to believe he can do whatever he wants, people remember tyrants with hatred and loathing. A generation before Joffrey, the people of Westeros rose up against the mad king Aerys Targaryen. This rebellion eventually led to Aerys's murder at the hand of Jaime Lannister. As season one of *Game of Thrones* comes to an end, Joffrey is fast following in Aerys's footsteps.[5]

With each act of cruelty, with each harm inflicted for selfish gain, Joffrey turns a potentially loyal ally into a lifelong enemy. Whereas Gyges gets to enjoy the benefits of appearing to be a good person, Joffrey is not so lucky. Before his rise to power, Joffrey's behavior was offensive enough to warrant a good beating from his uncle. Did you cheer the first time you watched Tyrion Lannister slap his nephew? I know I did. And being crowned king did nothing to improve Joffrey's behavior. A few short days after Joffrey takes the throne, Sansa, Joffrey's loving bride-to-be, is contemplating pushing him off a bridge. Joffrey's misdeeds all but guarantee that his time on the Iron Throne will come to a quick and bloody end.

Joffrey has clearly misunderstood what sitting on the Iron Throne means. But is Joffrey's mistake that he acts immorally? Or is it something else? Perhaps believing that he's invincible?

Joffrey believes that as king he can do whatever he wants and that there will be no negative consequences. This is hopelessly naïve. His fatal mistake is not so much that he behaves immorally, but rather that he incorrectly believes that he is invincible. After all, immoral behavior has given him a bad reputation and made many enemies. He'd be wise to start behaving better.

Members of Joffrey's court, such as Lord Petyr "Littlefinger" Baelish, are better at concealing their misdeeds. And, like Gyges,

Cersei and Jaime Lannister are capable of keeping their moral transgressions secret, even if it means pushing a child or two out a window. Maybe the real take-home lesson is that Joffrey just needs to be more careful about who *sees* him acting immorally.

The Truth Will Be What You Make It ("Lord Snow")

Cersei and Jaime Lannister are wise enough to keep their moral lapses secret. They act as if they're morally respectable when they're with other people, and they keep their love affair and political maneuvering in the shadows.

In a pivotal scene, Cersei advises Joffrey that "the occasional kindness will spare you all sorts of trouble down the road." ("Lord Snow"). Cersei is trying to teach her son the importance of keeping up the appearance of being a good person by acting as if he's a just ruler and cultivating the reputation of a moral person. Her advice is that it is fine to do whatever you want in secret, but to outwardly act a villain is to make quick enemies and set yourself up for a huge fall.

Cersei, of course, doesn't have a magic ring like Gyges. She has to resort to political doublespeak, her lover pushing children out windows, and other Machiavellian strategies for concealing her true motives. But assuming she's successful at maintaining the appearance of being a noble and just queen, does she have any reason to be moral in her private life? Given that Cersei's done her part to make sure she never has to face sanction, does she have any reason to be moral? Is fear of retribution the only real reason to be moral?

You've a Long Way to Travel and In Bad Company ("Fire and Blood")

Perhaps Cersei and Joffrey should be moral because of the social contract we're all part of as members of communities.

It's clearly in both their best interests to live in a society where people behave morally, where they respect the rights and interests of others. After all, if Cersei knew that everyone else at King's Landing was guaranteed to behave morally, provided she also behaved well, then she would have far less motivation to plot and scheme. Likewise, if the only way that Joffrey could ensure that his subjects would not try to usurp his throne was if he were a just and noble ruler, then he would also have a strong reason to behave morally.

The social contract theorist Thomas Hobbes (1588–1679) would agree. Hobbes worried about the danger of humans competing with one another to satisfy their own goals. He recognized that in a world without legal, moral, and social constraints on what we can and cannot do, there is nothing stopping us from deadly conflict. It's a grim reality that humans pursing their own goals and interests will inevitably come into direct conflict with one another. And it's an obvious truth that even the weakest of us can pose a threat to the strongest. Hobbes was well aware that an imp can always hire a sellsword, a queen can always resort to treachery or poison, and even a strong warrior like Drogo can be taken down by a mere flesh wound. When we all pursue our own goals and desires without the constraints of morality and society, we compete. And when we compete, we end up killing each other.

This fear of mutual destruction gives us a powerful motivation to find a way of ensuring that we all are on our best behavior. Rationally, we ought to be willing to do just about anything to ensure an environment without constant deadly competition. And one way to do this is to agree to live by a set of rules. If I agree to be a moral and just person provided you agree to be a moral and just person, and you agree to the same, we both have assurance that we're able to cooperate and live in peace. The reason that Joffrey and Cersei have to be moral, then, is to ensure the preservation of the social contract, to ensure that everyone else behaves morally as well.

At first glance, this seems to be a powerful answer to the "Why be moral?" question. It gives even the most warped and psychopathic person a compelling reason to be on her best behavior. If you step out of line and indulge in immoral acts, you're breaking the contract with your fellow citizens. And if you don't play by the rules, then they have no reason to either. Once you can no longer rely on your neighbors to behave morally, you're jumping at every shadow, expecting a knife in the back.

The men of the Night's Watch embrace a philosophy very much in the spirit of Hobbes's reason to be moral. The Night's Watch is a sort of prison colony made up of murderers, rapists, thieves, and those with nowhere else to go. Most end up joining the Night's Watch reluctantly. They've been given a choice between "taking the black"—pledging their lives to defend Westeros from the unspeakable horrors beyond the wall—or death. Clearly, when you're living among thieves and murderers, it's vitally important to have some assurance that your neighbor won't slit your throat while you sleep. The Night's Watch pulls this off by making sure its members understand that if they step out of line, they'll be killed.

But King's Landing is a place very different from the Wall, and Joffrey's court is far less honorable than the band of vagabonds that make up the watch. Even if Joffrey and Cersei were to agree with Hobbes that the desire for a stable, moral society gives us some motivation to behave well, that obligation lasts only as long as others keep up their end of the contract. And you don't need to be Eddard Stark to know that there is no contract in Joffrey's court. Behaving morally is not a good survival strategy at King's Landing.

King's Landing is more akin to the Dothraki civilization than to the honorable sort of community that the men of the Night's Watch inhabit. Behaving "morally" in both environments is viewed as a kind of weakness. Among the Dothraki, only the strongest survive. Drogo is Khal, the leader of his people, not because he is a pillar of virtue but because he is a ruthless, bloody killer who's willing to rip the throats out of his subjects if they challenge his authority or get in his way. Likewise, Littlefinger and Varys, two key players in the politics of King's Landing, have survived so long because both men are ruthless killers willing to squash any opponent. True, they use subtler, more indirect methods than pouring molten gold over the heads of those who annoy them, but the end result is the same. At King's Landing and in the Dothraki wilderness, you play for keeps. So King's Landing is not really the kind of environment that lends itself to respecting a social contract.

Even if King's Landing was a more morally respectable community, Joffrey wouldn't necessarily have a reason to behave morally. If you think about it, it's not really in Joffrey's interest to behave morally. What is really in Joffrey's interest is for *everyone else* to respect the rights and interests of others, and for them to think that Joffrey is behaving well.

If everyone else bought into the social contract theory, Joffrey would be at a distinct advantage. The citizens of his kingdom would be easy prey. Ned and Sansa were blindsided by his mother precisely because they thought Cersei would play by the rules. If Joffrey were to take his mother's advice and practice a little discretion, he could free-ride on the good behavior of his citizens and indulge his wildest immoral desires in private.

The social contract solution to the "Why be moral?" question doesn't really give Joffrey a compelling reason to behave morally. It might give a reason for why, in general, groups of people *should* behave morally, but that's not the sort of reason that would motivate an immoralist like Joffrey. Joffrey can grant that it's in his interest for everyone else to behave well, but what we really need is a reason why he also ought to behave well.

Our Way Is the Old Way
("Winter Is Coming")

According to Plato, immoralists like Joffrey are incapable of genuine happiness because happiness is about more than merely satisfying your desires and getting whatever you want.

It has to do with your inner life, the state of your soul. Joffrey should be a moral and just king, then, because he's missing out on happiness by refusing to embrace morality.

You might think there's some sleight of hand going on here. Sure, Joffrey looks like he's missing out on some good things in life, but is that because he's an immoral jerk? Joffrey's parents, Cersei and Jaime, both have fairly questionable motives as well (at least during the first season of *Game of Thrones*), but they both look like they've found some happiness with each other. They might push the occasional child out a window, or engage in the occasional incestuous romp, but are their souls and lives really a chaotic, disorganized mess because of these acts?

Joffrey and his family look like they have a lot of the good things in life, and a lot of those good things were surely gained through immoral actions. The Lannisters are an extremely wealthy family, and their accumulated wealth and power allow them to buy all sorts of pleasures. Whether it's lavish meals, easy access to prostitutes, or extravagant celebrations, the Lannisters look like they have a pretty comfortable life compared to many of those who live in the Seven Kingdoms. Is it really true, then, that immoral persons always miss out on happiness?

Perhaps Cersei and Joffrey have pleasurable lives, but this is different from genuine happiness. Plato has in mind a deeper kind of happiness. An immoral person, such as Joffrey, is an unhappy person, even if he gets what he wants and satisfies his desires. His soul is disordered, and his inner life is in chaos. His life is a small, selfish one. He is concerned only with himself and lacks the ability to connect in any meaningful way with other human beings. After all, in his view others are good only as a means toward satisfying his desires. Without any concern for morality, Joffrey lacks, or at least fails to display, the basic human emotions such as compassion, love, and concern that allow for real friendships and relationships. Joffrey is alone. If Plato is correct, Joffrey's immoral life prevents him from experiencing what is actually valuable in life. Genuine happiness, then, is something that might be out of the grasp of the immoral person.

Some philosophers are skeptical about Plato's view of happiness, but there's at least one person in Westeros who would agree with Plato. Eddard Stark seems to think that there's something to the moral life that makes living in an honorable and just way more important than any Iron Throne. Perhaps it's even worth dying for.

I Must Be One of the Few Men in This City Who Doesn't Want to Be King ("Fire and Blood")

In a telling scene, Ned confronts Cersei to let her know that he has discerned the truth that Joffrey isn't really the son of the king. He warns Cersei,

> "When the king returns from his hunt, I'll tell him the truth. You must be gone by then, you and your children. I'll not have their blood on my hands. Go as far away as you can, with as many men as you can, because wherever you go, Robert's wrath will follow you."
>
> "And what of my wrath, Lord Stark? You should've taken the crown for yourself. Jaime told me about the day King's Landing fell. He was sitting in the Iron Throne and you made him give it up. All you needed to do was climb the steps yourself. Such a sad mistake."
>
> "I've made many mistakes in my life, but that wasn't one of them."
>
> "Oh, but it was. When you play the game of thrones, you win or you die." ("You Win or You Die")

This conversation illustrates a key contrast between Ned Stark and Cersei Lannister. Cersei sees her life at King's Landing as a competition. She loves her brother Jaime and her children, and she is willing to do whatever it takes to seize power for herself and her family. She has no time for honor or morality. It's the Iron Throne and the power that comes with it that matters to her. Power, particularly the nearly limitless power that comes with sitting on the throne, comes with security. And to her, the stupidest mistake someone could make would be to pass up an opportunity to take the throne, to secure that privilege and safety for oneself and one's family.

Ned sees things differently. He might agree with Cersei that the game of thrones is played for keeps, but he's unwilling to play a game where the only way to win is to sacrifice your morality. To Ned there are more important things in life than power, and one's honor, one's morality, is of much higher importance than even a long and secure life.

This unwillingness to compromise his ideals is one of the main reasons Ned believes he was wise in refusing to take the throne. As a young man, Ned was aware that sitting on the throne and ensuring that he stayed there would mean compromising his honor again and again. It would be to live a life in constant fear of being overthrown, a life of constant competition and moral compromise. And for Ned, there's no happiness or even glory in that sort of life.

Ned's decision to reject the throne is in the spirit of Plato's answer to the "Why be moral?" question. After all, Ned rejected the throne to return to a life in the North with his wife. He remained steadfast in his commitment to honor and virtue and carved out a surprisingly happy and fulfilling life for someone in Westeros. He spent decades in a loving home, happily raising children and ruling his own corner of the kingdom justly and wisely. He cultivated deep and genuine relationships with those he most cared about and passed on his wisdom to his children. Were it not for Robert's insistence that he join him at King's Landing, Ned would have lived an honorable life until the end. This bliss is something that Cersei, her family, and all those struggling for position at King's Landing will never experience. It was Ned's commitment to morality that allowed him to find genuine happiness, despite his full awareness that winter is coming.

Because Ned recognized the futility of an immoral life, he was reluctant to take Robert up on the offer to become the King's Hand. Ned knew that his commitment to honor and justice made him particularly ill suited to compete with the den of vipers at King's Landing. Finally forced into the game of thrones, Ned plays it as he lived, with honor and justice. But an honorable man pitted against the likes of Cersei, Littlefinger, and Varys "The Spider" is a dead man. Ned was doomed the second he accepted Robert's offer. After a few short weeks at King's Landing, he finds himself imprisoned for treason, victim to the political maneuverings of those unencumbered by moral constraints.

After Cersei has Ned arrested, Varys pays Ned a visit to offer him a way to avoid execution. If Ned is willing to keep it secret that Joffrey is not really the son of the late king, Varys assures Ned that he'll be able to convince Cersei to let Ned take the black and join the Night's Watch. All Ned has to do is tell a little lie and keep Cersei's secret.

Ned responds "You think my life is some precious thing to me, as I would trade my honor for a few more years of, what? You grew up with actors, you learnt their craft and you learnt it well. But I grew up with soldiers. I learnt how to die a long time ago" ("Baelor").

The Spider tries one more tactic to persuade Ned to compromise his values. He asks, "What of your daughter's life, my lord? Is that a precious thing to you?" ("Baelor"). This veiled threat in the form of a question finally motivates Ned to compromise. He trades his honor to save his daughters and stay his own execution. In the end, though, it's futile. Ned sacrifices his honor, falsely claims that he conspired to steal the Iron Throne for himself, and proclaims Joffrey as the true and rightful heir. Joffrey dishes out his own warped sense of justice: Ned loses his head, and Sansa remains a prisoner with her life still in peril. Ned's death is tragic because he sacrificed his morality, his honor, for naught.

Despite his tragic end and his moment of weakness, Ned might actually be right about the value of morality. Perhaps Cersei and Joffrey are missing out on something that Ned's honor allows him to experience. Ned's answer to the "Why be moral?" question is similar to Plato's. The reason to be moral isn't to avoid punishment, scorn, disapproval, or being called to account for our misbehavior. Winter is inevitably coming, and we shouldn't be motivated to renounce morality out of fear of bad things happening to us. We should stick to morality because being moral is the only way to have the best that life has to offer. When faced with Cersei and Joffrey, then, Ned and Plato do have an answer. You miss out on the good life by being immoral. There's more to life than mere pleasure.[6]

NOTES

1. George R. R. Martin, *A Clash of Kings* (New York: Bantam Dell, 2005), p. 58.

2. Authors@google: George R. R. Martin, Aug. 6, 2011, www.youtube.com/watch?v=QTTW8M_etko.

3, Plato, *The Republic*, trans. G. M. A. Grube (Indianapolis: Hackett Publishing Company, 1974).

4. Ibid., pp. 31–34.

5. Martin, A *Clash of Kings*, p. 489.

6. Dedicated to Karen Haas, my mom, for raising me like a Stark and teaching me that there's more to the good life than always getting what you want.

THE MORAL LUCK
OF TYRION LANNISTER

Christopher Robichaud

"If you're going to be a cripple, it's better to be a rich cripple."

—Tyrion Lannister ("Lord Snow")

The world of A Song of Ice and Fire isn't pretty, but the ugliness isn't found in the setting itself. Westeros is filled with stunning locations, like the peaceful beauty of the godswoods and the vast greatness of the Wall. Rather, the ugliness of George R. R. Martin's world has to do with the *society* of the Seven Kingdoms. It's a nation of brutal social arrangements mired in a bloody civil war. And a chasm exists between the haves and the have-nots. Some of the have-nots eke out a meager life as farmers, tradesmen, or barkeeps, doing their best not to be conscripted to fight for a noble house in one of their never-ending conflicts. Other have-nots must turn to prostitution or thievery to get by. Life as a noble, in turn, brings with it a different set of concerns. Although the haves of the Seven

Kingdoms needn't worry about food, shelter, companionship, or anything of the like, at least most of the time, they do have to constantly be on guard against their food being poisoned, their shelter being invaded, and their friends turning foes. After all, everything is fair play in the game of thrones.

Enter Tyrion Lannister, one of the most complicated and compelling characters ever to appear in a fantasy series. Tyrion was born a dwarf,[1] offering reason enough for him to have been drowned at birth. A dwarf in the Seven Kings would normally be guaranteed a miserable existence, but luckily Tyrion was also born a Lannister. House Lannister is the richest in the Seven Kingdoms, and its political influence is vast. The patriarch of the family, Tywin Lannister, is a military mastermind. His daughter Cersei sits as the queen at the beginning of the story, and later she's the de facto ruler of the Seven Kingdoms while her eldest son, Joffrey, matures to an appropriate age to inherit the crown. Her beautiful twin brother, Jaime, a member of the Kingsguard, is an extremely skilled and deadly knight.

And then there's Tyrion. Grotesquely ugly (at least in the novels). Abnormally small. His birth killed his mother, a fact for which his father despises him. His mind is sharp, calculating, and exceedingly clever, which means his sister distrusts him, seeming to go so far as to order an attempt on his life. Yet Tyrion often shows compassion worthy of House Stark and displays heroism on the battlefield worthy of Jaime the Kingslayer himself. He reveals exceptional leadership qualities in running the Seven Kingdoms from behind the scenes, as the Hand of King Joffrey. And while he drinks and whores excessively, he nonetheless harbors a genuine love for the prostitute Shae.

What, then, do we make of Tyrion Lannister? Tyrion is both one of the luckiest and the unluckiest men alive. He came out of the womb with everything stacked against him physically, including killing his own mother in the process. And yet he was born with an intellect to be envied and into a noble house that guaranteed him wealth and political influence.

What do these facts have to do with the moral character of Tyrion? How should they affect our assessment of his actions as morally praiseworthy or blameworthy?

The Virtues and Vices of Tyrion Lannister

Let's begin by focusing first on Tyrion's moral character and the role that luck played in forming it. Is Tyrion a good guy or a bad guy? This question doesn't have a straightforward answer. But there's something worth noting about the question itself. When we think about whether a person is good or bad, we consider not only what the person has done, but what *kind* of person he or she is; that's how we put it, anyway. And what's behind that way of putting it is a concern about a person's moral character.

As with so much else in philosophy, there's a lot of disagreement over what we should understand a person's moral character to be. Most philosophers, though, agree that someone's moral character doesn't consist only in what that person does. Actions might reveal a person's character, but they don't constitute it. Here's an example: In *A Clash of Kings*, it becomes clear that Tyrion is quite a brave person on the battlefield, in addition to being a decent strategist.[2] He talks a good talk about not wanting to get into the bloody business of combat, but when push comes to shove—when Sandor "The Hound" Clegane flees due to fires on the battlefield—Tyrion leads a small number of men against a much larger number of Stannis Baratheon's army as they're rushing through the gates of King's Landing. What this reveals about Tyrion is that he is in fact brave. But it doesn't seem to make much sense to say that he suddenly became brave at that moment. Rather, the more appealing way to describe things is to say that he was brave going into the battle, but we learned that about him—and maybe he learned that about himself—only when an opportunity arose for him to act in a certain way. His actions revealed a certain virtue of his moral character—bravery. But he had that virtue regardless of whether the opportunity arose for him to demonstrate it.

In this way of seeing things, a person's moral character amounts to a set of dispositions that he has, dispositions to act in various ways under various circumstances. Those circumstances might never arise, and so we might never learn about certain virtues and vices—moral dispositions—that a person in fact has. That doesn't mean that he doesn't have those traits, though. In light of this, when we ask whether a person is good or bad, what we seem most interested in is what his moral dispositions are. Is he cruel? Compassionate? Generous? Stingy? And so forth. We usually base our answers to those questions on actions, because actions reveal character, even though actions alone don't make up a person's moral character.

So what of Tyrion's moral character? Well, from what we've learned of it, it runs the gamut of good and bad dispositions. In certain circumstances, he's prone to condescension, arrogance, and licentiousness. He also tends toward being a bit of a glutton and a drunk. Still, other situations reveal that he's understanding, compassionate, just, and brave. This makes for a complicated moral character. But how much of Tyrion's character is up to him? Is he mostly responsible for the kind of person he's developed into, or is luck—involving circumstances beyond his control—mostly responsible?

It's Out of the King's Hand's Hands

Despite what we might ordinarily think, Tyrion's moral character may be largely beyond his control. Consider his compassion and his empathy, two distinct but related moral virtues. Why do we think Tyrion is compassionate and empathetic? Tyrion's compassion toward those who are maligned and outcast—toward Sansa, kidnapped by Cersei and a victim of Joffrey's physical abuses, or toward Jon Snow, Ned Stark's bastard son—plausibly stems not from any formal training in good behavior that Tyrion devoted himself to, but simply from his own life circumstances. "What the hell do you know about being a bastard?" Jon Snow asks Tyrion. "All dwarves are bastards in their father's eyes," replies Tyrion ("Winter Is Coming"). Would Tyrion even attend to the plight of Jon as he is shipped off to the Wall, let alone care enough to give him some good advice on navigating his station in life, had Tyrion not been born into a similar position of being an outcast? Quite unlikely. Nor would he be clever and calculating were he not part of a family where a man of his physical limitations had to develop those traits to survive the machinations of his sister Cersei and the disdain of his father, Tywin. Nor would he necessarily be brave were his brother's exploits not held up to him as an ongoing example of knightly virtue.

Does this mean that no aspect of Tyrion's moral character is in his control? Of course not. But it does show that a lot more of it is beyond his control than we might have thought before reflecting on the matter. We like to think that we are the architects of our moral characters, but as Tyrion reveals, pure circumstance can play a substantial role in molding our moral characters.

The Many Faces of Moral Luck

At this point we might start to get a little worried about what these observations mean for moral responsibility. If so much of Tyrion's character is beyond his control, and yet his actions issue from his character, can we really praise him or blame him for what he does? Is he morally responsible for anything, if he's not causally responsible to a great extent for the moral character that gives rise to those actions?

It turns out that worries along these lines go beyond what we've explored so far. In his groundbreaking article "Moral Luck," philosopher Thomas Nagel calls the kind of luck we've been considering with regard to Tyrion's character "constitutive luck."[3] Nagel also explores areas where there seems to be a conflict in our way of assessing moral responsibility. One such area, which he calls "resultant luck," involves cases like the part in *A Clash of Kings* where Tyrion orders the massive production of "wildfire," a kind of combustible liquid, to be used to stave off Stannis's fleet. Tyrion takes great pains to ensure that this dangerous substance is produced with care and that those who will use it are properly trained. As it turns out, it is produced with great care, it is used properly, and much of Stannis's fleet is burned at sea because of it. But suppose instead that even though it was produced with care and used properly, a terrible accident happens in the course of battle, and instead of the wildfire destroying Stannis's fleet, much of King's Landing is set afire instead. Rather than triumphing, the Lannisters would have been defeated.

In the first case, we are prone to praise Tyrion for his role in the use of wildfire. (At least if we're Lannisters. Let's assume, for the sake of argument, that we have good reason to believe that the Lannisters are fighting a just war.) In the second case, we are prone to blame Tyrion *for the very same actions*. And that's the rub. In both cases, the part of the story that is in Tyrion's control is the same. He does the very same thing. Whether we judge him as praiseworthy or blameworthy depends, it seems, on results that are entirely beyond his control. Yet, and this is the crucial point, we think that we should praise or blame people only for things over which they exercise control. So here Nagel has alerted us to a deep tension in our moral thinking. There is a strong tendency to praise Tyrion in the first case and to condemn him in the second, all the while recognizing that we're praising him or blaming him for reasons outside his control. And that seems an incorrect thing to do, given that we think that having moral responsibility necessarily involves being in control of what happens.

It gets worse. Nagel also discusses what he calls "circumstantial luck," which is the kind of luck involved when we are put into certain situations where our virtues or vices have an opportunity to reveal themselves. Suppose Tyrion is disposed to being a very physically abusive person whenever he is put into a position where he is physically imposing. Luckily for him, his own features limit such situations from ever arising. As a result, we would not blame him for this vice, even though it's just happenstance that he never reveals it. Were he put into a situation where his vice were displayed through actions, we would blame him. Notice that this is not just a matter of us not knowing about the vice. It seems correct that even if we did know, somehow, that Tyrion is physically belligerent, we would be less prone to blame him for his belligerency if circumstances never, or rarely, cooperated in letting his vice act up; on the other hand, we would be more prone to blame him if they did cooperate in revealing his vice. But more often than not, it's purely a matter of luck whether those circumstances do or do not arise.

Circumstantial luck is a particularly powerful way to demonstrate the conflict that arises in our moral thinking. Many citizens of Nazi Germany found themselves in situations that led them to do horrible things. We blame them, rightfully, it surely seems, for their crimes. There's no comfort in this, though, for as we've learned from such episodes as the now-famous Milgram experiment, the disposition to blindly follow the orders of those in power, even when doing so induces us to do terrible things, is a vice that many, many of us have.[4] We just got lucky—and continue to be lucky—in not being thrown into circumstances where this vice comes to the fore. Yet even recognizing this, it still seems correct to hold certain Germans more blameworthy for the vice than those of us who also share it, but have never been put in circumstances where it's revealed. That's the tension that moral luck forces us to confront.

If chance pervades the circumstances of our moral choices, the consequences of them, and the very character that gives rise to them, it seems as though we shouldn't be praised or blamed for anything we do. But that would be absurd. We would have to abandon any notion of being morally responsible for what we do; we would be like cats, dogs, bears, and other animals that aren't considered appropriate subjects for moral evaluation. It would be encouraging at this point to turn to Nagel's article and find a resolution of this difficulty. But, alas, he offers none. Indeed, he observes, famously, that "[t]he area of genuine agency, and therefore of legitimate moral judgment, seems to shrink under this scrutiny to an extensionless point."[5] Not the most uplifting of observations, to be sure.

Kant to the Rescue?

Is there any way to salvage moral responsibility in light of these considerations? The German philosopher Immanuel Kant (1724–1804) offered one line of thought that divorces morality from luck. (Nagel, in his article, acknowledges Kant's attempts at this, but finds them largely unacceptable, for reasons we'll see in a moment.) Kant thinks that moral praise and blame should be determined by one and only one thing, namely, how well we exercise our *will*. Good willing, according to Kant, is the only thing that ultimately has moral worth, and it is the only appropriate subject of moral responsibility. Significantly, as Kant takes pains to emphasize, a good will is not held hostage to the consequences it brings about.

There's some intuitive force to Kant's position. When we evaluate individuals morally, we are often interested in why they acted as they did—what reasons they had for acting. And in certain circumstances, that's all we care about. For instance, Tyrion goes to great lengths in *A Clash of Kings* to keep Shae protected and out of the reach of Cersei. At some point it seems as though he fails at this, but it turns out that Cersei made a mistake in the prostitute she captured to hold sway over Tyrion—it's not Shae. Suppose, though, that it was Shae who's now in Cersei's clutches, virtually guaranteeing that bad things will befall her.

Is Tyrion blameworthy for this situation? Not, according to Kant, if he acted *for the right reasons*, even if, in doing so, circumstances conspired against him. Those right reasons, according to Kant, have to do with following the *categorical imperative*, one formulation of which states that we have an obligation to treat persons as ends in themselves and not as mere means. Tyrion's actions conform to this imperative, since, let us presume, he acted not only for personal reasons—keeping Shae safe certainly benefits him—but for Shae's well-being also. Tyrion shows his respect for her by recognizing that she doesn't deserve to be used by Cersei as a means in her campaign against him.

We're glossing over some important details in Kant's account. There's an ongoing disagreement among scholars regarding what Kant's moral psychology exactly amounts to—what he thinks has to be going on in our heads for us to count as acting for the right reasons and, thus, exercising a good will. In one interpretation of Kant, Tyrion would not be acting for the right reasons, since he had personal reasons for acting, in addition to recognizing his duty to keep Shae safe. This reading, though, is problematic, since it would mean that most of us rarely, if ever, act with a good will; most times, our choices are based on a number of motivating factors, moral considerations among them, but not exclusively. In light of this, in a different interpretation of Kant, Tyrion does count as acting with a good will, provided that he *would* have done what he did were he to have lacked any personal reasons for doing so.[6]

We needn't explore the details of these opposing interpretations of Kant, though, because it should be clear that they won't help us address all the problems associated with moral luck. Even if Kant is right, all he has tackled is resultant luck. He has offered us an understanding of moral responsibility that pushes back on the idea that we should ever count the consequences of an action in evaluating whether a person who performed it is praiseworthy or blameworthy. All that matters is the will itself, regardless of what happens. But even if Kant is correct on this count, and we think he gives us reason to correct our inclination, at least at times, to evaluate persons morally based on the consequences of their actions, this doesn't speak at all to the other forms of luck Nagel considers. Take constitutive luck. The disposition to act according to the categorical imperative—to have moral reasons guide and trump other reasons—is itself a contingent virtue that some persons have, and some don't, based as much on luck and circumstance as anything else. If this were not true—if this disposition were something entirely in our control—then it would be surprising that so many of us fail to act morally so often. But it's not surprising once we acknowledge that the disposition to let moral reasons guide our actions varies from person to person, and that life circumstances explain this better than anything else.

Moral Luck and the Last Laugh

The problem of moral luck isn't just a clever philosophical conundrum. It is, as Nagel recognized, a deep paradox that forces us to examine the very idea of persons being morally responsible for anything. We don't want to claim that no one is worthy of praise or blame, but at the same time, it seems that the only way to hold onto this idea is to abandon another idea that we cherish—that persons are morally responsible only for those things that are in their control. Finding a way to reconcile these two ideas has challenged philosophers for decades, without resolution. And Tyrion Lannister is the perfect character to force us to think about these matters as well. I doubt he'd be bothered too much by our inability to solve the problem. By his own admission, he is, in his words, a vile man whose crimes and sins are beyond counting ("A Golden Crown"). But he would no doubt have a smile on his face as we reflect on this and realize that perhaps, just perhaps, there's nothing for which he deserves blame. After all, how much of Tyrion is in Tyrion's control?

NOTES

1. Although I'm uncomfortable using the term "dwarf" to describe Tyrion, since we no longer refer to little people that way, I will nevertheless adopt the language used in the novels, for the sake of consistency.

2. George R. R. Martin, *A Clash of Kings* (New York: Bantam Dell, 2005).

3. In Nagel's book *Mortal Questions* (Cambridge: Cambridge Univ. Press 1979), pp. 24–38.

4. See Stanley Milgram's "Behavioral Study of Obedience" in the *Journal of Abnormal and Social Psychology* (1963), pp. 371–378.

5. Nagel, "Moral Luck," p. 35.

6. For a nice discussion of this issue, see Richard Hensen's "What Kant Might Have Said: Moral Worth and the Overdetermination of Dutiful Action," in the *Philosophical Review* 88 (1979), pp. 39–54; and Barbara Herman's essay "On the Value of Acting from the Motive of Duty," in her book *The Practice of Moral Judgment* (Cambridge: Harvard Univ. Press, 1993), pp. 1–22.

DANY'S ENCOUNTER WITH THE WILD: CULTURAL RELATIVISM IN *A GAME OF THRONES*

Katherine Tullmann

To Each His Own?

> As the hours passed, the terror grew in Dany, until it was all she could do not to scream. She was afraid of the Dothraki, whose ways seemed alien and monstrous, as if they were beasts in human skins and not true men at all.[1]

As Princess Daenerys watches the Dothraki people celebrate her marriage to their leader, Khal Drogo, she experiences a growing feeling of disgust and fear. All around her arguments turn deadly, and men and women alike gorge themselves on horseflesh and wine before giving in to their sexual urges for all eyes to witness. Like Dany, the reader is probably disgusted and appalled by this celebration. Surely this display of violence and sexuality is the sign of an immoral group of people.

Dany quickly learns that the wild regions beyond the Seven Kingdoms are not a land for the faint of heart. With her, we encounter a gritty, dark, and dangerous world where tempers flare, sexuality is unrestrained, and violence is commonplace. To a certain extent, audience members accept the foreign ethical codes and lifestyles that we encounter in the Seven Kingdoms. War is nearly constant because it was a different time; and women are treated poorly because they have not yet been "liberated." We sympathize with the characters of the Seven Kingdoms because their world is similar to our own—a slice out of the European Middle Ages with some magic thrown in for good measure. Dany and Eddard Stark, in particular, serve as our moral compasses in this world, shaping our reactions to the other characters' malicious deeds.

At what point, though, does our tenuous tolerance for these actions turn into disgust and moral outrage at the offenses they commit? There may not be a simple, cut-and-dry answer to this question. The further away some cultural practices are from our own, the less likely we are to condone them. This would suggest that moral practices vary by culture—and who are we to say that they're wrong?

But is this right? Consider the perversion of Cersei and Jaime Lannister's sexual relationship and the Dothrakis' pillaging compared to the Stark family's "honorable" rebellion—though even they are by no means innocents. Some moral transgressions are impermissible no matter what, it seems.

Moral Relativism

Since the time of the ancient Greeks, philosophers have proposed that certain moral truths are universal. This view is called *moral universalism*, as opposed to *moral relativism*, which states that moral truth is relative. Even moral judgments that seem to obviously true, such as "incest is wrong," are not independently justifiable beyond the beliefs of an individual, or perhaps a culture.

Cultural relativism is a descriptive theory, simply telling us that "different cultures have different moral codes."[2] Observing that moral codes vary between cultures, cultural relativism may help to explain why some actions in *A Game of Thrones* seem acceptable while others do not. For example, we are quicker to condone Tyrion for sleeping with whores than we are to condone his siblings for committing incest because the former action is somewhat acceptable in our culture whereas the latter is utterly unacceptable.

Although there are many examples of questionable morals in Martin's stories, several of the most philosophically interesting surround Dany's encounters with the Dothraki, whose transgressions strike the audience at a "gut" level—we know these actions are wrong, even if we can't exactly explain why. Cultural relativism provides a fruitful means of understanding both Dany's reactions and our own. Rape and murder seem like universal taboos, but that turns out not to be the case. Through Dany's eyes, and her moral stance, the audience experiences a different way of life and judges the Dothraki accordingly. But before examining Dany's experiences in more detail, let's first see how cultural relativism plays out in the world of *Game of Thrones*, and our own.

The Diversity of Ethical Codes

"Who are *they*?" Rickon asked.
"Mudmen," answered the Little Walder disdainfully.
"They're thieves and cravens, and they have green teeth from eating frogs."[3]

Different groups of people have different social practices, ranging from trivial dissimilarities in their choices of food and entertainment to more drastic differences in penalties for crimes and marital indiscretions. The men of the North scoff at the nomadic swamp-dwellers, the crannogmen, of the House Reed, who eat frogs and throw nets and poisoned spears in battle. The Starks live a Spartan lifestyle compared to the sumptuous frivolity of the Tyrells of Highgarden and the Lannisters in King's Landing—not to mention the differences between the Dothraki and the collective houses of the Seven Kingdoms. And the wildlings beyond the Wall differ from both the kingdoms and the Dothraki. In *A Clash of Kings*, for example, we see Jon and the other Black Brothers repulsed by Craster's custom of marrying his daughters and leaving his sons as offerings for the gods.[4]

Clearly, each of the different cultures in Martin's fictional world has its own way of life and its own way of handling social and moral problems. Such cultural diversity isn't restricted to the realm of fiction, however. In our own world, people from different backgrounds and cultures have different practices and laws as well. This suggests that different cultures also have different moral values.

Think about cannibalism, one of the strongest taboos in our society. In modern Western society, we view cannibalism as a morally repulsive practice, but other cultures did not always take such a negative stance. Historically, cannibalism was practiced by cultures all over the world, though in different ways and for different reasons. Mortuary exocannibalism, for example, is the eating of dead family members, whereas warfare cannibalism is the eating of members of other social groups after they are killed in battle. Contemporary philosopher Jesse Prinz argues that cannibalism may have been commonplace for most premodern societies, and that the practice tended to die out once groups began to organize into states.[5] The most notable counterexample to this was the Aztecs of North America, who belonged to a highly organized state but nevertheless practiced cannibalism until the Spanish takeover in the 1500s. Nowadays, cannibalism rarely occurs. But even the fact that it *did* occur, and may still occur in such places as Papua New Guinea, shows that the practice was not always universally considered to be immoral.

Love and Incest

"The things I do for love."

—Jaime Lannister ("Winter Is Coming")

Let's consider another example of the cultural diversity of morals found in *A Game of Thrones*: incest. Perhaps the reason why *we* are disposed to condemn incest is that we have been conditioned to do so by cultural practices and pressures.[6] We are exposed to stories or situations at a young age in which we learn that incest is disgusting and shameful. Other cultures, however, are much more tolerant of incest, at least in some respects. In America, it is morally blameworthy to marry your own first cousin, but this is a common practice in India, Pakistan, and parts of the Middle East. Among the Incas, those who committed incest had their eyes gouged out, while the Trumai, a native group in Brazil, merely discourage it. Sibling incest was common in ancient Egypt, but died out in Western cultures with the advent of Christianity.[7]

A Game of Thrones features incest between the twins, Cersei and Jaime Lannister. When Eddard Stark discovers the truth, he confronts the queen, who admits that Jaime is her lover, saying: "And why not? The Targaryens wed brother to sister for three hundred years, to keep the bloodlines pure. And Jaime and I are more than brother and sister. We are one person in two bodies. We shared a womb together. He came into this world holding my foot, our old maester said. When he is in me I feel . . . whole."[8]

The Lannisters' incestuous relationship has serious consequences for the kingdom. They have three children: Prince Joffrey and his younger siblings Myrcella and Tommen, all of whom are mistakenly thought to be sired by King Robert. After Robert is killed by a boar during a hunting trip, Joffrey becomes the illegitimate king. In fact, the true king should have been Robert's brother, Stannis! Thus, the cruel Lannisters gain control of most of the Seven Kingdoms, Joffrey being little more than a puppet for his manipulative mother.

Even if incest is not considered morally wrong, it still may have negative political and social consequences. This seems to be Eddard's view: he condemns Cersei and Jaime's relationship, but mostly due to its negative consequences for the realm he feels honor-bound to protect. In their confrontation, Eddard does not morally judge Cersei for *this* action. Instead, his thoughts are of Robert's blindness and the murders Cersei committed in order to hide the truth about her children. The incestuous relationship is a political indecency more than a moral one.

It seems that *some* of the citizens of the Seven Kingdoms have a more tolerant view of incest than we do. Cersei is correct in appealing to the Targaryens' long history of marriage between siblings: we see the truth of this from the Targaryen family line.[9] When he learns the truth, Eddard doesn't feel disgust, but rather dismay and indignation for the consequences of the coupling. We, on the other hand, likely feel a range of negative and condemnatory emotions when we first witness, through Eddard's son Bran's eyes, Cersei and Jaime having sex ("Winter Is Coming"). *We* think that this is as much of a moral transgression as a social or political one, and most of the people in the Seven Kingdoms share our view. After Stannis reveals that Joffrey is the son of Cersei and Jaime, people respond very negatively to this "abomination." Catelyn Stark muses that incest is a "monstrous sin to both old gods and new," yet recognizes that the practice was common for the Targaryens: "but they were the blood of old Valyria where such practices had been common, and like their dragons, the Targaryens answered to neither gods nor men."[10] The circumstances surrounding the Targaryens' incestuous relationships may make it more morally permissible than other deviant actions—the desire to keep the bloodlines pure, the lack of trust between warring families, etc. The Starks would never commit such an act themselves, and neither would we. But they can imagine situations in which incest might be permissible. Again, we find a case where the moral blame for an action varies, depending on the values of those committing it.

Moral Relativism

"It's not *my* law."

— Viserys ("A Golden Crown")

We've seen how the descriptive theory of cultural relativism helps explain our reactions to the diversity of moral practices, both in *Game of Thrones* and in our own world. As a normative theory, *moral relativism* goes further, claiming that not only do different cultures have different moral practices, but morality itself differs from one culture to another. In other words, there are no universal standards of right and wrong. There is nothing we could do to prove that our moral codes are better than any other culture's: they are merely different. There may be hundreds of different cultures with different moral values and stances on different issues, and we should be tolerant toward the customs of other cultures. Even if we are morally disgusted or outraged by instances of cannibalism or incest in another culture, moral relativism claims that we have no grounds to condemn those practices.

Despite the abundant diversity of ethical codes we encounter both in our world and in the Seven Kingdoms, moral relativism as a normative theory seems unsatisfactory. Surely there are *some* moral practices that should be blameworthy in every culture. While it makes sense to be tolerant of some of the different practices we encounter in other cultures, we certainly wouldn't want to be so for all of them. There might be cultures in which human trafficking, for example, is morally acceptable—or at least not as morally blameworthy as in others.[11] Moral relativism would tell us that since this is morally acceptable *for their culture*, there is nothing *really* wrong with it. Surely this is a negative consequence for the theory of moral relativism that will make us want to reject it. Dany's experiences with the Dothraki provide another example: the rape of innocent women during their plundering.

The Dothraki Wedding Ceremony

"A Dothraki wedding without at least three deaths is deemed a dull affair."[12]

—Magister Illyrio

Princess Daenerys Targaryen, the last of the line of the usurped rulers of the Seven Kingdoms, is married off to the leader of the wild Dothraki, a horse tribe that lives beyond the sea. We sympathize with Dany as she tries to accustom herself to the foreign ways of her new people. Dany did not grow up in the Seven Kingdoms since she and her brother, Viserys, who considers himself to be the rightful heir to the Iron Throne, were exiled from their land after Robert became king. Nevertheless, her values are similar to those of her ancestors as well as our own.

We first witness this strange culture in Dany's wedding ceremony to Khal Drogo, a strong and fearsome warrior. The celebration is an "endless day of drinking and eating and fighting."[13] Both the Dothraki men and women celebrate with bare chests, devouring horseflesh and guzzling wine. As the night progresses, a Dothraki warrior grabs a dancer and has sex with her in front of the crowd. Two other warriors fight over another woman, and one is killed.

Dany is frightened and appalled by the ceremony. This new culture is so different from her own that she cannot help but feel disgusted. Of course, the reader is also appalled by the celebration. Compare it to the last wedding reception *you* attended! Such overt sexuality and violence are strongly discouraged in our culture, but as the magister points out, it is commonplace for the Dothraki.

Though both Viserys and Dany seem to condemn these practices, moral relativism tells us that they are mistaken in doing so. Notice that Illyrio, who is acquainted with the Dothraki culture, does not seem surprised by the display. Likewise, the Dothraki spectators see no cause for alarm or outrage. In fact, they are exhilarated by the fighting and fornication. So, must we also accept that this strange celebration is morally permissible in this culture? *We* may be reluctant to do so, but for Dany, learning the Dothraki way of life is a necessity.

Pillage and Plunder

"This is the way of war."

— Khal Drogo ("The Pointy End")

At first, Dany listens to Ser Jorah's stories about the Dothrakis' ruthlessness with astonishment and fear. But as she grows accustomed to her new role, Dany learns to love her husband, and at least tolerate his followers. She adopts the Dothraki ways in her new role as *khaleesi*, the leader's wife, "talk[ing] like a queen" ("Lord Snow"), learning her people's language, donning their garb, and eating their food.

The shocking part comes after Dany discovers that she is pregnant with the Khal's son. During a ceremony to celebrate her pregnancy, she eats a bloody horse's heart ("A Golden Crown"). Only then does she fully join herself with the life force of the Dothraki people. Her brother Viserys does not adapt as Dany does, and he pays the price for it. In a way, the audience becomes accustomed to the Dothrakis' practices as well, at least to a certain extent, because Dany is our guide in this foreign land and her bravery and resilience make her a highly sympathetic character.

Dany adopts many of the Dothrakis' social practices, but her tolerance for their *moral* actions goes only so far. After Khal Drogo decides to overtake the Seven Kingdoms to restore Dany to her rightful place as queen, his people pillage the other horse tribes along the way. The Dothraki warriors brutally rape and murder everyone they encounter, not discriminating between men, women, and children. Dany is infuriated and disgusted by the violence, and she saves one of the women, a healer, who is about to be gang-raped by several of the warriors. Upon witnessing another rape, Dany orders Jorah Mormont, a follower from the Seven Kingdoms, to make the warriors stop their pillaging. He replies: "Princess . . . you have a gentle heart, but you do not understand. This is how it has always been. Those men have shed blood for the *khal*. Now they claim their reward."[14] One of Dany's servants, a Dothraki, says that the warriors "do this girl honor" and Khal Drogo himself says, "This is the way of war. These women are our slaves now, to do with as we like."[15]

Clearly this clash of moral codes causes tension between Dany and her people. The reader is likely just as horrified as Dany by the brutal way the warriors treat their captives. On the one hand, Dany realizes that this is the way things are done among the Dothraki—they don't consider rape wrong under these circumstances. But on the other hand, Dany cannot just ignore the rape. It's not something to get used to, like eating horse meat. It's something she believes is wrong, period.

The Morality of the Seven Kingdoms and Beyond

As we've seen, there are two important lessons that we can learn from cultural relativism. First, we should not assume that our moral practices are based on a universal, rational standard.

Second, we need to keep an open mind about other cultures' practices, even if we have a difficult time accepting them. We do not have to go so far as to adopt another culture's ethical codes, but neither should we be dogmatic about our own. This is especially true when we are confronted with a strange and mysterious world like the one we find in *A Game of Thrones*. There's a difference, however, between accepting that different cultures have different moral practices and a moral relativist's claim that we should therefore be tolerant of *all* differences we encounter. In the end, we must reject moral relativism. No matter what culture we're in, some actions are wrong. Which actions are those? Eating horse meat? Probably not. Sibling incest? Maybe—depends on the circumstances. Rape? Definitely.

NOTES

1. George R. R. Martin, *A Game of Thrones* (New York: Bantam Dell, 2005), p. 103.

2. James Rachels, "The Challenge of Cultural Relativism," in *Philosophy for the 21st Century*, ed. Steven Cahn (New York: Oxford Univ. Press, 2003), p. 595.

3. George R. R. Martin, *A Clash of Kings* (New York: Bantam Dell, 2005), p. 328.

4. George R. R. Martin, *A Storm of Swords* (New York: Bantam Dell, 2005), p. 444.

5. Jesse Prinz, *The Emotional Construction of Morals* (New York: Oxford Univ. Press, 2007), p. 224.

6. There may also be a biological disinclination toward interest. See Prinz, *Emotional Construction*, p. 255, for a discussion.

7. Ibid., pp. 188 and 233.

8. Martin, *A Game of Thrones*, p. 485.

9. Ibid., p. 833.

10. Martin, *A Clash of Kings*, pp. 497–498.

11. According to the United Nations Office on Drugs and Crime (UNODC), many nations do not have active laws in place to prevent illegal sex trade and human trafficking, which *may* suggest that the practice is less morally blameworthy there than in other nations. http://www.unodc.org/unodc/en/human-trafficking/index.html.

12. Martin, *A Game of Thrones*, p. 103.

13. Ibid., p. 101.

14. Ibid., p. 668.

15. Ibid., p. 670.

"THERE ARE NO TRUE KNIGHTS": THE INJUSTICE OF CHIVALRY

Stacey Goguen

The Dark Side of Chivalry

"It is chivalry that makes a true knight, not a sword. Without honor, a knight is no more than a common killer."

—Ser Barriston Selmy[1]

"Hodor doesn't like those much. . . . He likes the stories where the knights fight monsters."

"Sometimes the knights are the monsters, Bran."

—Bran Stark and Meera Reed[2]

Chivalry as an idealization and an ethical code is a strong theme in A Song of Ice and Fire. Sansa Stark, a highborn girl, is the primary embodiment of this idealization; she of all the characters in the series most thoroughly believes (at first, at least) in the valor, the romance, and the justice of chivalry.

Sansa's journey, however, from her home in Winterfell to the capital of King's Landing and then to the isolated Eyrie in the Vale represents another theme: the darker side of chivalry, where fully armored adults hit defenseless children, kings rape their queens, and anointed "knights" are not knights at all. Sansa, a teenager, starts off *A Game of Thrones* by being betrothed to a prince—her dream come true; however, by the end of *A Feast for Crows* she is smuggled away to a remote corner of the continent, the (arguable) kidnap victim of a man old enough to be her father, who has more than a familial interest in her.

Although Sansa, with her auburn hair, looks much more like her Southron mother from the Riverlands, she shares an important personality trait with her Northern father: naiveté in thinking that honor runs the world. But as we see Sansa's naive worldview crumble book by book, we also see that her flaws and the corrupt ethics of others are not the only cause of tragedy; chivalry itself holds something dark within its songs of strong knights and beautiful ladies.

Chivalry Is Misguided

"In the name of the Warrior I charge you to be brave. In the name of the Father I charge you to be just. In the name of the Mother I charge you to defend the young and innocent. In the name of the Maid I charge you to protect all women."

—Knighting Ceremony[3]

Sansa interacts frequently with a bodyguard named the Hound, who hates knights and knighthood as much as Sansa loves them. He tells her, "There are no true knights, no more than there are gods. If you can't protect yourself, die and get out of the way of those who can. Sharp steel and strong arms rule this world, don't ever believe any different." Sansa gives a standard teenage reply to this, shouting, "You're awful!" The Hound merely retorts: "I'm honest. It's the world that's awful."[4] Unfortunately for Sansa, the world of A Song of Ice and Fire sides with the Hound.

It's no coincidence that the Hound's brother, who is possibly the most ignoble, sociopathic character in the series (an impressive claim, given some of the other characters!), is also a knight. Sansa claims of Ser Gregor, "he was no true knight," but she must say the same of Ser Meryn Trant, who slaps her across the face at the behest of her king and betrothed, Joffrey Baratheon. And what of the Kingsguard of the Mad King Aerys—the most honored knights in the land, sworn to protect the royal family—who stood outside the king's door and did not stir as the queen screamed? Their duty was to protect her . . . but not from the king? There have been enough false knights throughout the history of the Seven Kingdoms to fill every castle from Dorne to the Wall.

So are we seeing systematic disregard of a moral code, or is the moral code itself part of the problem? Are there true chivalric knights who uphold justice, or is chivalry itself flawed as a moral code? There are upstanding men and women in Westeros, no doubt, and the irony should not go unnoticed that the knight who arguably adheres most to an ethical standard of knighthood is a woman—Brienne, the Maid of Tarth. A few virtuous knights, however, are not enough to save chivalry, for it does indeed fail as an ethical code.

Chivalry falls short in two main ways. First, it fails to accomplish what it sets out to do: protect those who cannot protect themselves. Knights are supposed to protect a lady's honor, but by focusing on protection as the paramount moral duty, chivalry exalts the sword that protects and (unconsciously) devalues the body that cannot protect itself, which leads to moral vulnerability. Chivalry explicitly claims that it does the opposite: it raises up the "fairer sex" on a pedestal of moral reverence. However, as the activist Gloria Steinem once pointed out, "a pedestal is as much a prison as any small, confined space."[5] The denizens of Westeros might put it: a pedestal is only three walls away from being a Sky Cell, and a prison counts as "protection" only in a twisted sense of the word.

Second, the injustice is not just that chivalry is an imperfect way of accomplishing a worthy goal; chivalry picks a flawed goal to begin with. It aims to protect the weak instead of empowering them to protect themselves. Moreover, since chivalry picks out women as a whole class of people who are in need of perpetual protection—even as adults—chivalry does not help people lead fuller, more flourishing lives. Instead, it creates rigid social roles that not only punish people when they try to step outside them but also cheapen social relations, turning them into caricatures. At the end of the day, chivalry treats many adult women like children, overvalues the role able-bodied men play as eternal protectors, and even slips in assumed heterosexuality here and there as part of the roles knights and ladies play.

Therefore, chivalry itself is unjust—regardless of the high moral standing of some people who adhere to it. It's not merely that some knights abuse the power given to them, but rather that the code of chivalry requires an unequal balance of power from the start. It propagates the vulnerability of women and further propagates oppressive frameworks of social relations and romantic love.

Some might object that in Westeros we see chivalry functioning within a homophobic, sexist, classist society. By this account, chivalry itself could be separated from these less savory social prejudices and distilled into a truly just ethical code. However, while the chivalry of Westeros has been influenced by its larger social values, we shouldn't forget that it also helps shape those values. Chivalry doesn't just soak up sexism; it inherently endorses and promotes it.

Moreover, this critique of chivalry extends well beyond Martin's fiction. The Western world—albeit somewhat different from Westeros—is not unacquainted with the ideal of modern "knighthood." A knight is a man who holds open doors for his lady, who woos her with romance, and who protects her. A good man is commonly described as a knight in shining armor or Prince Charming. But chivalry is as much a misguided ethical code in our world today as it is in Westeros. It too narrowly conceives the moral roles each person should play and, furthermore, fixes certain people into a status of vulnerability, which ultimately forces on them a status of inferiority. As Sansa learns, along with Martin's readers, chivalry does not promote human flourishing. There are no true knights because a knight adhering to chivalry is inherently being unjust.

Sansa and her Songs

"Life is not a song, sweetling."

—Petyr Baelish[6]

At the beginning of the series, Sansa thinks life is like a song. While various characters chide her for her naiveté, they rarely suggest that listening to such songs day in and day out is somehow inappropriate. Several characters remark that music is appropriate for girls, but girls alone. Petyr "Littlefinger" Baelish and the Hound come the closest to criticizing Sansa's upbringing. Littlefinger warns her, "Life is not a song, sweetling. You may learn that one day to your sorrow."[7] The Hound mocks Sansa for being like a little bird that sings songs to please other people; however, he also acknowledges that she has been taught these songs and trained to sing in this way. He derides her for being childish, but she has been encouraged to be childish in this manner. Then again, Sansa really is still somewhat of a child, and as the royal princess Myrcella once pointed out, "We're children . . . we're *supposed* to be childish."[8] But are even adult ladies supposed to be childish? According to chivalry, the answer in a sense is yes.

Chivalry treats (highborn) women as having a childlike status and then assumes that that status is a natural trait. Just as Sansa has been taught and encouraged to take on certain childish traits, chivalry encourages women to be vulnerable and dependent. It also encourages other people (especially knights) to treat women as if they are in a perpetually vulnerable state.

The postcolonial feminist philosopher Gayatri Spivak can help us here. Pointing out how imperialism and sexism can interact with one another, Spivak argues that when people from one country try to help people from another country, they run the risk of treating those people like children, even if they don't mean to. She argues that this problem often arises when people think they have a duty to right the wrongs befallen on others, while doubting that those others will ever be able to stand up for themselves and right their own wrongs. These "saviors" end up becoming oppressors; they start treating the people they're helping as forever dependent and vulnerable—subhuman and childlike. Perhaps not coincidentally, Spivak claims, "we reproduce and consolidate what can only be called 'feudalism.'"[9] Just as feudalism turns some countries and people into vassals, chronically dependent on their lieges for protection, anyone trying to help someone else can fall into this pattern of unconsciously treating them like children.

Spivak, however, isn't arguing that we shouldn't help people. Helping people is good. Helping people because it's your duty is also good. Immanuel Kant (1724–1804), for example, argued that morality stems from duty. So thinking you have a duty to help other people is not the problem. The problem arises, as Spivak says, when you think you are responsible for someone else because they are not responsible for themselves. The problem occurs when you perceive your role not as dutiful temporary guide but as dutiful eternal babysitter.

Knights do not perceive their guardian role as temporary. For instance, when fired, Ser Barristan proclaimed that he lived as a knight and thus would die as a knight. Furthermore, the people of Westeros do not perceive women as outgrowing their need for protection. For instance, Catelyn slit a man's throat and pried a dagger away from her own by grabbing the blade with her hands and biting her attacker, yet people still considered her as vulnerable as any other woman. Men and women are held to the ideals of knight and lady—the protector and the protected—regardless of an individual's need for such protection.

In her landmark work of feminist philosophy, *The Second Sex*, Simone de Beauvoir (1908–1986) discussed how social customs can be confused and entangled with physical facts. We consider many customs to be grounded in some fact that justifies them. To make this point, Beauvoir quoted George Bernard Shaw (1856–1950) on racism: "The white American relegates the black to the rank of shoe-shine boy; and then concludes that blacks are only good for shining shoes."[10] Likewise, chivalry relegates ladies to their pedestals, then from this concludes that ladies are fit only to stand on pedestals and not get their dresses dirty. The custom creates the narrative from which it was supposedly derived.

Some might object that women really are physically weaker than men. Most women just don't have the muscle mass to protect themselves against a hostile man, so women need knights for physical protection. To debunk this idea, consider Petyr "Littlefinger" Baelish, a man of small stature. He was even smaller as a teenager, when he tried to fight Catelyn's betrothed one-on-one for her hand in marriage. He lost. Badly. And yet Petyr is more than capable of protecting himself. He knows there is more than one way to skin a cat, and there is more than one way to overpower your enemies. He points out to Ned Stark (poetically while in a brothel) that since he can't win by fighting his enemies, he will fuck them (over) instead ("You Win or You Die"). Similarly, when Syrio Forel is teaching Arya sword-fighting, he points out that the "knight's dance" of using brute force is not the only way to fight. Strength and muscle mass are not the only ways to protect yourself; agility, speed, cunning, intelligence, and stealth (the Water Dance) will also do the trick. No one has ever denied that women can excel at these things, least of all fucking people over. It is said in Westeros that poison is a woman's weapon, and Cersei points out to Sansa that crying and sex are also weapons for manipulating people.

And yet, chivalry sets women up as an entire group of people who, by virtue of being women, need protection. Always. For example, Grand Maester Pycelle discusses the "frailty" of the female sex in reference to Cersei, the queen regent, who is as ruthless and ambitious a leader as any. Or again, when Lord Stark finds Arya's sword Needle he remarks, "This is no toy for children, least of all for a girl," even though she had disarmed Prince Joffrey, who was not only bigger than she, but better trained.[11] In the HBO series, when his sons make fun of Bran for being a bad shot, Lord Stark asks which of them were marksmen at ten. Meanwhile, Arya, only slightly older than Bran, scores a perfect bull's-eye. Yet no one seems to consider what Arya could do if she had been given formal training like her brothers.

On the issue of power and vulnerability, consider the riddle Varys poses to Tyrion in *A Clash of Kings*: Between a king, a rich man, and a septon, who will a sellsword fight for? Does power ultimately rest in wealth, legal status, or social/religious status? Does power ultimately lie within sellswords, or within the person who commands them? The Spider concludes, "Power resides where men believe it resides. No more, no less."[12] The issue with chivalry is that it does not encourage anyone to believe it could reside within a woman, unless she was, like Arya, Brienne, or Daenerys, truly exceptional. But even then, an exception as such does not disprove the rule.

Within Sansa's songs, all knights are gallant, maids are always beautiful, the season is always summer, and honor always rules. Chivalry is unproblematic because no one is unhappy with their role. There are no Aryas or Briennes or Daeneryses in the songs; there are only Sansas—women who want nothing more than to be the ideal lady.

But life is not a song, and thinking this way does not help women flourish. Even Sansa realizes this eventually. After she suffers a severe beating from the Kingsguard at her King's command, a kind maester patches her up and tries to comfort her. Before, Sansa would have taken these gentle words to heart, as when her Septa told her, "A lady's armor is courtesy."[13] At this point, though, Sansa disregards this coddling as worthless prattle in the face of real injustice. She realizes how vulnerable she is when there are no "true knights" to protect her. When the maester tells her, "Sleep a bit, child. When you wake, all this will seem a bad dream," she thinks to herself before passing out, "No it won't, you stupid man."[14] Sansa has come full circle from thinking that chivalry dictates the proper role each person should play. Now she concludes of the men around her, "They are no true knights . . . not one of them."[15]

The Death of Modern Chivalry: Good Riddance

> "I like dogs better than knights. . . . A hound will die for you, but never lie to you. And he'll look you straight in the face."
>
> —The Hound[16]

Homosexual love is another thorn in chivalry's side. Martin approaches this topic mostly through Renly and Loras, who are knights and lovers. Overall, though, not much commentary is made on homosexuality throughout the series, and that is precisely the point. The people of Westeros often forget that homosexuality exists, and when they are reminded, they often remark that it is strange, or abnormal, or very rare. The chivalric love stories are always about knights and ladies.

Knights and ladies play specific romantic roles; the knight who wins a tourney places a laurel on the lap of the woman he crowns the Queen of Beauty. Loras crowned Sansa, who swooned at the romantic gesture, but in the TV series, we see Loras has eyes only for Renly. Loras could not, however, crown Renly King of anything in the tourney because a knight is supposed to woo a lady, as Florian wooed Jonquil. It is known.

Medieval chivalry was homophobic, sexist, classist, able-ist,[17] and probably racist, too. This is one reason why chivalry, as it has been historically construed, is not a just ethical code. The chivalry of Westeros also adopts many of these prob-lematic ideologies from its culture at large. One might think, however, that "modern-day chivalry" is able to avoid these oppressive pitfalls and be an honorable code of ethics.

Modern-day chivalry promotes rigid expressions of sexuality as well, though. Chivalry dictates gender roles, and heterosexuality is woven throughout the chivalric interpreta-tion of gender. Even if someone claims that being nice to other people or defending those who can't defend themselves is a chivalrous ideal, we should recognize that the ideal comes at a price. Modern-day chivalry is invoked primarily as an ethics for how people romantically attracted to each other should interact. How people should act depends on their gender, however. Additionally, chivalry specifies rules only for inter-acting with someone of the opposite gender. For instance, if two women were out on a date, chivalry couldn't dictate who should pay for the meal, or whether one should hold a door open for the other. Likewise, if two men were in a relation-ship, chivalry would be unable to explain how the two men should support each other. Modern chivalry presents itself as a universal code of ethics, but really, it offers guidance only for heterosexual men and women.

Simone de Beauvoir argued that modern chivalry wove itself into the heterosexual narrative of romance that many French girls in the 1940s imagined for themselves. In this narrative, men played a specific, chivalrous role: "He [a man] is the liberator; he is also rich and powerful, he holds the keys to happiness, he is Prince Charming. She [the girl] anticipates that in his caress she will feel carried away by the great current of life."[18] Girls imagine a specific role for themselves: waiting for Prince Charming to carry them away. Girls who dream of a "Princess Charming" find these dreams and desires ignored and unacknowledged.

Clearly, George R. R. Martin understands that people are not always satisfied with the roles their society encourages or dictates. Arya claims that she will not grow up to be a lady, and Brienne was so dissatisfied with her role as a highborn lady that she asserted that no one could marry her until they bested her in combat. (No one ever did.) Likewise, Daenerys proclaimed herself Khaleesi and Queen even though neither Westeros nor the Dothraki were accustomed to having women leaders. Each of these women had to struggle against social norms in order to live the kinds of lives they wanted for themselves.

This is not to argue that societies shouldn't be in the business of helping people understand and choose different social roles. The argument against chivalry isn't an argument for social anarchy. The Southron religion in Westeros, for instance, worships the Seven: the Father, the Mother, the Smith, the Warrior, the Maiden, the Crone, and the Stranger. Focusing on these as seven societal roles/positions is not necessarily unjust or oppressive, since the roles are distinct but not mutually exclusive. A person can be a father and a smith. A single woman could be maiden, mother, and crone in her life. Therefore, it's possible for Catelyn to see the image of her maiden daughter Arya in the warrior. When she does, Catelyn muses on a piece of theology: "Each of the Seven embodies all of the Seven. . . . There was as much beauty in the Crone as in the Maiden, and the Mother could be fiercer than the Warrior."[19] Societal roles can help us form identities, build communities, and understand our strengths and weaknesses.

Societal roles are not oppressive unless groups of people are categorically denied access to roles of value (like being a warrior, valiant and honorable). Bran's case is a little more complicated; he is crippled and so cannot fulfill his dream of being part of the Kingsguard. This fact in itself isn't oppressive; the oppression comes when Bran thinks he will not be able to fulfill any valuable role in life. His father's bannermen encourage this thought by whispering that it would be more honorable for Bran to kill himself. It is not until Jojen comes along that Bran realizes being a knight is not the only way to be a hero—cripple and hero are not mutually exclusive categories.

Recognizing that people do not function in only one social role their whole lives can help us understand the extent to which our societies encourage us to take on different roles, to explore and change our social identities. Chivalry missteps when it presumes to know which roles are best for us based on our gender and based on its presumption of our sexual orientation. In this way, chivalry is akin to a well-meaning but too-restrictive parent. It needs to let its children grow up and find their own way in the world.

Women, Not Wards: What Has Humanity Made of the Human Female?

Beauvoir argues that even if there are biological differences between men and women, it is cultures and societies that put certain values and meanings on those differences. Gender has primarily a cultural meaning (not a biological one), and so if we want to see why Beauvoir thinks that "one is not born, but rather, becomes a woman,"[20] then we must ask ourselves "what humanity has made of the human female."[21]

Chivalry has made the human female into a Lady. Well, historically, it made certain women into ladies (specifically, highborn European women). Even if we try to strip chivalry of its classist and ethnocentric trappings, it still clings to its sexist framework. The chivalric lady is a kind of ward and not an autonomous human adult. This is not to say that it's unjust to have anyone ever be a ward under someone else's protection; many people consider their children to be their wards. However, children eventually outgrow their roles as wards. The problem is having someone as a ward permanently when they are able to function as an autonomous person.

Feminist philosophy, therefore, sees chivalry as oppressing women by formulating a specific role that not all women want for themselves, and, further, by devaluing the role that women are supposed to play. Of course, some women fit naturally with the ideal of what being a "lady" entails, but many don't. By propping up the lady as the best and most proper image of a woman, chivalry silences many other forms of womanhood, demanding that all "proper" women look and act a certain way. Under chivalry, a lady can be seen as honorable, but never quite as honorable as a knight, since a knight can help others besides himself. The ward is never as valuable as the sword that protects him or her, or as the man who wields the sword. Men are also limited by chivalry; being a "knight (in shining armor)" or a "prince (charming)" may offer a bit more breathing room to express one's personality, but not if a man wants to do anything ladylike, such as singing, dancing, or—heaven forbid—sewing.

Some might object that thinking of chivalry along gender roles is too simplistic. Even in Westeros there are myriad subcultures in which gender roles are tweaked and changed. For instance, in Dorne, it is not out of the ordinary for a woman to have martial training. The Dornish were descended from the Rhoynar and their warrior-queen Nymeria, after all. However, this means that other regions of Westeros categorize women from Dorne based on their ethnicity. Dornish women are known for being not quite like "regular" women of Westeros. For instance, when Tyrion is asked about the strangest thing he's ever eaten, he asks if a Dornish girl counts. Ethnic exceptions exist for gender roles, but in being exceptions, they leave the rule untouched.

In the end, power dynamics can be hidden in how we conceive of ourselves as men, women, citizens, adults, children, and nations. As a result, we can imprison people when we believe we are actually helping them. Instead, we should examine the cultural connotations of what being a knight or a lady means, and try to understand that if we are seeking a just ethical code, chivalry is not a good choice. If a knight is a follower of chivalry who upholds justice and promotes human flourishing, then "there are no true knights."

NOTES

1. George R. R. Martin, *A Dance with Dragons* (New York: Bantam Books, 2011), p. 878.

2. George R. R. Martin, *A Storm of Swords* (New York: Bantam Dell, 2005), p. 339.

3. George R. R. Martin, "The Hedge Knight," in *Legends*, ed. Robert Silverberg (London: Voyager, 1998), p. 518.

4. George R. R. Martin, *A Clash of Kings* (New York: Bantam Dell, 2005), p. 757.

5. "Women's History: Gloria Steinem Quotes," *About.com*, accessed June 2011, womenshistory.about.com/cs/quotes/a/qu_g_steinem.htm.

6. George R. R. Martin, *A Game of Thrones* (New York: Bantam Dell, 2005), p. 473.

7. Ibid.

8. Martin, *A Clash of Kings*, p. 47.

9. Gayatri Spivak, "Righting Wrongs," *South Atlantic Quarterly* 103 (2004), p. 542.

10. Simone de Beauvoir, *The Second Sex* (New York: Alfred K. Knopf, 2009), p. 12.

11. Martin, *A Game of Thrones*, p. 220.

12. Martin, *A Clash of Kings*, p. 132.

13. Ibid., p. 50.

14. Ibid., p. 490. In a small way, a lady's courtesy can be her armor; Sansa's composure and politeness do save her from beatings in a handful of circumstances; however, it's not foolproof armor. As polite as Sansa is, Joffrey is sometimes just in a foul mood and so she amasses a collection of bruises from Ser Meryn and Ser Boros (since it is not kingly for a king to hit his lady . . . himself).

15. Ibid., p. 490.

16. Ibid., p. 288.

17. "Ableist" refers to manifestations of a discriminatory attitude toward people who are not considered able-bodied, that is, people with disabilities. When the bannermen

in Winterfell whisper that Bran would have more honor if he killed himself rather than living as a cripple—that's ableist.

18. Beauvoir, *Second Sex*, p. 341.

19. Martin, *A Clash of Kings*, p. 497.

20. Beauvoir, *Second Sex*, p. 283.

21. Ibid., p. 48.

PART FIVE

"STICK THEM WITH THE POINTY END"

FATE, FREEDOM, AND AUTHENTICITY IN A GAME OF THRONES

Michael J. Sigrist

"Never forget what you are, for surely the world will not. Make it your strength. Then it can never be your weakness."[1]

"Winter is coming." For centuries these well-worn words may have expressed little more than the stern mind-set of the North, but they take on a prophetic and fatalistic force as the drama of *A Game of Thrones* unfolds.

Fatalism is the idea that the future has been set in advance and cannot be changed. "Winter is coming." Nothing can be done to avoid this. The best one can do is to prepare. Let's call this idea—that the future is already determined—"metaphysical fatalism."[2] *Metaphysical fatalism* is an ancient idea that endures to this day. Any notion that the future has already been written, that certain events are destined to happen, or that one's future has been predetermined assumes the truth of metaphysical fatalism.

We can link that sense of fatalism to two other concepts—*freedom* and *authenticity*—in order to better understand the dramas and destinies that conspire in Westeros. Many philosophers believe that fatalism poses an insuperable challenge to human freedom. If the future is already written, then nothing can be done to change it; therefore human freedom is an illusion. This view implies its converse: if we *are* free, then it is fatalism that is the illusion. These two views vie uneasily throughout A Song of Ice and Fire. It seems that one can believe *only* in freedom *or* in fatalism, but that may be the real illusion. Perhaps you can believe in both.

The Freedom to Be or Not to Be

Take the story of Daenerys Targaryen, a tale that begins well before the first chapter of *A Game of Thrones*. Her father, the Mad King Aerys II, was slain by Jaime Lannister. Fleeing King's Landing, her mother, Rhaella, gives birth to Dany and Viserys aboard a ship and then dies. Daenerys and her brother, born of the dragon blood and heirs to the House Targaryen, spend their childhood as paupers on the streets of Braavos, only to end up as wards of the mysterious Illyrio Mopatis. When we first meet Dany, she is a shy young girl, only vaguely aware of the intrigues in which she herself unwittingly plays a central role. If fate is at work at this point in Dany's life, it seems to come at the cost of her own freedom and self-determination. Her youth, her gender, and the machinations of her brother and Illyrio are forces shaping her life in ways she can scarcely recognize, let alone control. Her fate appears to be out of her hands.

Readers will know that the Dany who emerges from the fires of Khal Drogo's funeral pyre—and the Dany who unleashes herself on the East in the later books—is anything but the shy, meek girl we meet at the start. This later Daenerys owns the stage like perhaps no other character in the series—a woman in full control of her actions, upending the world, waging war, trampling on convention, responsible only to herself. And yet, her resolve and fortitude are made possible by her sense of fatalism, not despite it. It is only when she is certain that fate is somehow in control that she feels truly free.

The coincidence of fate and freedom is not solely a privilege of Dragon princesses. Most of us intuitively understand that fate and freedom are not really as opposed as may first appear. Many of us struggle to find a meaning or purpose that has been, as it were, decided for us, and we believe that discovering this purpose will prove profoundly liberating. But should we take this as anything more than an inspiring sentiment? Could it really be that a purpose one has not chosen is the key to one's freedom? Consider again the case of Dany: perhaps her belief in her own fate is mistaken, though it provides the resolve she needs in order to succeed in her freely chosen mission. Or conversely, perhaps her sense of autonomy is the illusion needed in order for her to fulfill her destiny.

The French philosopher Jean-Paul Sartre (1905–1980) believed that human beings, and human beings alone, were utterly free of fate. He coined a pithy slogan to explain this idea: "Existence precedes essence."[3] Everything besides humans, according to Sartre, has an essence or nature. An essence is that which makes a thing the kind of thing that it is. For example, while there are vastly many different kinds of trees, there is something that is true of each one by virtue of which it is a tree. This essence need not be some ethereal property "treeness" that is there in addition to bark, leaves, root systems, or cell structure. A thing's essence might just be a set of necessary and sufficient properties. Sometimes a thing's essence—this is especially true of artifacts and tools—is just the use or purpose for which it is made, as the essence of a hammer is to drive nails, and of a watch to tell time.

Philosophers from ancient to modern times have tried to discover the human essence, in the hope that this would reveal the meaning of human life. For example, the Greek philosopher Plato (424–348 BCE) believed that the human essence is reason, and therefore that the best life for a human is a rational life devoted to wisdom. By contrast, another Greek philosopher, Epicurus (341–270 BCE), believed that humans, like all animals, are essentially pleasure-seeking beings, and he argued that therefore the best human life is one dedicated to achieving an optimal amount of pleasure.[4]

Westeros is a world where a person's purpose or essence is determined by the categories of class, status, and tradition. Robb's purpose in life is to succeed Ned as the head of House Stark. Robb can either live up to this purpose or fail; it is not something that he can choose for himself. Similarly, a woman cannot rule a kingdom in Westeros, which is why Lady Lysa may only rule in regency for her son, Lord Robert, just as Cersei may wield power only in regency for Joffrey. Cersei, of course, laments this fact, and Arya Stark consciously struggles to overcome it, but nearly every character takes gender to be an essential fact. (Brienne is the exception that proves the rule.) More generally, *what* one is determines *who* one is. Station is not something one can rise above, nor sink below. Jon is a bastard, and no matter what he achieves, he will never be heir to Winterfell.[5]

Sartre tried hard to dispel this kind of essentialism. He believed that humans were very different from anything that has an essence. Sartre's pithy slogan notwithstanding, it is not so much that human existence precedes essence as that human existence *precludes* essence. Sartre argued that if anything defines human beings, it is our unconditioned and absolute freedom to choose to be the kind of beings that we are.[6] And since we are free to be anything, then we are in fact nothing, which is just another way of saying that human beings have no essence.[7] No person is *essentially* a man or woman, lord or liege, just as no person is essentially a rational being or a pleasure-seeking being.

How does Sartre know this? He believes that absolute freedom reveals itself through reflection and in certain moods. Before any action, one can always pause and reflect upon *why* one is about to act. What does one find in these moments of reflection? We discover motivations, desires, attitudes, and goals, *none of which can force us to act*. To act, you must choose, and this choice itself has no ground or cause other than the fact that you make it. The individual is always responsible for each and every choice. Cersei, for example, may try to excuse her actions on grounds of necessity: she *must* arrest and silence Ned because what he knows will bring ruin to the House of Lannister and Joffrey's Kingship. She might think that her own desires or preferences have nothing to do with this. But of course this is wrong. She *does* have the choice; in fact, she has chosen.

We are also aware of our freedom through certain moods, the most important of which is anguish (*Angst*, as it is sometimes referred to in the original German). Think of Eddard as he faces the choice to become Robert's Hand. He surely knows the likely consequences. He knows well the fate the Hand has held for those before him, and is likely to hold, not only for himself, but also for the entire House Stark. We may never be asked to serve as the King's Hand, but each of us has experienced moments of decision where we know that our choice, whatever it is, will lock in one future while foreclosing others. To feel that one's entire life is at stake in the moment is anguish, which Sartre, following the German philosopher Martin Heidegger (more on him later!), interprets as a fear not in the face of some threat coming from the world, but the fear that accompanies the knowledge that one must decide one's entire life.

Ned must decide whether his primary loyalty is to the realm or to his family. Later, when Cersei demands his confession of treason, he faces an even starker choice: is it my family, or my honor, for which I live? Facing these choices in full awareness that in so choosing, you are choosing a life (will I be a traitor to my country, or to my family?) is what Sartre, again following Heidegger, calls "authenticity."

Anguish, Sartre says, rips us from our everyday existence—our being as father, friend, worker, and so on—and forces us to decide for that existence as a whole. We can do so authentically or inauthentically. If we are inauthentic, we push the enormity of such moments off onto forces we claim to be unable to control—such as fate! Sansa, as she stands before King Robert and is forced to choose between her fiancé and her family, chooses, as we know, the former. Surely Sansa is one of the most frustrating—and therefore most artfully drawn—characters in *A Game of Thrones*. Despite the manifest evidence, Sansa refuses to believe that Joffrey is anything other than a chivalrous prince, or that the Lannisters are anything but regal and upstanding wards. Sansa's inauthenticity shows itself in "bad faith," as Sartre calls it, by refusing to take ownership of herself and her situation.[8] To Sansa's mind, it is as if she has no choice but to lie about Joffrey's attack against Mycah, as this is what loyalty as a fiancée requires.

Authenticity thus defined is the very opposite of fatalism. To accept fate is to relinquish one's freedom. Daenerys, if this theory is correct, may believe that fate is guiding her actions, but in reality it is only her choices and her freedom that drive her. If she does not recognize this, she is, in Sartre's view, inauthentic.

Que Sera, Sera (What Will Be, Will Be)

Fate is often associated with justice. If not in this life, then in the next, the good shall be rewarded and the evil punished. Fate and justice do not seem to align in this familiar way in Martin's books. Some argue that this is what makes Martin's books unique, bestowing a sense of realism on a series otherwise firmly within the fantasy genre. If fate is operating in A

Song of Ice and Fire, it does not seem to be a force for justice, but rather something cold and pitiless, sometimes allowing good characters to needlessly die while bad characters succeed.

What sort of fate, then, might be operating in Westeros, if not the fate of cosmic justice? Metaphysical fatalism says nothing about the moral order of the universe. It says only that the future has already been determined. The Macedonian philosopher Aristotle (384–322 BCE) worried that the truth of metaphysical fatalism would nullify human freedom. In a treatise on the logical form of language, Aristotle considers the following argument in support of fatalism: Suppose that someone were to say, "There will be a sea battle tomorrow," and someone else were to assert the opposite, "There will not be a sea battle tomorrow."[9] Since the second statement is only the negation of the first, one of these statements must be correct. Why is that? Aristotle was the first systematic logician and had elsewhere established that every proposition must be either true or false. For very many propositions, of course, we may never know which is the case. "There are exactly seventeen extraterrestrial civilizations," "Caesar ate three eggs one morning in 45 BCE," "Every even integer greater than two can be expressed as the sum of two primes"—we may never know, for any one of these propositions, whether it is true or false. All the same, Aristotle reasoned, surely each proposition has to be one or the other, true or false. He called this principle "the principle of bivalence." A commitment to bivalence left him in a bind when it came to propositions about the future. If "There will be a sea battle tomorrow" is true, then it must be the fact that there is a sea battle tomorrow that makes it true. Hence we can infer that if the statement is true, the fact it describes *must* be the case, for otherwise the statement would not be true. But to say that something in the future *must* be the case is to endorse fatalism. If it's true that there will be a sea battle tomorrow, then *necessarily* there will be a sea battle tomorrow, and nothing can be done to change that fact.

Aristotle worried that if this argument were sound, human freedom would mean nothing; it would mean that we are powerless to affect the future. The truth of fatalism thus would mean that we neither have control over our lives nor possess individual responsibility. To avoid this conclusion, Aristotle decreed that for this one class of propositions (propositions about the future), the law of bivalence should be suspended. Thus, if you say to someone, "Tomorrow it will rain," that statement, according to Aristotle, is neither true nor false. Some may take comfort in the fact that this means that one could never be wrong with a claim about the future, but of course it equally follows that one could never be right.

The Roman orator and politician Cicero (106–43 BCE) spelled out more explicitly the threat that metaphysical fatalism seems to pose to human agency. It is called the "Idle Argument," for it concludes that if fatalism is true, then there is no reason to do anything. Take the following example:

1. If Daenerys is fated to rule Westeros, then she will rule Westeros regardless of whether she leaves Mereen.
2. Hence, whether she leaves Mereen is idle with respect to whether she will rule Westeros.
3. Hence, Dany has no reason to leave Mereen.

It should be apparent why this argument is problematic: clearly Daenerys will *not* be able to rule Westeros if she remains in Mereen. If we look again at the premises, we will see why this and any argument like it is unsound: it could be the case that Daenerys comes to rule Westeros only *because* she leaves Mereen.

Philosophers use the term "practical" to refer to the sorts of deliberations we perform when acting. To say that a certain argument or fact matters practically is to say that it should figure in one's deliberations about what to do. The Idle Argument, we can now say, makes exactly that claim about metaphysical fatalism—it claims that metaphysical fatalism matters for deciding what to do. But that, we now see, is false. It hardly follows from the arguments we have seen in favor of metaphysical fatalism that what you do does not affect the future; in fact, the future in large part is the result of what you do! So fatalism does not pose a threat to agency in the way that Sartre may have maintained. Remember that for Sartre, fatalism is anathema to human freedom if one uses it as an *excuse* for remaining in bad faith. In that much he is correct: because there are no practical consequences that follow from metaphysical fatalism, it would be in bad faith to use a commitment to fatalism as an excuse for not acting. Suppose, as a further example, that Jon believes the Others are fated never to enter Westeros. It would be wrong for him to do nothing. Fate might have it that the others fail to invade Westeros *only because* he stands firm in his duties at the Wall.

Fulfilling Fate

There is something of a paradox emerging here. It is wrong, we have just seen, to think of fate as an external force coercing agents this way or that. One's fate is largely one's own doing. Dany is fated to marry Khal Drogo, just as Jon is fated to don the Black, yet these are clearly things that each of them does. At the same time, metaphysical fatalism tells us that only *one* future is possible. It seems, then, that one's fate is largely the result of one's own doing, and yet, it is something that one can do nothing about. What notion of freedom could make sense of this?

To answer, let's return to Martin Heidegger (1889–1976), who first introduced the term "authenticity" to systematic philosophy. "Authenticity" normally connotes something real as opposed to something fake. No replica of Ice, Lord Eddard's sword, no matter how exact, will ever be the "authentic" Ice. In this sense, being "real" is a way of being unique or singular.

Heidegger appropriates this common understanding of authenticity to develop an alternative to the usual concept of human freedom as autonomy. While *autonomy* is defined in terms of control—I am autonomous if I can control what I do, free from any external or internal compulsion—*authenticity* is defined in terms of ownership and singularity: freedom as "owning" oneself and being one's own.[10] The challenge Heidegger wants to meet with the concept of authenticity is as follows: while acknowledging that we are wholly shaped by our past and that this will decide our future, how can one ever be free—how can one take possession of one's own life? I think we can all appreciate this problem: while on the one hand we feel as if we are in control of ourselves and our lives, we understand that had we been born to a different time or in a different place, we would be very different from the person we are now and would make very different life decisions. How can we acknowledge this fact while still retaining any notion of freedom, any notion, that is, that we are responsible for who we are?

Return to the moment when Eddard must decide, do I confess to treason and spare my family, or do I stand on principle and forfeit the lives of my daughters? The discerning reader, when aided by a writer as gifted as Martin, already knows the answer. Eddard has proven time and again that his honor matters more to him than his life or his status. But this honor is anchored in an even deeper sense of responsibility. He knows that it was his mistakes that put Arya and Sansa in danger, his decisions that endangered Winterfell, and his acquiescence that could thwart war. If Eddard can make matters right by laying down his honor before King's Landing, then we already know what Eddard will do. When you know a person's character, you know the sorts of choices that person will make. One's choices at any moment do not, contrary to Sartre, float free of one's past. We are determined by our history, and most importantly, by our character. The Greek philosopher Heraclitus

(c. 535–c. 475 BCE), whom Heidegger greatly admired, expressed this point by saying that "character is destiny."

Freedom, as Heidegger interprets it, is, rather than a potentiality confined to the moment, something that characterizes one's life as a whole. Contrary to Sartre, this freedom does not mean being cut off from one's past, but rather fulfilling it. Heidegger says that normally we exist in a state of "average everydayness." In this mode of existing, we go about our day doing what "one" does, being a father, brother, colleague, and friend. Our average or everyday existence is dispersed among many different projects and roles, only some of which cohere with one another. For example, Jon's obligations as a brother to Robb conflict with his obligations as a brother of the Night's Watch. He cannot live a life committed to both. He must choose. By his choice he does not escape those obligations. Rather, the obligations bind him even were he to choose to ignore them. What he must do instead is choose to fulfill one obligation or the other. Notice that in fulfilling an obligation, Jon is fulfilling a *purpose* he did not choose for himself, and in this sense, he is choosing his fate. Jon did not decide to be born a bastard in House Stark, nor did he decide that brothers of the Night's Watch have no family but one another. But by choosing to fulfill one purpose rather than another, Jon is choosing himself, and in this sense, by becoming an individual, is free.

Becoming Who You Are

We began by asking, are fate and freedom compatible? Or does fatalism nullify freedom? Intuitively perhaps, we understand that they can be compatible—that finding one's purpose or living up to one's fate can be liberating. The challenge is to find a philosophical justification for that feeling. We have found it, I think, in Heidegger. Over the course of a life, one becomes who one is. Struggling to make something of one's life is the struggle, in Heidegger's terms, for authenticity. Life presents each of us with any number of incompatible possible lives that we might equally fulfill. Many options are open, but to live authentically, to be an individual, one must choose one and forfeit others. Good characters do this: Dany has chosen the rights to the House Targaryen, Jon has chosen the life of Watch, Robb has chosen to be the King of the North, and Tyrion has chosen to be a Lannister, no matter how much his father, his sister, and the world protest that that is a place to which he has no right. In choosing these lives, these characters are fulfilling purposes or fates that themselves were not chosen. Pindar (522–443 BCE), a Greek poet, expressed this point in the following words: "Become who you are." How can a person become that which he or she already is? The answer is that who one is, is decided by how that person fulfills the purposes that fate—one's past, one's history, one's character—has assigned.

NOTES

1. George R. R. Martin, *A Game of Thrones* (New York: Bantam Dell, 2005), p. 57.

2. The philosophical term "metaphysics" is nearly the opposite of its other meaning when used to denote spiritual or otherworldly things. In philosophy, "metaphysics" refers to the study of reality. For example, the theories of space, time, and causality are "metaphysical." In the present context, "metaphysical fatalism" says that the future, in some sense, *really* exists and cannot be changed. This is in contrast to what might be called "psychological fatalism," that sense of powerlessness or passivity that follows from the belief that nothing can be done to change the future. A belief in metaphysical fatalism is often said to entail psychological fatalism, but I dispute this in the present chapter.

3. Hence the name of the school in philosophy that Sartre more than any other perhaps represents: *existentialism*.

4. It is worth pointing out that Epicurus did not believe that one should try to maximize pleasure at all times. In fact, Epicurus exhorted his followers to lead as abstemious and moderate a life as possible. A demand for great pleasures too easily leads to great disappointment, whereas a life of simple, rustic pleasure is easily achieved and its disappointments less severe.

5. Several characters self-consciously struggle against this essentialism. One is Petyr Baelish, who, we are led to believe in *A Feast of Crows*, perhaps desires to run House Arryn, and maybe even Westeros itself, or maybe even something grander. Many readers admire Davos for similar reasons. It does not appear to take much for Lord Manderly to revivify the smuggler in him in *A Dance with Dragons*. And of course, in counterpoint

to Jon, there is Ramsey Bolton, whose deformed character seems to betray his unfitness for his false station as Lord Bolton's heir.

6. A clever reader might be asking herself at this point, "Is Sartre not saying that freedom is the human essence, something each human has, by virtue of which each of us is a person? And is not this just admitting that humans do after all have an essence?" "Yes and no," is the right answer. If we wish to insist that freedom is the human essence, then we may do so, so long as we recognize (a) that this essence is different from all other essences and (b) that since one *could be* anything one *is* nothing, and if our essence is nothing, then it really is not an essence at all.

7. Sartre does not mean by this that we can *succeed* in becoming anything we choose. No human will ever succeed in becoming a god, and it's probably safe to say that no human will achieve immortality. On a more mundane level, most of what we choose to do or be meets with only partial success. So Sartre is not saying that I *can* be whatever I want to be. His point is that I can *try* to be anything I can conceive, while of course recognizing that both the world and other people constrain my chances of success.

8. It's worth remarking here that if we accept the Sartrean terminology, "taking responsibility" and "taking responsibility for oneself" are two quite different things. Responsibilities are something that the world puts on you. Sartre might admit that there are responsibilities, but these responsibilities have no power over you unless you choose to let them. You are, however, absolutely responsible to yourself; in fact, it is the only true responsibility that you have and one that you cannot evade.

9. See Aristotle, *Categories and De Interpretatione*, trans. J. Ackrill (Oxford: Oxford Univ. Press, 1963).

10. The term for *authenticity* in German is *Eigentlichkeit*, drawing on the root word *eigen*, meaning "own." *Eigentlichkeit* might more literally be translated as "ownedness."

NO ONE DANCES THE
WATER DANCE

Henry Jacoby

"Who are you?" he would ask her every day.
"No one," she would answer, she who had been Arya
of House Stark.[1]

It's a long journey from being a nine-year-old tomboy playing
with wooden swords, to learning the Water Dance, to escap-
ing King's Landing after her father's beheading, to hiring an
assassin in Jaqen H'ghar, to becoming an apprentice assassin
herself with the Faceless Men at the House of Black and White
in Braavos. It certainly makes Arya Stark one of the most
compelling characters in A Song of Ice and Fire. She faces all
that life throws at her with a fierce determination that's rare,
especially for one so young. Some readers may see Arya as
one who becomes a crazed killer, perhaps even a psychotic,
driven mad by her thirst for revenge. I see her, however, as a
strange mixture of moral virtues and Zen sensibilities. How
can this be? What do moral virtues and Zen have to do with

each other? And what does either of them have to do with our favorite skinny girl from Winterfell?

This chapter is about Arya's journey and what it can teach us about how to lead a good life. It's also about stabbing people— you know, sticking them with the pointy end. Interestingly, as we will see, they turn out to be much the same.

Virtues and the Good Life

In moral philosophy, a distinction is often made between an ethics of *doing* and an ethics of *being*. Roughly, the idea is that while some ethical theories attempt to tell us what to do and what makes our actions right or wrong, other theories focus more on *how we should live* and *what we should be like*. These latter theories comprise the field known as *virtue ethics*.

The goal of all virtue theories is to instruct us on how to lead a good life. The theories disagree, though, on what constitutes "a good life" as well as on the necessary means for achieving it. Many of the ancient Greek philosophers held that the good life equals the life of reason. By contrast, the great spiritual and philosophical traditions of the East tend to distrust reason, and instead would have us focus on living authentically. In Zen, this means having direct experience of reality and finding the true self, whereas in Taoism it means living in harmony with nature in an effortless way. Arya's journey—from Water Dance beginner to apprentice assassin in Braavos—encompasses all of these. After all, I'm not just writing this because she's my favorite character (well, maybe).

If you're going to map the tricky path to the good life, and thus present any virtue theory of ethics, the first thing you need to do is explain what a virtue is. Aristotle (384–322 BCE) was the first to do this in any sort of systematic way in his *Nicomachean Ethics*,[2] so that's a good place to start. He explained that virtues were character traits; but not just any character traits are virtues. After all, Littlefinger is devious; Sandor Clegane, the Hound, can be vicious; and Joffrey, well, Joffrey needs to be slapped. The point is that these character traits are not virtues. A virtue, said Aristotle, is a character trait that is good for you to have. "Well, isn't it good for Littlefinger to be devious and the Hound to be vicious?" you might ask. These traits serve their purpose, that is true, but they are not good for them in the sense that they do not bring them true happiness. Certainly these traits don't bring them *eudaimonia*, the Greek word sometimes translated as *happiness*, but better translated as *well-being* or *flourishing*.

In discussing happiness and the good life, Aristotle is not talking about pleasure. Like his teacher Plato (428–348 BCE), Aristotle denied that pleasure was "the good." He is talking instead about a life lived with the rational part of the mind controlling our desires and appetites, a life in which we fulfill our proper function as rational beings, living what Socrates (469–399 BCE) called "the examined life." Virtue is thus not some prize to obtain; it is a process that one works through in an entire lifetime. The person without reason in control—or any immoral individual, for that matter—might obtain various pleasures, but such a person could never attain true happiness. On this point, Socrates, Plato, and Aristotle all agreed.

Since the proper virtues are needed when engaged in the process of living a good life, the next thing we need to know is how these virtues are obtained. Aristotle thought that the moral virtues could be acquired only through practice, and not through instruction. So, for example, Maester Luwin's having Bran read all about brave knights is not sufficient to make Bran himself brave. He might come to understand the concept of bravery in this way, and thus recognize it in his brother Robb. But for Bran to actually possess the virtue, he must practice performing brave acts until it becomes natural for him to react bravely. It must become a habit.

This leads us back to Arya's beginnings with the Water Dance. As we will see, the martial arts are a good way to illustrate what Aristotle had in mind. But since the martial arts originated in the East, they are infused with, and help illustrate, the philosophies of Zen and Taoism as well.

Martial Arts and Virtues

Before he leaves to "take the Black" and join the Night's Watch, Jon Snow gives Arya a special present: a thin sword, made of the finest Valyrian steel, which she names "Needle" (special swords need to have names, of course). Arya Stark may be a very young girl, but unlike her older sister Sansa, who dreams of being a princess, Arya has no time for such foolishness. She'd much rather be a knight. She is already aware that the training she receives from Septa Mordane is not the sort of training that is needed for the life of well-being; she needs a different sort of "needlework." Jon Snow's present, on the other hand, resonates with her, and sets her on her path of self-discovery.

At first, all Arya knows of swordplay is that "you stick 'em with the pointy end." "That's the essence of it," her father agrees, but seeing that she's genuinely interested, he arranges a proper teacher for her ("Lord Snow"). And not just any teacher, we learn, but the Dancing Master from Braavos himself, Syrio Forel. What she learns from Syrio—the Water Dance—is not just how to hold the sword and how to position her body to avoid attacks, but something much more. Indeed, she begins to learn how to live. Just so.

True martial artists will tell you that martial arts are not just about self-defense, but are also about health and well-being. Studying martial arts can help us acquire moral virtues while teaching us how to live, and like Aristotle's life of virtue, the martial arts stress the importance of the process over the prize. When studied seriously, a martial art is a spiritual practice as well. More on this later.

When I first began studying martial arts, I asked my *sensei* (the head instructor—literally, "one who has gone before") how often one should train. He replied that you never stop training; everything you do is part of it. What you learn in the *dojo*—the place of training—obviously has application on the outside, if you ever have to defend yourself, for instance. But it's not just about defense. The awareness you learn, the respect and compassion you show for your training partners, and how you learn to conduct yourself all carry over to the rest of your life. If you think of every action in your life as part of your training, then all your interactions, with people, animals, and the environment, require the same care and focus you must have in the dojo.

Now, let's return to Aristotle's idea of virtues as habits. Aristotle wants us to practice honesty, courage, justice, and so on until they become a natural part of us. In martial arts training, something very similar takes place. For example, in karate, students practice various movements, like upward blocks, endlessly. An upward block is an unusual sort of movement—not something that one routinely does—but over time it becomes a simple automatic movement. And that's a good thing, because if someone attempts to strike the martial artist over the head, you want the block to be an automatic response. If it was not so—if it was instead the case that you first had to think about how to respond to the attack—it would be too late. The same is true for all the movements Arya learns in practicing the Water Dance. The sword thrusts and blocks, the graceful movement of the body, chasing cats through the castle, as well as standing on one leg or walking on her hands to create a new sense of balance, are all meant to train Arya to respond instantly and appropriately to any dangerous situation.

Similarly, the honest person responds automatically with the truth in every situation; he doesn't have to think about what the proper response should be. This idea, that the "proper response" does not involve thinking, is not only shared by martial arts and Aristotle's virtue ethics,[3] but is also an essential part of the philosophies of the East. And further, the common theme in each is that character is developed through discipline, practice, and attention. In martial arts, without this training of the mind, you're just learning how to fight. With this training of the mind, though, you're learning how to *live authentically*.

The Water Dance

> "This is not the dance of the Westeros we are
> learning. . . . This is the Braavos Dance, the Water
> Dance."
>
> —"Lord Snow"

Virtue theories such as Aristotle's are concerned with how we should live. Since martial arts share this goal, they can be put in the same category. But there are many differences. For Aristotle, to lead the good life, reason must be in charge. The rational part of the mind must control the irrational part so that we are not ruled by our desires. For the martial arts path to the good life, we must also control our desires, but this is not accomplished by living "the examined life" of Socrates or "the life of reason" recommended by Aristotle. It instead requires an egoless presence with a "mind like water."

It's not for nothing that the sword style Arya is learning is called the Water Dance. For one thing, water is a very important concept in Taoism. Taoism's main work, the *Tao Te Ching*, attributed to the great sage Lao Tzu, is full of passages encouraging us to "be like water."[4] What does this mean?

In their first lesson, Syrio explains to Arya: "All men are made of water; do you know this? If you pierce them, the water leaks out . . . and they die" ("Lord Snow").

Water is essential to life. The Water Dance mirrors the very dance of life. Water flows and adapts to its surroundings, filling containers of any shape, going through holes or cracks, and moving around an obstacle when it can't go straight through. In martial arts, there must be a flow as well—a dance, if you will. The martial artist adapts to the situation, using only the amount of force necessary, and never more. To lead a good life, we too must be able to adapt, and go with the flow.

Several characters in A Song of Ice and Fire adapt well to their surroundings, and their lives, while still containing tragedies and suffering, are the better for it. Tyrion and Daenerys come to mind as excellent examples, while Daenerys's brother Viserys illustrates the opposite. But no one is a better example of harmonizing with one's surroundings than Arya. From working in the kitchens at Harrenhal, to becoming "Cat of the Canals" in Braavos, she learns to accept her situation for what it is, and thereby to do what is required. This involves, at Harrenhal, enlisting the help of Faceless Man Jaqen H'ghar to assassinate some of her enemies and lead a revolt, and killing a Night's Watch deserter in Braavos. Using Needle is sometimes, unfortunately, what the situation calls for.

Another feature of water is its flexibility, which enables it to withstand great force; the martial artist can likewise withstand attacks by being flexible. An important skill in martial arts involves redirecting an attacker's own energy against him. Doing this properly requires little energy of your own. If you're struggling to make it work, using all your strength, you're not doing the technique properly.

This idea of avoiding struggle involves one of Taoism's key concepts: *wu wei*. This is the idea of responding to every situation in life effortlessly and naturally, like water. Lao Tzu tells us that "the way of the sage is to act without struggling."[5] When you achieve this, you are in harmony with the Tao itself—the flow of nature, or the very dance of life. In martial arts, this is nicely illustrated by performing a Tai Chi form, which is a series (sometimes quite long) of choreographed movements done very slowly. To the outside observer, it looks like a graceful dance; in reality, it consists of a series of deadly self-defense blocks, strikes, and kicks. To do it properly, thinking must be put aside; one *becomes* the form. Again at her very first Water Dance lesson, Arya complains that her wooden sword is too heavy to hold in one hand. "What if I drop it?" she asks. Syrio replies "The steel must be part of your arm. Can you drop your arm? No" ("Lord Snow"). That's the idea.[6]

Zen and the Sword Master from Braavos

"There is only one god and his name is death. And
there is only one thing we say to death: Not today."

—"A Golden Crown"

To be able to respond effortlessly, and to be able to become one with the dance around you, requires that your mind be like water. But Zen has us go further, as we strip away the ego in order to find our true self. Indeed, a famous Zen koan asks, "What was the face you had before you were born?"[7] Slaying the ego—which, as we will see, is perhaps the most important part of Arya's later training at the House of Black and White— is also crucial in Zen.

Zen is a way of seeing the world, and a way of authentically being in the world. It can be thought of as a philosophy of life, yet it has no theory. And unlike most philosophical systems, it deemphasizes the intellect in favor of intuitive action. As its approach to life is often illustrated in the interaction between student and master, Arya and Syrio will thus do just fine.[8]

Syrio Forel tells Arya that he was first sword to the Sealord of Braavos. He explains how this came about:

On the day I am speaking of, the first sword was newly dead, and the Sealord sent for me. Many bravos had come to him, and as many had been sent away, none could say why. When I came into his presence, he was seated, and in his lap was a fat yellow cat. He told me that one of his captains had brought the beast to him, from an island beyond the sunrise. "Have you ever seen her like?" he asked of me.

And to him I said, "Each night in the alleys of Braavos I see a thousand like him," and the Sealord laughed, and that day I was named the first sword. [9]

At first, Arya doesn't understand, but Syrio explains to her that the others saw what they were expecting: a fabulous beast. Whereas he saw what was there: just an ordinary tomcat. He continues:

Just so. Opening your eyes is all that is needing. The heart lies and the head plays tricks with us, but the eyes see true.[10]

This idea, this "seeing with your eyes," is an essential part of Zen; we might even call it "Zen seeing." Recognizing the flow of all things—the Taoist idea alluded to above—is also part of this. For example, earlier in the lesson when he explains how he became First Sword of Braavos, Syrio was calling out his moves, indicating which direction Arya should move to be able to defend herself. One time, though, he doesn't go where he says, sends her a stinging blow with his wooden sword, and says, "You are dead now." When Arya protests that it was unfair because he had lied, he replies:

"My words lied. My eyes and my arm shouted out the truth, but you were not seeing."

"I was so," Arya said. "I watched you every second."

"Watching is not seeing, dead girl. The water dancer sees."[11]

Watching and seeing are clearly two different things. Zen is an attempt to train the mind in order to bring it into contact with ultimate reality. Partly, this is done by using your senses to perceive what is there without any preconceived notions, as in the tomcat example. Another example occurs much later when Arya first enters the House of Black and White in Braavos.

She sees old people lying around in alcoves who appear to be sleeping; but, as she reminds herself to "look with your eyes," she realizes that they are either dead or dying.[12] She will soon learn that this is why they come to the temple.

Seeing rather than just watching also requires that one must be fully present. In one of their lessons, the training isn't going very well. Lord Eddard has been seriously injured, and Jory, the head of his guard, has been killed. Arya is naturally worried about her father. Syrio says to her:

> You are troubled. . . . Good! Trouble is a perfect time for training. When you are dancing in the meadow with your dolls and kittens, this is not when fighting happens. . . . You're not here; you're with your trouble. If you're with your trouble when fighting happens . . . more trouble for you. Just so! ("A Golden Crown")

If your mind is somewhere else, you cannot "see with your eyes," and you're likely to get hit, kicked, or whacked with a stick. When you are doing a technique, you must do the technique and nothing else. The idea is to be able to have this level of presence—being in the now, or what the Buddhists call "mindfulness"—throughout your everyday life. Again, every encounter in life is part of your training.

Without mindfulness, negative emotions can gain control: "Fear cuts deeper than swords." Arya's familiar mantra reminds us that our fears must be conquered before we can lead lives of well-being. Prominent among these fears, of course, is the fear of death. "*Valar morghulis*"—all men must die—as they say in Braavos. Because of its certainty, Syrio refers to death as "the one true god." But until we die, we must live, and so we say to death, "Not today."

In her training with the Faceless Men, Arya learns about their "Many-Faced God," and learns a good deal more about death. Her training in part prepares her to bring death to others; but there is also the death of the self alluded to earlier.

While Arya's entire journey illustrates this key idea of Zen (think of the different identities she has, the different roles she plays; yet none of them is *her*), her training at the House of Black and White takes this stripping of the self to a frightening extreme, as her face is literally removed at one point before it is later returned to her. The Faceless Men can magically change their appearance; Arya witnesses Jaqen H'ghar do this. To be able to do this requires that you become "no one." This idea parallels what occurs in another sort of martial arts training from the East known as *Ninjutsu*.

Ninjutsu and the Faceless Men

In *The Spiritual Practices of the Ninja*, Ross Heaven tells us that the word "Ninjutsu" (the Way of the Ninja) is often translated as "the art of stealth" or "the art of invisibility." The word implies two things: first, the use of stealth to uncover the hidden self so we can discover our inner truth and know what our real purpose is. Second, the skill of remaining true to ourselves but blending so effectively with the prevailing ways of society that we remain almost unseen, leaving no footprints in the sand, while still achieving our purpose.[13]

From the movies, we picture Ninjas as secret assassins, clad in black, performing amazing, acrobatic feats. But as we see from the definition above, Ninjutsu is more than just deadly martial arts training. Like all martial arts, when done properly, it is also a spiritual practice.

"Spiritual" here must be understood in a naturalist way. It refers to a specific sense of self and a felt connectedness to everything that exists. The spiritual person, like the Taoist sage or the Zen master, lives in the present moment, in harmony with nature, and in possession of a self-awareness that leads to effective living.

Arya doesn't seem to fit the mold of the spiritual person—she is still very young and has a long way to go. But her training at the House of Black and White closely mirrors both

Ninja training and the rituals and trials common to initiation processes found in many cultures. Such initiation processes usually involve three stages:[14] First, the initiate must leave behind the past; Arya's main teacher, the kindly man, makes her throw away all of her possessions, which are the only remaining ties to her past identity as Arya of House Stark. (While she mostly acquiesces, she can't bear to part with Needle and hides it.) Second, challenges are presented that must be overcome in order for growth to take place. Arya is being trained to fully experience reality, and to do this, she must use all her senses. Therefore, she is given a potion that temporarily renders her blind. And third, there is a celebration of rebirth, which requires the initiate to remember her true self. Arya has not yet reached this stage, but the master is impressed with her ability to carry out her mission—an assassination—successfully, and she is then ready to begin her true apprenticeship as a Faceless Man.

The Faceless Dance of Virtue

Needlework—the traditional kind—and being a lady are not for Arya. Her journey begins long before she must flee King's Landing with Yoren; it begins with Jon Snow's gift, which empowers her. Learning the Water Dance serves her well, as she is introduced to a new way of being in the world. She survives and eventually reaches Braavos. While there, Arya continues her quest for awareness, and against this Eastern backdrop she can still be considered virtuous, even though we've now left behind traditional ideas of good and evil. Even an assassin can avoid the suffering that comes from living according to who we think we are, rather than who we really are. She now dances faceless. "Who are you?" the kindly man continues to ask. "No one," she continues to reply.

Each of us takes part in rituals and processes on our individual paths of self-discovery. Usually, these don't involve temporary blindness or assassinations, and that's a good thing;

but drastic measures are often needed to break from the past and remember who we truly are, which is necessary for enlightenment. We each have our own version of the Water Dance as well. The "Zen" part of it isn't about learning the moves, and that's why I haven't written about them. I also haven't really written a lot about Zen, because Zen isn't *about* anything— you have been paying attention, right? You can't teach Zen; one can only point at some stuff designed to make you stop thinking so you'll spend more time just *being*. What's being pointed at must be experienced; like Aristotle's virtues, it can't be taught. But I can tell you this: the secret to living a good life is to dance faceless like a Zen-Ninja-Aristotelian. Sort of like Arya. Got it? Now try not to stab anyone.[15]

NOTES

1. George R. R. Martin, *A Feast for Crows* (New York: Bantam Dell, 2005), p. 446.

2. In Richard McKeon, ed., *The Basic Works of Aristotle* (New York: Random House, 1941).

3. I don't mean to suggest that Aristotle is anti-thinking! Reason, of course, is crucial for him in obtaining the virtues initially, but once one has the virtues, the responses, like those of the martial artist, should be instinctive and automatic.

4. There are many wonderful versions of this great spiritual masterpiece. One I especially like is *Lao-tzu's Taoteching*, translated by Red Pine (San Francisco: Mercury House, 1996). The commentaries it contains are highly recommended.

5. Ibid., verse 81.

6. Even though their practice swords are wood, he refers here to steel swords that would be used in a real battle (although Syrio himself does pretty well with just a wooden one!).

7. Koans are mind puzzles designed to challenge our normal modes of thinking. For an excellent discussion of this and all things Zen, see Roshi Philip Kapleau, *The Three Pillars of Zen* (New York: Anchor Books, 1980).

8. The classic text on this approach is Eugen Herrigel, *Zen in the Art of Archery* (New York: Random House, 1999).

9. George R. R. Martin, *A Game of Thrones* (New York: Bantam Dell, 2005), pp. 531–532.

10. Ibid.

11. Ibid., p. 531.

12. Martin, *A Feast for Crows*, p. 137.

13. Ross Heaven, *The Spiritual Practices of the Ninja* (Rochester, VT: Destiny Books, 2006), p. 2.

14. Heaven, *Spiritual Practices*, pp. 15–16.

15. I am grateful to R. Shannon Duval, who kindly and generously shared her wisdom and insights with me and helped make this chapter much better than it otherwise would have been.

THE THINGS I DO
FOR LOVE: SEX, LIES,
AND GAME THEORY

R. Shannon Duval

And I shall say: "games" form a family.
—Ludwig Wittgenstein, *Philosophical Investigations*[1]

"When you play the game of thrones, you win or you die," Cersei Lannister whispers to Ned Stark in the godswood at King's Landing.[2] These words might serve as the Lannister siblings' unofficial credo as Jaime, Cersei, and Tyrion Lannister pursue their family's forbidden games and lovers' logics in George R. R. Martin's *A Game of Thrones*. As we'll see, the field of game theory has traditionally been limited to rational play only, but it can be adapted to offer compelling insight into House Lannister's games of cunning artifice.

What Is Game Theory?

Any situation where agents employ strategies toward a desired end can be considered a game. Game theory mathematically models the architecture of rational choice and suggests the best strategy based on a player's preferred outcomes. In philosophy, game theory has become particularly relevant as philosophers attempt to resolve the tension between self-interest and cooperation in moral, social, and political settings. In essence, game theory can serve as each player's personal Hand—advising the best course of action, predicting the likely actions of others, and crafting the most successful strategies. Though game theory was originally both defined by and expressed in specifically mathematical terms, it is possible to set the specific calculations aside while applying the principles of game theory to particular options faced by players in *A Game of Thrones*. We can further profit from the insights game theory provides into the choices of our most favorite, and least favorite, characters.

While game theory is effective in seeking a certain outcome, game theory itself is not concerned with whether the outcome is right or wrong. In other words, game theory can tell us how to support our favorite contender for the Iron Throne—Baratheon or Targaryen, for example—and even tell us which contender it may be most to our advantage to support, but aside from those considerations it has nothing to say about whether Robert Baratheon or Mad King Ayres would be the "better" king, unless we add additional information from outside game theory itself. Like the maesters who are sworn to serve the realm regardless of who is king, game theory serves the stated outcome but does not make any judgment on its worthiness or its morality.

House Rules

In a world where "might makes right," game theory can help us to understand the successes of unlikely players as well as the downfalls of promising heroes. Tyrion Lannister makes this point to Jon Snow when Tyrion reflects,

> Well, my legs may be too small for my body, but my head is too large, although I prefer to think it is just large enough for my mind. I have a realistic grasp of my own strengths and weaknesses. My mind is my weapon. My brother has his sword, King Robert has his war-hammer, and I have my mind . . .[3]

Game theory offers a means to model humans' interactions and to predict future moves based on three criteria: rationality, self-interest, and investment. If it is true that when playing the game of thrones Lannister-style, "you win or you die," then all players have an important stake in the game. It is also safe to assume that players are ultimately concerned with their expected payoffs, although discovering a player's true endgame is often half the game itself. The first criterion, however—that players are rational—turns out to be a critical element in evaluating game theory's usefulness as a predictive tool.

A Game of Thrones is steeped in the chivalric milieu of knighthood with its ideals of courtesy, honor, and fair play. "Give me an honorable enemy and I will sleep better at night," quips Jaime Lannister.[4] And well he might. An honorable enemy is a predictable one. An honorable enemy does not lie, cheat, steal, or poison. An honorable enemy will not break an oath or turn his cloak. In other words, an honorable enemy's sense of fair play is not altered by love or war. Game theory is considerably simplified if our enemies are honorable, but we must ask: "Is honor *rational?*"

Knights are honored because they have chosen service above self-interest and thus can be entrusted with the protection of the interests of others. Opponents may not always be as true as Ser Barrison Selmy, however, because they may have calculated that it better serves their interests, and thus is more rational, to lie. Although game theory may sometimes advise a lie, it can also help us spot deception if we know enough about a player to understand his goals. If a promise is not rational—if it does not support a successful strategy toward an opponent's goal—then it should not be believed. A talented liar may be difficult to detect, however, especially if he is able to mask his true endgame. This strategy is perhaps best articulated by Littlefinger when he advises Sansa Stark:

> Always keep your foes confused. If they are never certain who you are or what you want, they cannot know what you are like to do next. Sometimes the best way to baffle them is to make moves that have no purpose, or even seem to work against you. Remember that, Sansa, when you come to play the game.[5]

Because prodigious liars can be difficult to recognize before the damage of the lies is realized, the penalties to turncloaks and oathbreakers are severe. In explaining to Bran why he must behead the Black Brother who deserted his post at the wall, Ned Stark tells his young son that an oathbreaker is the most dangerous of all criminals. Having lost the currency of his good name, there is no crime an oathbreaker will not commit.[6]

Games of complete information in which all moves are known by all players are easier to control than games of incomplete information in which players may not even know which game they are playing.[7] Deception obscures the true nature of the game, thus rendering the deceived player disadvantaged at best. In effect, lying makes a game difficult and dangerous. Reliable information is worth more than Lannister gold in the game of thrones, because without it, players cannot form an effective strategy.

Eros's Aim

If liars are unwelcome participants in the game of thrones, lovers are even more poorly received. The Greek philosopher

Plato (428–348 BCE) described love as a type of madness.[8] Game theory agrees with the ancient philosopher in this respect and recommends taking a preemptive stance toward lovers. Women, historically considered to be most vulnerable to the sway of love, were traditionally excluded from the games of politics, law, and war because they were thought to be too enmeshed in emotion to be reasonable. This sentiment is echoed in the wisdom of ancient Westeros. "Love is the bane of honor, the death of duty,"[9] Maester Aemon tells Jon Snow when explaining why the Black Brothers take no wives and sire no children. The men who formed the Night's Watch "knew that they must have no divided loyalties to weaken their resolve."[10] In the cases where the most extreme forms of loyalty and honor may be required, marriage and families are forbidden. Not only do the Black Brothers not marry, but neither do the Kingsguard, maesters, septas, or septons.

Yet even when love is outlawed, it cannot be exiled. Black Brothers do love, Kingsguard forswear their oaths, and maesters, septons, and septas are not always the chaste practitioners that duty demands. If the very rules of rationality and fair play that govern game theory are truly inapplicable in love, not to mention war,[11] it would seem that game theory has to remain feckless at the keep during the most important game of all. However, the German philosopher Friedrich Nietzsche (1844–1900) amends Plato's view, claiming, "Always there is a drop of madness in love, but always there is a drop of reason in madness."[12]

Nietzsche's remark reminds us that if we can detect the drop of reason in madness, we can envision a world in which the lover is sane and his actions therefore predictable. In game theory, the objection to love is that it is irrational, and the objection to irrationality is that it is erratic and therefore cannot be systematized. If we are able to see our opponents' outcomes as they do, however, seemingly irrational behavior often resolves into a coherent strategy. "Irrationality" usually signals that we have misidentified either the type of opponent we face, the opponent's endgame, or both. This information can be invaluable in restoring our position in the game. Consider the following example. After the mystifying attack on Bran Stark's life at Winterfell, Robb Stark expresses the senselessness of the event:

> "Why would anyone want to kill Bran?" Robb said. "Gods, he's only a little boy, helpless, sleeping . . ."
>
> Catelyn gave her firstborn a challenging look. "If you are to rule in the north, you must think these things through, Robb. Answer your own question. Why would anyone want to kill a sleeping child?"[13]
>
> "Someone is afraid Bran might wake up," Robb said, "Afraid of what he might say or do, afraid of something he knows."[14]

By placing a seemingly irrational action into a rational context, Catelyn is able to use a process that game theory calls "reverse induction" to reveal information that would have otherwise remained hidden.[15] After swearing her closest advisers to secrecy, she tells them,

> "It comes to me that Jaime Lannister did not join the hunt the day Bran fell. He remained here in the castle." The room was deathly quiet. "I do not think Bran fell from that tower," she said into the stillness. "I think he was thrown."[16]

Jaime is a knight of the Kingsguard, Cersei is queen of the realm, and it may seem irrational to suppose they would need to harm an eight-year-old boy. Lady Stark's own master at arms, Rodrik Cassel, is shocked at the notion that even a knight as dishonored as the Kingslayer would stoop to an attempted murder of an innocent child. Yet by starting with the irrational act and using reverse induction to hypothesize a game in which that action made a type of strategic, if not moral, sense, Catelyn is able to plan a future strategy that is both more informed and more likely to succeed. If we expand our understanding of rational actions to embrace people in relation to others and all the emotional, psychological, and social commitments that entails, we can expand our understanding of rationality itself and thus of predictable behavior. When unpredictable events occur, they need not be seen as destabilizing the game. In fact, it is just such events that can guide players in asking the right questions and thus gaining the information needed to put a game of incomplete information aright. Recognizing a diversity of commitments, each of which may be reasonable from some player's point of view, allows players to adapt and adjust their own strategies with the agility that high-stakes games such as the game of thrones demand.

The Nature of the Game

Games of incomplete information, such as the game of thrones, are the most complex form of games. When invested in such a game, strategies for gaining information are of the utmost importance. In *A Game of Thrones* no single player knows all the players populating the game, what their payoffs are, and which strategies they are most likely to employ. Consider the situation surrounding Cersei and Jaime Lannister's children, Joffrey, Myrcella, and Tommen. As long as the children are assumed to be legitimate, they are first in line to succeed King Robert to the Iron Throne. Everyone who assumes the children's legitimacy is playing a game of incomplete information. The payoffs of King Robert's death, for example, are very different for various players if it is known that Cersei's children are truly Lannisters and not Baratheons. Lords Stanley and Renly, the king's brothers, would benefit greatly from this information, as would King Robert himself.

The information that players have, and their confidence in its reliability, make a profound difference to their strategies.

The more complete a player's information, the stronger that player's strategy becomes. That is why in complex games like the game of thrones the strongest players may be those who are the best advised rather than the best armored, especially if one player has access to information that is unavailable to the other players. The advantages proffered by secrets and spycraft account for the rise of players such as Petyr Baelish and Lord Varys, whose power resides in their ability to broker information to more prominent players.

The Dwarf's Gamble: Non-Zero-Sum Games and Repeated Play

Tyrion Lannister is one of the most gifted players in the game of thrones. Lacking the shelter of physical strength, stature, or beauty, Tyrion has learned that it is never to his advantage to avoid a hard truth. Denial is dangerous and leads to undue vulnerability. As the dwarf advises the bastard Jon Snow upon their first meeting, "Never forget what you are, for surely the world will not. Make it your strength. Then it can never be your weakness."[17] This attitude is a key virtue, because substituting wishful thinking for reality always produces flawed strategy. Sansa Stark's misplaced loyalties to Joffrey Baratheon and Cersei Lannister stand as excellent examples of the dismal failure of a damsel's wishful thinking to produce sound results. Tyrion is a keen observer of the nature of others and uses that knowledge to both his own advantage and, if they will heed his advice, to the advantage of his friends as well. When Jon Snow challenges Tyrion's wisdom, asking what the heir to Casterly Rock could possibly know of being a bastard, Tyrion replies, "All dwarves are bastards in their father's eyes."[18] This observation indicates Tyrion's expertise in reading others' signals and typing those players and their strategies to ensure his own survival. These strategies see him through many dangers and hardships and make this most unlikely hero a giant in the game of thrones.

One of Tyrion's particular strengths is his ability to convert either the strictly win-lose "zero-sum game" or an all-or-nothing one-shot game into a win-win situation; or at the very least, into a repeated game where he is likely to come out, if not ahead, then at least *with* his head. By forging alliances and reframing payoffs, the dwarf masterfully improves his position in the game, as the events that follow his capture by Catelyn Stark and subsequent trial at the Eyrie leave little doubt. Tyrion begins his long and perilous journey to the Eyrie as a captive. By reading the motives of his captors, Tyrion is able subtly to begin to lay the groundwork for coalition with Bronn, one of the sellswords currently serving Catelyn Stark. Tyrion understands that those of his captors who joined Lady Catelyn out of duty and honor will not offer him any aid, because any help given undermines their endgame of fealty. The sellswords, however, are another matter. Their endgame is reward, and that is a field of play on which Tyrion and his Lannister gold have an advantage.

The Lannisters are known not only for being the richest family in the Seven Kingdoms but also by their motto, "A Lannister always pays his debts." When Catelyn Stark's tattered group reaches the Eyrie, Tyrion is able to transform what looked to be his immediate summary execution into a public trial by calling into question the honor of house Arryn. By introducing house reputation, Tyrion forces the game to move from a one-shot to a repeated-game scenario. Even if Tyrion is executed—the ultimate one-shot game for any player—Lysa Arryn is still left to answer for the events. Thus for her the game becomes a repeated one. Tyrion's cleverness underscores why publicity is crucial to justice. What may be carried out as a one-shot game in private becomes a repeated game when a player is associated by name with those events each time they are mentioned by others.

For her part Lady Lysa agrees to a trial without concern, as the judge will be her own seven-year-old son. Little Lord

Robert has already declared his desire to "see the bad man fly," indicating that any trial would be a mummer's farce at best.[19] Thus, Tyrion's next play must take Lord Robert out of the equation. Having gained an audience for his maneuvers, Tyrion has improved his bargaining position and is able to demand his right to a trial by combat. On the surface this move may seem to have improved Tyrion Lannister's position little or none at all. However, trading now on the precarious coalition he has cultivated with Bronn and the type of player Tyrion believes Bronn to be, the dwarf engineers a situation where both his own and Bronn's positions improve dramatically if Bronn agrees to champion Tyrion—assuming he emerges victorious!

Tyrion has typed Bronn correctly. The sellsword volunteers to serve as Tyrion's champion and wins the day, thus ensuring both Tyrion's freedom and a handsome payment for Bronn from Tyrion's father. Tyrion's maneuver turns out to achieve further gains as well, because in order for Bronn to collect his reward, the sellsword needs to deliver Tyrion safely to Tywin Lannister. Tyrion has thus earned not only a champion, but also an armed escort back through the mountains and to his father's encampment.

Tyrion uses this strategy and again meets with success when Conn and the mountain clans accost Tyrion and Bronn on their way home. Tyrion convinces the raiders that whatever they got by robbing and killing Tyrion in the woods would not be nearly so valuable as the new weapons and armor that Tywin Lannister would provide as reward for his son's safe return. Tyrion thus completes the journey he began as a captive with a small army of his own. Each time Tyrion's situation seems destined to lead to his demise, he is able to rewrite his destiny by recognizing the endgame of his opponent and offering a revised strategy, a strategy where it is in everyone's interest that Tyrion stays alive, if only a little longer.[20]

Through the Eyes of Love

Alliances, temporary or permanent, are critical within the game of thrones. Tyrion Lannister demonstrated how temporary alliances based on mutual gain can dramatically improve a player's position. The more players have invested in an alliance, the more important that alliance becomes, and perhaps none more so than those alliances forged through love or marriage. It's just a happy coincidence when love and marriage go hand in hand in the Seven Kingdoms. More typically, marriages are arranged so that lords can unite their houses in order to strengthen the position and commitment of both families. In the marriage of Cersei Lannister to Robert Baratheon, the Baratheons gained the power, wealth, and prestige of House Lannister, while the Lannisters gained access to the Iron Throne. Their coalition seems mutually beneficial as both parties receive their desired payoff. Any children the king and queen have together reinforce the alliance, because as the legitimate heirs to the throne, the children ensure the succession, and therefore the success, of both houses.

The marriage appears to King Robert to be a non-zerosum game, but in fact it is not. There is game within a game. The Lannisters are playing to eliminate the king and sit a Lannister upon the Iron Throne. This subgame changes the nature of the original game from beneficial alliance to deathly trap. One of the reasons Cersei Lannister's pronouncement "You win or you die" strikes the reader as particularly sinister is that this outlook reduces what is normally a much more complex game, with multiple payoffs and possibilities for cooperation, to a simple zero-sum scenario.

King Robert and Queen Cersei's alliance is based on mutual gain, and not on shared love or affection. Does the equation change when the players' self-interest includes compassionate commitment to the best interest of another player? This question truly reaches the heart of the matter. The game theory one uses must be robust enough to accommodate a self-interest that privileges the interest of another in order to model many of our most important decisions—that is, the things we do for love.

Consider the familiar game of "I Cut, You Choose." The logic driving the game is that in the division of a limited set of goods, such as a piece of cake, each player will want the better portion. Thus it is in the cutter's interest to divide the pieces equally because the chooser will have the first selection. Yet if we put that game to Septa Mordane's test, we would likely come to a very different result. Practical experience teaches us that in social situations the choosers often select the smaller, and not the larger, of the offered pieces of cake. What deviant reasoning could possibly underlie such irrational decisions? Perhaps a guest takes a smaller piece because it is more important to be seen as polite than to enjoy the larger portion, or because she is watching her weight or wants to appear to be health-conscious. Or perhaps the smaller portion is chosen because the "chooser" knows how much the "cutter" enjoys cake and would like the cutter to enjoy the larger portion. None of these strategies is actually irrational, but all deviate from the mathematically predicted outcome. What we learn is that "I Cut, You Choose" may be an effective strategy for modeling fairness, but *fairness is but one of many rational preferences*. Furthermore, fairness understood as *equality* is only one of many rational models of fairness. These insights will take us far in adapting game theory to games ruled by love.

Game theory has typically discounted strategies in which fairness is not paramount, but the logic of love may actually accept and promote them. Far from seeing her as a "free rider," the chivalrous knight will assume all the duties of rowing his lady across the river and take satisfaction in allowing her simply to enjoy the ride. Parents regularly take on the greater share of work in a village so that children are not overburdened and still share in the benefits of living in a community. Lovers willingly sacrifice their own interests so that their beloved can have a greater share of something treasured. Allowing for the fact that love merges and binds our interests with our loved ones', we can see that players may formulate multiple coherent strategies. This recognition compels us to assess which of a plurality of possible rational choices are in play.

Recognizing multiple rational possible moves by an opponent demands that the successful player be able to sympathetically inhabit the other player's position to determine which rationality is operative. It is not enough to know what *you* would do if you were in the other player's position—you must understand what *your opponent* would do in that position. This sympathetic identification with another's preferences in and of itself demands that we acknowledge and regard the humanity and potential uniqueness of that player. The ability to see other players' outcomes as *they* see them, and not simply how we would see them, is the basis of "brotherly love" and is a prerequisite for honoring the dignity of other persons. The Golden Rule in game theory evolves from "Do unto others as you would have done unto yourself" into the more discerning "Understand others as they understand themselves."

Games thus understood *demand* that we attend to each player as a uniquely situated person and not simply as an abstract rational agent automatically moving toward a predetermined rational end. Such insight improves our ability to predict, understand, and foster the actions of others, as well as to further our own ends as we play the expanded game of thrones we call the game of life. It is in heeding the call of love that game theory transcends its previous applications and becomes effective in the arenas of moral and social philosophy.

NOTES

1. Ludwig Wittgenstein, *Philosophical Investigations*, trans. G. E. M. Anscombe (New York: Basil Blackwell, 1958), p. 32, ¶67.

2. George R. R. Martin, *A Game of Thrones* (New York: Bantam Dell, 2005), p. 488.

3. Ibid., pp. 123–124.

4. Ibid., p. 82.

5. George R. R. Martin, *A Storm of Swords* (New York: Bantam Dell, 2005), p. 841. Thank you to Henry Jacoby for reminding me of this quotation.

6. Ibid., p. 16.

7. In a game of complete information, such as chess or its Westerosi cousin *cyvasse*, all players are aware of each move up to the current point of the game. In games of incomplete information, however, one player has private information that is relevant to her game play or strategy. For an excellent introduction to game theory, I recommend Ken Binmore's *Game Theory: A Very Short Introduction* (Oxford: Oxford Univ. Press, 2007).

8. Plato, *Phaedrus* , 249d5–e1.

9. Martin, *A Game of Thrones*, p. 662.

10. Ibid., pp. 662–663.

11. "The rules of fair play do not apply in love and war." John Lyly, *Euphues*, 1578. This quotation is believed to be the source of the nonlogically equivalent popular adage, "All is fair in love and war."

12. Friedrich Nietzsche, *Thus Spoke Zarathustra*, "Reading and Writing," part 1, Chap. 7, trans. Alexander Tille (New York: The Macmillan Company, 1896).

13. Martin, *A Game of Thrones*, p. 135.

14. Ibid.

15. Reverse induction is the process of reasoning backward from a conclusion through a sequence of actions to determine the most likely starting point.

16. Martin, *A Game of Thrones*, p. 136.

17. Ibid., p. 57.

18. Ibid.

19. Ibid., p. 437.

20. The technique of generating a change in strategy in which one player is better off and no payers are worse off is called a Pareto improvement, after the Italian sociologist and philosopher Vilfredo Pareto (1848–1923). Pareto optimal outcomes are outcomes in which Pareto improvements are no longer possible. In other words, there are no possible outcomes to be sought that would not cause at least one party to be disadvantaged.

STOP THE MADNESS!: KNOWLEDGE, POWER, AND INSANITY IN A SONG OF ICE AND FIRE

Chad William Timm

"I am no maester to quote history at you, Your Grace. Swords have been my life, not books. But every child knows that the Targaryens have always danced too close to madness. Your father was not the first: King Jaehaerys once told me that madness and greatness are two sides of the same coin. Every time a new Targaryen is born, he said, the gods toss the coin in the air and the world holds its breath to see how it will land."[1]

—Ser Barristan Selmy to Daenerys
Targaryen in *A Storm of Swords*

In A Song of Ice and Fire, George R. R. Martin introduces us to a world full of murder, brutality, and death, a world seemingly full of insanity. At one time or another more than a dozen significant characters have their sanity questioned, from the Mad King Aerys to Patchface, the lackwit fool in Stannis Baratheon's court. Upon closer examination, though, the actions of those labeled "mad" are not much different from those assumed to be of sound mind. As a matter of fact, the line between sanity and insanity in Martin's books is so blurred that it barely exists at all. Ser Barristan Selmy, former knight of Robert Baratheon's Kingsguard, claims madness is hereditary, as it apparently runs in the Targaryen family right alongside greatness. But why are one person's actions deemed great while another's are labeled mad? Who gets to determine insanity and decide what is done with the mentally ill? The French philosopher Michel Foucault (1926–1984) can help us answer these questions with his investigation of the relations among knowledge, power, and madness.

The Archaeologist and the Mad Fool

While traditionally philosophers have sought knowledge of universal truth, Foucault and other postmodern philosophers have questioned the existence of universal truth and have sought instead to uncover the circumstances that lead to thinking something is true.[2] Foucault called his method of historical excavation "archaeology." In *The History of Madness*, he worked to show how the definition of madness, as well as the knowledge used to determine sanity, has changed historically, depending upon who had the power to define and determine it. According to Foucault, "One simple truth about madness should never be overlooked. The consciousness of madness, in European culture at least, has never formed an obvious and monolithic fact. . . . Meaning here is always fractured."[3] Instead of madness having a universal definition or absolute truth, the way European society defined madness changed constantly depending upon social, economic, and political circumstances. As we shall see, much the same is the case in Westeros.

According to Foucault, knowledge of insanity has depended upon those with power to name it, whose power in turn increased with their ability to designate certain people as insane. For example, both Stannis Baratheon and Joffrey Lannister surround themselves with entertainers known as mad fools. Patchface, the fool in Stannis Baratheon's court, is a boy who was lost at sea for two days before washing up on shore "broken in body and mind, hardly capable of speech, much less of wit."[4] Everyone except Shireen, Stannis's daughter and only child, sees Patchface as "mad, and in pain, and no use to anyone, least of all himself."[5] The fool in King Joffrey's court at King's Landing, Moon Boy, is described as a "pie-faced simpleton" who often acts strangely.[6] On one occasion he "mounted his stilts and strode around the tables in pursuit of Lord Tyrell's ludicrously fat fool Butterbumps."[7]

So what's the big deal? It's obvious that Patchface and Moon Boy deserved their label as mad fools, right? But what if they aren't crazy? What if it's just that the kings are powerful enough to label people mad and force the named to comply with the king's decree? By labeling the fool mad, the king creates an identity for the person as insane. Because of the king's power and authority, everyone associates madness with the person named mad. This clearly occurred when King Joffrey named Ser Dontos Holland a mad fool. Within a matter of minutes Ser Dontos went from being a knight in the king's tournament to a crazy fool in his court. In *A Clash of Kings*, after being late for his joust and making King Joffrey wait, "The knight appeared a moment later, cursing and staggering, clad in breastplate and plumed helm and nothing else . . . his manhood flopped about obscenely as he chased after his horse."[8] Dontos, too drunk to get on his horse, sat down and said, "I lose . . . fetch me some wine."[9]

King Joffrey initially responded by ordering Ser Dontos's execution, stating, "I'll have him killed on the morrow, the fool."[10] Upon Sansa Stark's recommendation, however, Joffrey decided to turn Dontos into a fool. Joffrey declares, "From this day on, you're my new fool. You can sleep with Moon Boy and dress in motley."[11] In naming Dontos a fool, Joffrey used his power as the king to construct a new identity of Dontos, an identity as a lackwit idiot.

Foucault called this the power/knowledge nexus. Because you have named the category, you are perceived as knowledgeable or an expert in the subject. As a result, your expertise in the realm of madness gives you additional power to continue naming and categorizing. Foucault further argued that we must vigilantly tease out these knowledge/power relationships so "we can grasp what constitutes the acceptability of a system, be it the mental health system, the penal system, delinquency, sexuality, etc."[12]

Pointing a Finger at the Crazies

Kings aren't the only ones with enough power to decide who is crazy in Westeros. Madness also manifests itself through other examples of naming and sorting the mad. Quite often this sorting is seemingly harmless and is used as a means of explaining a person's abnormal behavior. For example, Tyrion Lannister characterized Ser Loras Tyrell's response to the murder of Renly Baratheon by saying, "It's said the Knight of Flowers went mad when he saw his king's body, and slew three of Renly's guards in his wrath."[13] Catelyn Stark's sister, the Lady of the Vale, Lysa Tully, was believed to have gone insane with grief after having five miscarriages and losing her husband, Lord Jon Arryn. King Robert Baratheon stated, "I think losing Jon has driven the woman mad,"[14] and Grand Maester Pycelle remarked, "Let me say that grief can derange even the strongest and most disciplined of minds, and the Lady Lysa was never that."[15] In these instances, naming madness seems like no big deal. After all, we are constantly describing people's actions and valuing them as appropriate or inappropriate, reckless or crazy, logical or illogical. It becomes a big deal, though, when this naming is done in a systematic way as a means of marginalizing an individual or a group in order to justify one's own questionable actions. This is exactly what occurs with Aerys "The Mad King" Targaryen.

Meet the Mayor of Crazytown

As Catelyn Stark notes in *A Clash of Kings*, "Aerys was mad, the whole realm knew it."[16] Granted, King Aerys's mannerisms were enough to raise eyebrows. According to Jaime Lannister, King Aerys's "beard was matted and unwashed, his hair a silver-gold tangle that reached his waist, his fingernails cracked yellow claws nine inches long,"[17] and he was seen "pacing alone in his throne room, picking at scabbed and bleeding hands. The fool was always cutting himself on the blades and barbs of the Iron Throne."[18]

Furthermore, Mad King Aerys had a reputation for brutality. When talking to Hallyne the Pyromancer, the Imp Tyrion Lannister thought to himself, *"King Aerys used you to roast the flesh off enemies."*[19] Aerys also had Ser Ilyn Payne's tongue cut out for no more than claiming that the King's Hand, Tywin Lannister, actually ruled the kingdom.[20] Perhaps most brutally, after being held captive by Lord Denys during the Defiance of Duskendale, Mad King Aerys went on a killing rampage: "Lord Denys lost his head, as did his brothers and his sister, uncles, cousins. . . . The Lace Serpent [Denys's wife] was burned alive, poor woman, though her tongue was torn out first, and her female parts, with which it was said she enslaved her lordly husband."[21]

According to these accounts King Aerys was an incredibly dangerous individual due to his madness. This is a phenomenon that Foucault similarly traced to the nineteenth century and the birth of psychiatry, contending, "Nineteenth-century psychiatry invented an entirely fictitious entity, a crime that is insanity, a crime that is nothing but insanity, an insanity that is nothing but a crime."[22] Foucault demonstrated how psychiatrists, using their credentials as medical experts, defined certain instances of mental illness as criminal and certain criminal behaviors the result of insanity. Being able to identify the criminally insane gave psychiatrists more power, because their diagnoses claimed to reduce crime and make cities safer.

This seems to apply to the Mad King, since he murdered and brutalized people. But think of it this way: Jaime Lannister, among others, defines Aerys's brutality to be a result of his madness. Is he one to talk? In *A Game of Thrones* Jaime Lannister threw Bran Stark, a child, out a window because he caught Jaime having sex with his own sister, Cersei.[23] And remember Jaime's also the Kingslayer, responsible for murdering King Aerys, even though he was a sworn brother of the Kingsguard.

This is only the tip of the iceberg. The series is full of examples of brutally violent behavior, yet only a select few individuals have their violence attributed to madness. Is this because some acts of brutality and violence are justified or logical? Was it logical for Jaime to throw Bran out the window to preserve his incestuous secret, but illogical for Aerys to cut out Sir Ilyn Payne's tongue for undermining his power?[24] In the world of Westeros, this is exactly the case: one instance of brutality is justified and the other is not. This is because by naming the acts of others mad, a person places himself within the group of the sane, or logical. Such a person's sanity isn't scrutinized then, no matter how crazy the person's actions might seem. For how can the person who has the power to name what it means to be insane actually be insane her/himself? As we'll see, this is well illustrated by the heated debate between Eddard Stark and Robert Baratheon over whether to send assassins to murder Daenerys Targaryen and her unborn child.

We Had to Murder the Mad Murderer!

In *A Game of Thrones*, King Robert Baratheon received word that the last of the Targaryens, Daenerys, daughter of Aerys, was pregnant with "the stallion that mounts the world," future son of Khal Drogo. Ned Stark, Hand of the King, disagreed with Robert's command to have Daenerys and the unborn child assassinated. "Your Grace, the girl is scarcely more than a child. You are no Tywin Lannister, to slaughter the innocent."[25] Here Ned referred to the fact that upon usurping the throne from Mad King Aerys, Tywin Lannister (Aerys's own Hand) presented Robert with the corpses of Aerys's heirs, Rhaegar's wife and children, "as tokens of fealty."[26] Ser Gregor Clegane had dashed the children's heads against rocks and raped Rhaegar's wife, Elia. Robert replied, "Seven hells, *someone* had to kill Aerys!"[27] Whereas Robert saw the killing of Daenerys as justifiable and logical given his hatred of the Targaryens, Ned drew the line at killing children, stating "the murder of children . . . it would be vile . . . unspeakable."[28]

King Robert's argument is that the death of Mad King Aerys and his family, along with Daenerys and her unborn child, is justifiable based on the necessity of preventing the mad Targaryens from holding the throne. In truth, Robert's feelings for the Targaryens stemmed from his hatred of Rhaegar for naming Robert's betrothed, Lyanna Stark, "the Queen of Love and Beauty" after a tournament victory at Harrenhal where Rhaegar subsequently ran off with her.[29] Instead of announcing it in those terms, which would have made the error of his logic obvious, Robert's excuse rested on the supposed madness of the Targaryen family. Robert, from his position of power and authority as the King of the Seven Kingdoms, defined the acts of Aerys as mad in order to justify his own actions. In response to Ned's question, "Robert, I ask you, what did we rise against Aerys Targaryen for, if not to put an end to the murder of children?" Robert replied, "To put an end to *Targaryens!*"[30]

Robert frames the knowledge or facts of Targaryen insanity in such a way as to link Aerys's acts of violence to madness. We might think that ordering the murder of a child is completely insane, but Robert considered it justified in order to prevent another mad king from eventually taking the throne. Foucault claimed that the early psychiatric movement sought to solidify its position of power and authority in European society by proving its own necessity. Likewise, Robert tried to demonstrate his power and authority by killing Daenerys and her unborn child. Early psychiatrists demonstrated their own necessity by linking crime with insanity, and insanity with crime. As Foucault says, "Crime, then, became an important issue for psychiatrists, because what was involved was less a field of knowledge to be conquered than a modality of power to be secured and justified."[31] In other words, instead of psychiatrists seeking to learn all they could about what it meant to be insane, they were more concerned with establishing and maintaining their position of power and authority.

By linking madness to despicable crimes, especially murder and death, psychiatrists made it clear that all mental illness was to be feared. Since you never know when the insane will turn to murder and crime, you should be wary and thank psychiatrists for institutionalizing them! As Foucault wrote, "It must not be forgotten that . . . psychiatry was then striving to establish its right to impose upon the mentally ill a therapeutic confinement. After all, it had to be shown that madness, by its very nature . . . was haunted by the absolute danger, death."[32]

Technologies of the Self

As we've seen, Foucault believed that knowledge influences our actions by serving as a form of power. Linking madness with crime and inevitable death, for example, served as a powerful means of social control: it justified the institutionalization of those socially awkward individuals deemed insane. Subjective morality influenced notions of insanity, yet psychiatry pretended to rely on knowledge of objective truth about madness. This process reflected a change in the manner in which governments wielded power in the seventeenth and eighteenth centuries. Whereas the primary means governments used to maintain their control over people up to that point involved outward and open punishment or confinement (what Foucault referred to as sovereign power), the psychiatric asylum represented a shift to a more subtle form of control, or disciplinary power.

Disciplinary power is more subtle because the point is to encourage subjects to govern themselves. This type of power is evidenced in *A Storm of Swords* when Jon Snow falls in love with the wilding Ygritte. Periodically Jon hears a voice in his head reminding him he is a member of the Night's Watch and that his actions violate his vows. Jon didn't fear physical torture or punishment, examples of sovereign power; instead he feared not living up to the code of the Night's Watch. By ensuring that members of the Watch remained loyal to their vows, the code itself served the function of disciplinary power, encouraging individuals to regulate themselves.

Similarly, rulers in eighteenth-century Europe realized that if they pushed people long enough and abused their power through public punishment or torture, the people would eventually push back with revolution. The key to disciplinary power, then, is that the criminal, or in our case the insane person, is encouraged to see himself as insane. By convincing persons that they are not "normal" or that they need rehabilitation, the expert exerts power over the patient externally in the form of an expert diagnosis, but also internally in the form of a self-image. Foucault referred to this as the "technologies of the self," "which permit individuals to effect by their own means or with the help of others a certain number of operations on their own bodies and souls, thoughts, conduct, and ways of being, so as to transform themselves in order to attain a certain state of happiness, purity, wisdom, perfection, or immortality."[33] By diagnosing and labeling a person as mad or insane, the expert begins the process of disciplining the patient's mind. Patients are encouraged to critically analyze themselves, change their conduct or way of being, in the hopes of being seen by themselves or others as rehabilitated.

Am I Sane? I Think I Am. . . . I Think I Am. . . . I Think I Am. . . .

Power is wielded in A Song of Ice and Fire primarily through sovereign power. The Seven Kingdoms of Westeros and beyond are full of outward and open struggles for power. There are games of thrones and clashes of kings; there are public executions, like Ned Stark's beheading and Viserys Targaryen's golden crowning. There are also, though, examples of disciplinary power in which characters question and sometimes change their behavior in an attempt to govern themselves according to arbitrary social or political rules.

For example, upon being named a mad fool in King Joffrey's court, Ser Dontos internalizes his new identity and genuinely behaves as a mad fool. On a number of occasions Dontos lived his new identity, galloping around on his horse broomstick while he "made farting sounds with his cheeks and sang rude songs about the guests" or pretending to beat Sansa Stark with a melon-headed Morningstar, "shouting 'Traitor, traitor' and whacking her over the head with the melon."[34] In the case of Dontos, King Joffrey had the power to decide what we know of him. No visitor to the king's court would ever know Ser Dontos the knight. This labeling wasn't based on objective truth but on a subjective opinion. The identity imposed on Dontos encouraged him to change his behavior to meet societal (or royal) expectations. According to Foucault, "He is mad because that is what people tell him and because he has been treated as such: 'They wanted me to be ridiculous, so that is what I became.'"[35]

Another example of disciplinary power, where a character internalizes an imposed subjective identity, is found with

Daenerys Targaryen. As the quotation at the beginning of this chapter suggests, Daenerys was used to hearing about her family's mental illness. After all, "Every child knows that the Targaryens have always danced too close to madness."[36] On a number of occasions Dany questioned her own actions based on this constructed identity. This was especially true when Khal Drogo died and Dany struggled with how to move forward. After ordering the preparation for Drogo's funeral pyre, "She could feel the eyes of the *khalasar* on her as she entered her tent . . . they thought her mad, Dany realized. Perhaps she was. She would know soon enough."[37] Remembering her brother Viserys, Dany thought, "*He must have known how they mocked him.* Small wonder he turned so angry and bitter. In the end it had driven him mad. *It will do the same to me if I let it.*"[38] Dany's self-identity had been influenced by the dominant discourse surrounding her family.

As a final example of the effects of disciplinary power as it relates to madness, consider Catelyn Stark's freeing of the Kingslayer Jaime Lannister in *A Storm of Swords*. Catelyn secretly freed Jaime and sent him to King's Landing with Brienne of Tarth to return her captive daughters, Arya and Sansa. Robb Stark's bannermen responded with anger, until the Castellan of Riverrun, Ser Desmond, attributed the decision to her mental state. "The news must have driven you mad . . . a madness of grief, a *mother's* madness, men will understand."[39] As she sat confined to her sick father's bedchamber, Catelyn asked him, "What would you say if you knew my crime, Father. . . . Would you have done as I did if it were Lysa and me at the hands of our enemies? *Or would you condemn me too, and call it a mother's madness?*"[40]

Everything Is Dangerous

Is someone who acts unreasonably or illogically mad? After all, Catelyn's decision to free Jaime in order to free her two daughters seems like a logical decision, whereas Aerys's love affair with fire is illogical.[41] On the other hand, a person might make illogical decisions based on stupidity or naiveté, as Sansa Stark's naive trust in Dontos Hollard gets her sent off to live in captivity with Petyr "Littlefinger" Baelish.

Foucault's point is that any process of sorting and categorizing individuals is an act of power. When we self-sort and identify ourselves as a student, a Democrat, or a Chicago Bears fan, it's probably no big deal; we use these labels to reflect our membership in certain communities with like-minded individuals. But when we use our positions of authority to arbitrarily place people into categories, we are walking on thin ice. When discussing this issue, Foucault famously said, "The point is not that everything is bad, but that everything is dangerous, which is not the same as bad. If everything is dangerous, then we always have something to do."[42]

Because madness and mental illness have been defined and treated arbitrarily throughout history, we should question the power that allows experts to determine what it means to be insane. Just as we should question the foundation of madness in A Song of Ice and Fire, we should also question the foundation for our present understandings of mental illness.[43] Our awareness of the danger of categorizing someone as mentally ill due to subjective social norms could prevent gross abuses of power. As Foucault said, "My role . . . is to show people that they are much freer than they feel, that people accept as truth, as evidence, some themes which have been built up at a certain moment during history, and this so-called evidence can be criticized and destroyed."[44] Thus we should question the truth of claims about mental illness in order to expose potential abuses of freedom, as there may be a fine line between sanity and insanity. As Daenerys Targaryen climbed down off of Khal Drogo's funeral pyre, the witch, Mirri Maz Duur, shouted, "You are mad!" Dany responded with a question: "Is it so far from madness to wisdom?"[45] Based on what we know about power and knowledge in Westeros, we can confidently respond, "No."

NOTES

1. George R. R. Martin, *A Storm of Swords* (New York: Bantam Dell, 2005), p. 987.

2. For a great introduction to postmodernism, see J. Jeremy Wisnewski, "Killing the Griffins: A Murderous Exposition of Postmodernism," in *Introducing Philosophy through Pop Culture: From Socrates to South Park, Hume to House*, eds. William Irwin and David Kyle Johnson (Oxford: Wiley-Blackwell, 2010), p. 24.

3. Michel Foucault, *The History of Madness* (New York: Routledge, 2009), p. 163.

4. George R. R. Martin, *A Clash of Kings* (New York: Bantam Dell, 2005), pp. 7–8.

5. Ibid., p. 8.

6. George R. R. Martin, *A Game of Thrones* (New York: Bantam Dell, 2005), p. 299.

7. Martin, *A Storm of Swords*, p. 820.

8. Martin, *A Clash of Kings*, p. 45.

9. Ibid.

10. Ibid., p. 46.

11. Ibid.

12. Michel Foucault, "What Is Critique?" in *The Essential Foucault: Selections from the Essential Works of Foucault, 1954–1984*, eds. P. Rabinow and N. Rose (New York: New Press, 2003), p. 275.

13. Martin, *A Clash of Kings*, p. 530.

14. Martin, *A Game of Thrones*, p. 45.

15. Ibid., p. 253.

16. Martin, *A Clash of Kings*, p. 798.

17. George R. R. Martin, *A Feast for Crows* (New York: Bantam Dell, 2005), p. 331.

18. Martin, *A Storm of Swords*, p. 158.

19. Martin, *A Clash of Kings*, p. 311.

20. Martin, *A Feast for Crows*, p. 561.

21. Ibid., p. 191.

22. Michel Foucault, "About the Concept of the 'Dangerous Individual' in Nineteenth Century Legal Psychiatry," in *The Essential Foucault*, p. 213.

23. Martin, *A Game of Thrones*, p. 85.

24. Martin, *A Storm of Swords*, p. 156.

25. Martin, *A Game of Thrones*, p. 112.

26. Ibid.

27. Ibid., p. 115.

28. Ibid., p. 112.

29. Martin, *A Storm of Swords*, p. 586.

30. Martin, *A Game of Thrones*, p. 353.

31. Michel Foucault, "About the Concept of the 'Dangerous Individual' in Nineteenth Century Legal Psychiatry," in *The Essential Foucault*, p. 214.

32. Ibid., pp. 215–216.

33. Michel Foucault, "Technologies of the Self," in *The Essential Foucault*, p. 146.

34. Martin, *A Clash of Kings*, p. 487.

35. Foucault, *History of Madness*, p. 343.

36. Martin, *A Storm of Swords*, p. 987.

37. Martin, *A Game of Thrones*, p. 801.

38. Martin, *A Clash of Kings*, p. 578.

39. Martin, *A Storm of Swords*, p. 34.

40. Ibid., p. 35.

41. Ibid., p. 505.

42. Michel Foucault, "On the Genealogy of Ethics: An Overview of Work in Progress," in *The Essential Foucault*, p. 104.

43. Of course, mental illness is real, and today there are better criteria for determining whether or not a person is sane. To diagnose mental illness, psychiatrists today use the criteria in the following: American Psychiatric Association, *Diagnostic and Statistical Manual of Mental Disorders* (4th ed., rev.) (Washington, DC: American Psychiatric Association, 2000).

44. "Truth, Power Self: An Interview with Michel Foucault," in *Technologies of the Self*, eds. L. Martin, H. Gutman, and P. Hutton (Amherst: University of Massachusetts Press, 1988), pp. 9–15.

45. Martin, *A Game of Thrones*, p. 803.

CONTRIBUTORS

The Learned Lords and Ladies from beyond the Seven
Kingdoms

Albert J. J. Anglberger is a postdoc research fellow at the
Munich Center for Mathematical Philosophy (LMU Munich)
and has published papers in logic, ethics, philosophy of science, and philosophy of religion. He earned his Maester's
chain at the University of Salzburg, under the guidance of
Maester Alexander Hieke, amongst others. Just recently Albert
was sent away to the Citadel of Munich to earn further links
for his chain by doing research in mathematical philosophy.
Although he claims not to be a nerd, he still immerses himself
in all kinds of nerdish stuff: from pen-and-paper role-playing,
to an addiction to graphic novels, to fantasy and science fiction, to always having to buy the latest gadgets. Sometimes
he is quite self-confident and believes he could even outsmart
Tyrion Lannister and outdrink Robert Baratheon.

Richard H. Corrigan is currently in exile from his fair native
land, Ireland, due to the dark tyrannies of economics and
opportunity, and is presently suing for support in the Kingdom
of Gloucestershire. He has served under many lords and
houses, including the Open University, the University of
Reading, the University of the West of England, and

Malvern College, having first gained his doctoral letters at University College Dublin. He has scribed numerous tomes dedicated to philosophy and religion, including *Ethics: A University Guide, Divine Hiddenness, Divine Foreknowledge and Moral Responsibility, The Self-Revelation of the Judeo-Christian God*, and *Philosophical Frontiers*. He has written in various learned journals. The Corrigan House's emblem is a lizard and two shamrocks, and its words are *Never mind, it could be worse!*

Edward Cox was born in Oklahoma and apprenticed at the University of Chicago, which is much like Winterfell without the natural hot springs to keep the bathrooms warm. He earned his Maester's chain, or PhD, in philosophy from the University of Oklahoma. Like Tyrion Lannister, he is rarely to be found without a book, most of them on philosophy of mind and metaphysics. He has taught at several universities and is currently a lecturer at Georgia State University. He lives with his wife, Erika Tracy, a published fantasy author, a young son named after his favorite fantasy character, and a pack of direwolves (or German shepherds, as they are called in America).

R. Shannon Duval is an associate professor of philosophy at Mount Mary College, a second-degree black belt in tae kwon do, and a national champion in kali arnis. Daughter of houses Yin and Yang (House Words: The Obstacle Is the Path), fostered to House Fulbright, she traveled to distant lands and learned that while the pen is mightier than the sword in all of them, swords are still an awful lot of fun. Known as "The Wonderninja" for her dual careers as philosopher and martial artist, she is the editor of *The Encyclopedia of Ethics* and a coauthor of *Engineering Ethics* and publishes in the areas of comparative philosophy and philosophy of contemporary culture. She is sure she could be busier, but somehow the ravens keep "getting lost." Whilst awaiting their return, she spends her time pondering the original nature of snowmen, attending the three wildlings posing as her heirs, practicing water dancing, and avoiding red weddings.

Don Fallis is associate professor of information resources and adjunct associate professor of philosophy at the University of Arizona. He has written several philosophy articles on lying and deception, including "What Is Lying?" in the *Journal of Philosophy* and "The Most Terrific Liar You Ever Saw in Your Life" in the forthcoming *The Catcher in the Rye and Philosophy*. He has always felt that it is just too easy to tell which side someone is on in Middle Earth and in Narnia. His sigil is a coyote, brown, on a red field. His words are "Trust Me on This."

Stacey Goguen studies philosophy at Boston University, where she works on feminist philosophy, philosophy of race, and philosophy of science. She takes every opportunity to incorporate pop culture and video games into her work (whenever she is not playing video games or slavishly devouring pop culture). Her house words are "Dinner Is Coming."

Daniel Haas descends from House Haas, a small but notable family with most of their land holdings situated north of the Wall, in the frozen wastelands of Canada. Upon hearing that winter is coming, he fled south to Florida State University, Tallahassee, where he is currently a philosophy graduate student. His research interests include Valyrian-steel forging, Dothraki language and culture, and the philosophy of action. When teaching, he always makes it a point to stress that you stick 'em with the pointy end.

David Hahn is a maester in training, working at forging his philosophy link at the University of Buffalo's PhD program. Currently in his second year, most of his work is about not getting sent to the Wall. At the Trident, he made a mark for himself in *The Sopranos and Philosophy*, *Poker and Philosophy*, and

Final Fantasy and Philosophy. In his free time he makes sure that his daughter stays away from all Needles.

Alexander Hieke has been teaching philosophy at the University of Salzburg, Austria, for twenty years now. During this time he also received his Maester's chain. He was recently appointed head of his department. His research focuses on the areas of ontology, epistemology, and philosophy of language. He has been lucky in having quite a few very talented young apprentices, one of whom is his coauthor Albert Anglberger, who just left for the Citadel of Munich to continue his research there. Fifteen years ago, one of Alexander's Maesters introduced him to the scholars from a school beyond the big sea, located in Portland, Oregon. He was invited to teach their students at their Salzburg Campus, and he still enjoys educating the young sophomores in ethics there. When not busy with administrative duties, teaching, or research, Alexander loves to read about lands and ages far, far away (which some people claim to be only imaginary). And sometimes he meets with friends, armed with pen and paper only, to fight the forces of evil in those distant realms. That is also where he first encountered the wondrous world of Westeros.

Ser Henry, the Zen Maester of House **Jacoby** (House words: Everybody Lies) teaches philosophy at East Carolina University in Greenville, North Carolina. He has published articles on philosophy of mind, language, and religion, and on the nature of moral perception. He also contributed to the volume on *South Park and Philosophy*. He is the editor of *House and Philosophy* (now in nine languages!). Known throughout academia unfortunately as "The Deanslayer" (well, it *was* necessary), he, alas, has no evil twin sister.

The **Greg Littmann** are a savage clan of sea raiders who sail out from their craggy fastness in the Iron Islands to attack ships and plunder coastal towns. Their fleet has ranged as far as the coast of North Carolina, where they laid siege to the University of North Carolina at Chapel Hill until it yielded up much booty and awarded the clan a PhD. Emboldened by this success, the Greg Littmann raided the Americas with increasing frequency, plundering Southern Illinois University Edwardsville once a semester, doing great slaughter and teaching critical thinking, media ethics, metaphysics, and the philosophy of mind. Eventually, the clan declared itself assistant professor over the university. From this stronghold, they have published in metaphysics and the philosophy of logic and have written philosophy and popular culture chapters relating to *The Big Bang Theory*, *Breaking Bad*, *Doctor Who*, *Dune*, *Final Fantasy*, *The Onion*, *Sherlock Holmes*, *The Terminator*, and *The Walking Dead*.

Christopher Robichaud is Lecturer in Ethics and Public Policy at Harvard University's Kennedy School of Government. A fan of fantasy fiction his whole life, he started gobbling up George R. R. Martin's series A Song of Ice and Fire and has never looked back. It's been suggested to him that he might be taking things too far by asking his policy students to start a campaign to elect Tyrion Lannister for president. All the same, he's pushing forward. The platform's simple, really. Elect Tyrion. He'll be indebted to the country. And a Lannister always pays his debts.

Jaron of the House **Schoone**, the First of His Name, currently occupies a PhD position in the small but proud Kingdom of the Netherlands, across the Narrow Sea. The position was awarded to him after winning a jousting tournament as the squire of Lord-Professor Knoops of Amsterdam. Jaron spends his days in the Philosophers Tower of the Utrecht University, enjoying honeyed wine from the Arbor while researching the philosophy of science and religion. Whenever the gods grant him the pleasure of teaching a philosophy class, Jaron never fails to remind his students that "those who slack, have to take the Black."

Marcus Schulzke is an ABD PhD candidate in political science at the State University of New York at Albany. His primary research interests include political theory, comparative politics, political violence, applied ethics, digital media, and video games. In addition to his many scholarly articles and book chapters, he has written chapters for *Catcher in the Rye and Philosophy* and *Inception and Philosophy*. Marcus is currently writing a dissertation about how soldiers make moral decisions in combat. He hopes that the soldiers he interviews act more like Ned Stark than like Bronn, and he will advise all of them to avoid angering any Lannisters.

Abraham P. Schwab (House words: Nobody knows) left the urban indifference of Chicago and Brooklyn, New York, for the urbane ignorance of Fort Wayne, Indiana, where he serves as an assistant professor in the Philosophy Department at Indiana and Purdue University's joint campus. He continues to labor as the cartographer of the intersecting rivers of epistemology and medical ethics, work that has led to publications in the *Journal of Medical Ethics*, *Social Science and Medicine*, the *American Journal of Bioethics*, and the *Journal of Medicine and Philosophy*. He remains unsure whether George R. R. Martin's Song will end in the fires of desire or the cold hatred of ice, but is confident that either will suffice.

Michael J. Sigrist teaches philosophy at George Washington University in Washington, DC. His love for fantasy began in the fourth grade, when he discovered the Iron Tower Trilogy by hometown author Dennis McKiernan in the local library. Michael's research focuses on the philosophy of mind, and recently he has written on the nature of time and temporal perception, fatalism, and personal identity. Naturally Michael admires the wit of Tyrion, the valor of Robb, and the resourcefulness of Arya, but if you ply him with enough wine, he will admit that, all things considered, Tywin might have been the least bad option for Westeros. Michael's House words are randomly selected on a weekly basis from the lyrical songbook of the rock band Cinderella. This week: It's gonna be a long cold winter.

Eric J. Silverman is assistant professor of philosophy and religious studies at Christopher Newport University in Newport News, Virginia. His conquests include a dozen publications, such as chapters in *Battlestar Galactica and Philosophy* and *Twilight and Philosophy*. His first monograph is entitled *The Prudence of Love: How Possessing the Virtue of Love Benefits the Lover*. In spite of these accomplishments, Silverman is best known for his House words: Never pay the gold price, pay the Silver price instead.

Matthew Tedesco is associate professor of philosophy at Beloit College in Wisconsin, where the words "winter is coming" are spoken ominously each autumn. His interests are in ethical theory and practical ethics, and he has contributed essays to both *James Bond and Philosophy* and *Facebook and Philosophy*. He is sometimes referred to, with only minimal respect, as "The Molehill That Jogs."

Chad William Timm is an assistant professor of education at Grand View University in Des Moines, Iowa. He has chapters forthcoming in *The Girl with the Dragon Tattoo and Philosophy* and *The Hunger Games and Philosophy*. While spending a year North of the Wall living among the wildlings, he learned to question the role that power played in constructing his personal identity. As a result he moved back south with his direwolf "Bandit" and now encourages future teachers to use postmodern philosophy in their classrooms.

Scoffing at the prospect of life as a noble lady, **Katherine Tullmann** struck out to achieve greatness in the Kingdom of Manhattan. Once there, she had to make a decision between earning her keep as a rogue knight-errant dedicated to keeping the peace or a humble scholar devoted to a life of the mind. In the end she chose the latter; Katherine is currently forging her Maester's chain at the City University of New York Graduate Center, completing links in the philosophy of mind and philosophy of art. In her free time, she wrote a chapter for *Inception and Philosophy* and other essays on art and emotions. When Katherine finishes her training, she hopes to be placed somewhere in the North, where she can spend her time quietly reflecting in the weirwoods.

INDEX

From the Archives at Oldtown

social control and, 271–273
values and, 267–268
intellect, happiness and, 65
intention
    just war theory and, 52–53,
        59–60
    lying and, 20–21
    power and virtù, 42
investment, game theory and,
    252
Iron Throne, social contract
    theory and, 5–6. *See
    also individual names of
    characters*
irrationality, game theory and,
    254–255

James I (King of England), 12
Jefferson, Thomas, 30
Johns Hopkins Hospital,
    104–105
Jojen, 216
Jonquil, 214
Jordan, Robert, 137
Jory, 245
justice, fatalism and, 228–231
justification
    epistemology and, 148–151
    insanity and, 270–271
    justifiable conduct and just
        war theory, 55–56
justified true belief,
    epistemology and, 147–148
just war theory, 49–60
    cost-*versus*-gain ratio and, 55
    defined, 49–50
    discrimination between
        combatants and
        noncombatants, 56–57

idealism and, 85
intention and, 52–53,
    59–60
legitimate authority and,
    50–51, 53
moral luck and, 188
motivation and, 51–52
probability of success and,
    54–55
reprisal and, 58
rights of state's own citizens,
    58–59
treatment of prisoners of war
    and, 57
war as last resort, 53–54

Kant, Immanuel
    chivalry and, 210
    lying and, 23–24, 26, 29
    moral luck and, 190–192
Kingsguard, chivalry and, 207
King's Landing, morality and,
    176–177
knighthood
    chivalry and, 206–209,
        216–218
    game theory and, 252–253

Lady (direwolf), 19, 170
Lannister, Cersei (Queen), 16,
    41, 43, 50, 52, 83, 84, 88,
    89, 93, 99, 131, 184, 186,
    190–191, 257, 260
    authenticity and, 227–228
    chivalry and, 212
    cultural relativism and, 195
    egoism and, 91–92
    game theory and, 250,
        255–256